A Directory of York Pubs 1455-2003

by

Hugh Murray

John Ward Knowles, 1838-1931, better known as a stained glass and ecclesiastical artist, paints a sign for the Old White Swan, Goodramgate, in 1862.

Published by VOYAGER PUBLICATIONS

British Library Cataloguing in Publication Data
The Catalogue Record for this book is available from the British Library.

ISBN No. 0 9525392 5 X

Printed by J W Bullivant & Son
296 Bishopthorpe Road, York
Tel: 01904 623241

Cover: Licensee Sarah Weston stands in the doorway of the Crown and Harp in Mount Ephraim 1906.

By the same author:

The Horse Tramways of York 1880-1909	1980
Dr Evelyn's York	1983
Servants of Business	1984
Heraldry and the Buildings of York	1985
Photographs and Photographers of York:	
The Early Years 1844-1879	1986
Outside Micklegate Bar	1988
Nathaniel Whittock's Bird's Eye View of the City	
of York in the 1850s	1988
Opportunity of Leisure	1989
York through the Eyes of the Artist	
(with S. Riddick and R. Green)	1990
This Garden of Death	1991
The Yorkshire Architectural and York	
Archaeological Society:	
A Sesquicentenary Retrospect 1842-1992	1992
The York Graveyard Guide	
1994	
The Great Chamber at Gilling Castle	1996
Scarborough, York and Leeds: The Town Plans	
of John Cossins 1697–1743	1997
A Directory of York Goldsmiths, Silversmiths and	
Associated Craftsmen	1998
Where to go in York: The History of Public	
Conveniences in the City of York	2000
Monuments in York Minster	
(with Ian R. Pattison)	2001

For Ken and Rita Booth

Acknowledgements

The inspiration for this book stems from the regular Friday night meetings between Ken Booth, Robin Bell and myself which started in 1981 and still continue today with, now, only two participants. Before Ken's death in January 2002 those meetings took place in the pubs which Ken knew so well, having been a lifetime patron of such houses. Many were the stories told and retold, on those occasions, of his adventures in the pursuit of alcoholic refreshment. To give us another, perhaps more elevating, purpose at our meetings, we decided, for reasons of historical research, to visit every public house within the then boundaries of the City of York. This aim we achieved, probably several times over, before the advent of cafe bars and the political manoeuvrings which enlarged the city, although it must be said that during the longer summer evenings we visited the hinterland as well, though not so systematically.

Ken's other interest, photography, had led him to amass a collection of historic pictures of York, including public houses, which his wife, Rita, used as the basis for anecdotal slide shows with which she entertained many groups of people. These were enlivened with stories gleaned from Ken as well as from the results of her own delvings into the history of York. Ken and Rita were a great team, and after Rita's death in June 1993, I proposed to Ken that a book on York pubs would be a fitting memorial to her. With Ken's death occurring before my researches were completed, it is thus a tribute to both of my friends.

The book is immeasurably improved by 243 pictures of public houses, many from Ken's collection, supplemented with others from my own and other collectors' albums. I have been assisted in my researches particularly by Rita Freedman and her staff in York City Archives, Amanda Howard at York Reference Library, Chris Webb at the Borthwick Institute of Historical Research and Peter Young, the York Minster archivist. Others who have helped to improve this publication are Alwyn Fletcher, Geoff Hodgson, Susan Major, David Poole, Chris Titley (aka Joshua Titley) and my wife, Jill. My acknowledgements would not be complete without mentioning the arduous task of proof reading such a difficult manuscript undertaken by Kath Hatfield and Van Wilson. To Van Wilson and Mike Race I have to offer a very sincere thank you for undertaking the editorial and production tasks which have allowed this book to come to fruition.

A Directory of Pubs in York 1450 - 2003

Introduction

To the drinker and non-drinker alike, public house signs are a familiar sight in the streets of Great Britain, used, along with churches, as the most popular means of giving directions to strangers. Another use is a game to keep children amused during long boring car journeys – pub sign cricket – in which the legs appearing on the signs are equated to runs, and inanimate objects, e.g. The Bell, The Windmill, to wickets. The public houses of today, places where anybody can be served, during permitted hours, with intoxicating beverages, have their beginnings in a number of different establishments originally founded for disparate purposes; particularly alehouses, coffee houses, inns and taverns. To these can be added bars, change-houses, hostelries, host-houses, hotels, lushing-kens, post houses, shebeens, tipling-houses and wine-houses amongst others.

Alehouses, places where beer could be bought, had established an unsavoury reputation by the middle of the 8th century. Archbishop Egbert of York decreed that priests were not to eat or drink in them and also prescribed over-indulgence as 'none of us who is numbered among the priests cherish the vice of drunkenness nor force others to be drunk by his importunity'. That the taverns, too, were not of an appropriate standard can be seen from his requirement that hospitiums should be built in the vicinity of churches to provide accommodation for strangers.

By the reign of King Alfred (871–899) there were many alehouses in towns, villages and alongside the roads providing beer, probably brewed on the premises. They could be identified by an ale-stake, a long pole, erected outside and accompanied, if they sold wine, by a bush of evergreens, a sign used by the Romans and derived from the ivy and vine leaves associated with Bacchus. King Edgar (959-75) was concerned by this over provision and closed many alehouses, allowing only one per village. He was also responsible for having pegs fitted at regular intervals inside drinking horns. A drinker was required not to go beyond the next peg at each draught but the legislation back-fired as it gave rise to drinking contests! A code of laws about breaches of the peace was issued by King Aethelred (979-1013) in 997. One was concerned specifically with trouble in alehouses - 'six half marks shall be paid in compensation if a man is slain, and twelve ores if no one is slain'.[1] This is the earliest use of the phrase ale-house listed by the Oxford Dictionary.

In the main, documents recording local government in York do not start until 1272 with the earliest extant roll of Freemen.[2] The House Books, recording the proceedings of York City Council, do not exist before 1461.[3] Thus it is in the former, together with charters that the earliest appellations for members of the hospitality trade can be found. William the innkeeper appears in the 1250s,[4] William de Castelford and Adam de Pontefract became free as taverners in 1277,[5] a number of hostelers are mentioned in a list of transgressors against the 1301 Civic Ordinances,[6] while Ketell Braciarius, brewer, predates them all by several decades appearing in a charter made between 1180 and 1240.

The 1301 Civic Ordinances laid down trade practices 'for the relief and remedy of those coming to York, and staying in the city, both on the king's business and on that of others, who complain of the extortions and oppressions imposed by the citizens, both by failing to observe the Assize of Bread and Ale and by the intolerable cost of other victuals and necessities agreed between the citizens'. The Assize of Bread and Ale had been introduced in 1266 by Edward III and was the means whereby these two necessities, both corn based, were to be controlled for the next 300 years.

Brewers and ale-wives
Ale shall be brewed from good grain and malt. If it is sweet, well brewed and blended, and put in tuns, two gallons shall sell for a penny. When it is well prepared and put in casks, a gallon of the best shall cost 1d, and a gallon of the second quality ¾d. If a brewer or ale-wife sells ale contrary to the assize, by false measure, the measure shall be burned. For the first and second offences they shall be heavily fined, and for the third shall go to the tumbrel. If they go to the tumbrel three times by indictment, the brew-house, if they own it, shall be destroyed, and they shall abjure their calling for ever. If the ale is made of bad grain, badly malted and ill brewed, so that it is not worth the assized price, it shall be forfeit, and three or four gallons sold for 1d. The money shall be used for the common profit of the city as above. This ordinance is not to prevent men in the city from brewing their own ale, provided that they do not put it on sale in taverns contrary to the assize. If the price of grain goes up or down, the assize is to be set accordingly.

Taverners
Taverners, wine sellers and sauce makers shall not keep bad or putrid wine or vinegar in their houses. If convicted, their vessels shall be broken up, and those who break them shall keep the wood. For the first offence they shall be fined 6s. 8d., for the second 13s. 4d. If they offend a third time, and do not want to be beaten, they are to be fined 20s. and are to abjure their calling for ever. Good old wine is to be sold at 4d. a gallon, and new at 5d. Anyone offending against this assize shall be punished like those found keeping bad wine in their houses, but if there is a great scarcity of wine, or an improvement in trade, a new assize is to be set by the justices and keepers of these ordinances.

Hostelers
It is agreed that hostelers who take in strangers, and those who rent out houses, rooms, stalls or other accommodation, shall not take more than ½ d for stabling a horse for a night. If the guest has no horse, the hosteler shall be content with 1d. a night for his bed and a room, but this is not to apply to boys and other poor people who cannot pay. Hostelries, rooms and stalls rented out are to be viewed by the keepers of the ordinances, and set at the rents used to be paid before the king's court came to the city, save in the case of a newly-built hostelry or one repaired to enhance its value since the arrival of the court, when the rent shall be set at its true value. For the first offence, a hosteler shall be fined 6s. 8d., for the second 13s. 4d., and for the third 20s. and abjuration of his calling. Anyone who rents out houses, outhouses or stalls shall lose the rent for a year if it is too high. The money is to go to the common profit of the city.

From these ordinances it is clear that there is a distinct difference between inns, taverns and alehouses. Hostelers (or innkeepers) provided accommodation for travellers. Taverners bought wine from the wholesalers, the vintners, to sell to their customers for consumption on their premises. Brewers of ale sold it to the alehouse keepers for resale there. It is interesting to note that no specific trade was mentioned at this time in the various records whose sole function was the selling of ale, although in later centuries first tipler and later ale-draper were used to designate the licensee of an alehouse. Both the hostelers and the taverners were organised into trade gilds by 1415 when the part in the Mistery Play Cycle for which they were responsible was recorded: the former for the performance of the Coronation of the Virgin Mary and the latter for the Marriage at the Feast of Cana.[7] It would appear that the alehouse keepers, custodians of such unsavoury establishments, did not merit the dignity of a gild and an appearance in the Pageant. In later years the corporation had to use the ward or parish constables when they wanted information about the activities of alehouse keepers rather that using the searchers that were responsible for good practices in trade gilds.[8]

Alehouses

Apart from the setting of standard measures for wine, ale and corn in the Magna Carta in 1215 there was no new country-wide legislation enacted until 1393 to control, the ale-houses which were noted for the unruly and intemperate behaviour on their premises and were still a source of concern. In that year Richard III ordered that a sign must be exhibited on alehouses; 'whosoever shall brew in the town with the intention of selling it must hang out a sign otherwise he must forfeit his ale'.[9] This was the first formal requirement that a house selling ale should be capable of being easily recognized by its intending customers and, perhaps, also by the authorities responsible for ensuring the keeping of the peace. While the provision of signs on alehouses was required by law many other tradesmen began to realise the advantages of displaying a sign, at first, usually a simple implement or product of their trade, but later, as signs became more common, by bigger, more colourful and individualistic designs. The advantage of this signage was not lost on the prominent citizens whose house could be more easily found if intending visitors were told that 'Mr ..... lived at the sign of the ......'

No doubt amongst a proliferation of signs the alehouse keepers regained some anonymity and hoped to avoid some of the attentions of the law but their premises still required official regulation if they were to be brought under some measure of control. This did not occur until 1496 when a statute designed to clamp down on 'Vagabonds, Idle and Suspected Persons' included at the end a clause relating to the sale of ale. Any two justices of the peace were empowered to 'rejecte and put away com[mon] ale-selling in townes and places where they shall think convenyent, and to take suertie of the keepers of alehouses of their gode behavyng, by the discrecion of seid justices, and in the same to be advysed and aggreed at the time of their sessions'.[10] That this provision appears in legislation dealing principally with vagrancy, is an indication of the stigma associated with ale-selling.

Nevertheless, in spite of the reputation which alehouses had not unjustly gained, it was nearly 60 years before the first formal attempt was made to licence keepers of such establishments. In 1552 a law was put on the statute books 'for keepers of Alehouses and Tipling Houses to be bound by Recognisances'. Tipling houses were, apparently, places where beer could only be sold and not brewed. The preamble to the Act defined the problem 'forasmuch as intolerable Hurts and Troubles to the Commonwealth of this Realm doth daily grow and increase through such Abuses and Disorders as are had and used in common alehouses and other houses called Tiplinghouses'. The Justices of the Peace, or at least two of them, could close any alehouses they wished and no future alehouse could be opened without a Bond and Surety, on payment of 12 pence, that good order would be maintained on the premises and no unlawful games would be played there. The recognisance entered into was to be certified at the next Quarter Sessions and remain there on record. However at fairs it was to be lawful for anybody to sell ale from booths 'for the Relief of the King's Subjects that shall repair to the same'.[11]

To implement this Act the Corporation of York on 27 May 1552 ordered the parish constables to make diligent enquiries to find all alehouse and tipling houses in their parishes and then, by 1 June, provide the Lord Mayor with a list which would enable him and his brethren to decide who should be authorised to continue in their occupation. At the same time the constables were to provide lists of bowling alleys, and, with the help of the clergy, to provide a list of every inhabitant and householder living in the parishes, drawing particular attention to the impotent, aged and needy – an early example of census taking.[12]

Having agreed who should be allowed to keep alehouses in the city the Corporation required each successful individual to enter his recognisance in a special register, the full wording being laboriously rewritten for each entry. Anyone admitted to keep a common alehouse or tipling house, was not to allow the playing of dice, cards, bowls or shovegroat (a non-inflation linked precursor of shove-halfpenny) or any other unlawful games in his house or garden after 9 p.m. and on Sundays or other festival days during divine service. No person behaving suspiciously or inordinately was to be allowed to remain on the premises and good and quiet rule and honest order was to be kept there at all time.[13]

The alehouse keepers were apparently slow to bring their houses into order as required by the Act since on 9 June the Corporation required all clerics to read out a bulletin in their churches reminding their congregations that it was illegal to frequent any tavern, alehouse or tipling house on Sundays and other holy days during divine service, between Matins and Communion or after 9 o'clock at night on pain of at least three days in prison. They were also warned against playing dice, cards, bowls and other unlawful games at such houses, a warning that was obviously not heeded as on 24 November that year the constables of the wards were sent to search all the establishments every holy day to ensure that no unlawful games were being played and that the ambience within them was not unruly.[14]

But, however diligently the Corporation applied the Act, evasion was widespread and there were some brewers and tiplers trading without having entered into a recognisance. On 27 February 1561/2 the Corporation required the constables of each of the four wards to make a list of all persons occupied officially or unofficially in brewing or tipling (selling ale) and to consider, after consultation, which of them should be allowed to continue their trade. By 10 April the lists were completed and, from St George's Day next (23 April 1562), 139 innholders, brewers and honest citizens were authorised to brew or tiple ale, at a price set by the Lord Mayor, in the city and its suburbs on pain of the punishment decreed in the statute.[15]

The activities in alehouses continued to be a running sore in the side of the Corporation who continually had to review or revise the measures it had in force to control them. Even the regular visits to alehouses by constables had failed to prevent the excesses on Sundays and other holy days. A limitation of hours was the only answer and so, on 15 February 1571/2, the Corporation directed that none of the taverners, innholders, keepers of alehouses and tipling houses or victuallers in the city and suburbs should allow anybody into their premises to drink between 7 and 11 am on these days on pain of a fine of 6s 8d. Any person found drinking was to be fined 12d. Searchers were to be appointed to check that these restrictions were being properly applied.[16]

The real problem was the large number of alehouses in the city and the character of their keepers. The Council of the North, permanently established in York in 1561 as the monarch's representative in the north, wrote to the corporation on 12 April 1572 with a long list of requirements for stricter enforcement of the law in the city in which it and all its supporting staff were now living. Included was an item dealing with the excessive numbers of alehouses:

> Also that all superfluous alehowses be avoided and non to be suffered to be kepte at outesydes or in corners, but the same to be in the townes and open stretes thereof, and none suffered to kepe alehowses but suche as be of honest and good conversacon, an upon good bond, with sureties for kepyng of good order in the same; and that ye enquyre every moneth .... of the defalts of the said alehowses.[17]

From this it can be seen that some of the offending alehouses were more in the nature of booths in any hole and corner rather than permanent buildings.

A further problem in the conduct of alehouses would seem to have been the refusal of their proprietors to serve all customers. They were thus reminded by the Corporation on 11 Dec 1594 that all tiplers were required to 'serve all the Queen's people without refusal for their ready money'. The Corporation also took the opportunity at this time to remind the tiplers that they were not allowed to brew and neither should they keep in their houses any dice or cards nor allow anybody to play any unlawful games, for which they must presumably have brought in their own gaming implements.[18]

Ale or Beer is not directly mentioned in the 1552 Act, only in its role as a catalyst for disorder is its influence hinted at. This omission was covered in 1604 with an Act to restrain the inordinate Haunting and Tippling of Inns, Alehouses and other drinking places. While drinking houses were said to be for the 'Receit, Relief and Lodging of Wayfaring People travelling from Place to Place' and to supply victuals for those not able to do so for themselves, they were not intended for 'Entertainment and Harbouring of lewd and idle People to spend and consume their Time in lewd and drunken Manner.' In other words local customers who would only waste their time in drinking houses and drink to excess, were not to be encouraged.[19]

However well-meaning were the intentions of the 1604 Act, it continued to be ineffective. From the number of people who were willing to breach the law by brewing and keeping of an alehouse without a licence it can be seen that they were obviously profitable businesses. At a trial held in May 1606 19 persons were committed to prison for these offences. One of the offenders escaped from prison but on being recaptured said he 'cared not for my Lord Mayor a pin nor a fart'. He had, of course, known before he made this remark that his return to prison was inevitable and thus could afford to be rude.[20] On 17 November 1608 the Corporation made yet another of their regular attempts to ensure that only licensed alehouses were allowed to trade in the city. All alehouses were to be examined with a view to determining which were fit for their purpose and who were the fit persons to run them. It was reiterated that all alehouse keepers were to be bound by a recognisance and, further, that they were to be licensed at the Quarter Sessions.[21]

To try and remedy matters nation-wide the Privy Council wrote a letter to all civic authorities. It was dated 19 October but it was not until 19 November 1622 that it was laid before York Corporation who were required to suppress all alehouses 'not needful for the ease and conveniency of His Majesty's people'. The alehouses in the kingdom had grown to a very great number and, for the most part, were places of 'disorder and entertainment for lewd and ill governed persons'. The letter also included a requirement that the strength of ale and beer to be brewed and sold should be moderated. While this measure may have had a beneficial effect in controlling drunkenness it was really brought about by the currently high price and scarcity of corn.[22]

The 1552 Act had been designed to deal with the problems of drunkenness and social disorder occasioned by alehouses and was short on detail on a number of important points particularly the length of time for which a licence could be granted, although it was usually regarded as an annual requirement especially after a Royal proclamation in 1618. While any two justices had the power to grant licences they could do this on demand at any time of the year. After 1729 licences could only be granted at special licensing meetings of the bench of justices called the Brewster Sessions. Justices were restricted to granting licences only to alehouses within their division. This was designed to remedy the problem of licences being granted by justices living remotely from the applicants and 'may not be truly informed as to the Occasion or Want of such Inns or Common Alehouses, or the Characters of the Persons applying for Licences to keep the same'.[23]

Over a period of ten years starting in 1743 the Government, by a series of Acts, strengthened the power of the justices in an attempt to prevent the return to the earlier scenes of wickedness experienced in alehouses. Licences, which were not to be granted to grocers, chandlers or distillers, could only be held by keepers of public houses and for that one house only.[24] Licensed premises had to be of sufficient size for their purpose and justices were given summary powers of search. Licences were only to be granted at Brewster Sessions and at no other time of the year. The licensee, who had to a person of higher personal standing than previously, had to produce sureties of his good behaviour.[25] All previous statutes relating to the granting of licences were consolidated into a single Act in 1828. The Licensing Justices were to hold not more than eight and no less than four special sessions each year at which licences could be transferred from one holder to another (Transfer Sessions). The withdrawal of the financial bond or surety against good behaviour was surely an indication that the government had finally brought alehouses under control. Licences were subject to certain conditions: liquors were not be adulterated, all measures were to be properly stamped, drunkenness, disorderly conduct and unlawful gaming were not to be permitted on the premises, and the premises were not to be opened during Divine Services on Sundays, Good Friday and Christmas Day.[26]

Taverns

While in alehouses unruly behaviour was the major problem, in taverns, however, it seems to have been that there was no control over the quality of wines sold. Consequently in 1330 an Assize of Wine was introduced 'because there are more taverners in the realm than were wont to be, selling as well corrupt wines as wholesome because there was no punishment ordained for them as hath been for them that sell bread and ale, to the great hurt of the people'. It was decreed that wines were to be tested twice a year, at Easter and Michaelmas, and corrupt wines were to be poured away and the vessels containing them destroyed.[27]

Eventually taverns were to gain the same unwholesome reputation of the alehouse. The preamble of an Act of 1553 defined the situation at that time. The Act was primarily intended

> 'for avoiding the many Inconveniences, much evil Rule and common Resort of misruled persons used and frequented in many Taverns of late newly set up in a great number in Back-lanes, Corners and suspicious Places within the City of London and in divers other Towns and Villages within this Realm.'

As well as defining the prices of wines and the licensing authority the most Draconian provision of the Act was to severely limit the number of taverns or winesellers that could be authorised within the kingdom: London could have 40, York eight, Bristol six, Kingston-upon-Hull, Exeter, Norwich, Cambridge, Newcastle-upon-Tyne, Gloucester, Chester and Winchester four each, Westminster, Oxford, Lincoln, Shrewsbury, Salisbury, Hereford, Worcester, Southampton, Ipswich, Colchester three each. All other cities and towns were limited to two taverns each but the liberties of the Universities of Oxford and Cambridge were not to be impaired. York's position as the second city was thus well and truly established.[28]

York Corporation decided on 13 December 1553 to have a special meeting two days later to decide who would be the lucky eight who could keep taverns and retail wines in the city. Only two vintners were chosen, the remaining six were all merchants, including one alderman.[29] In 1567 13 vintners, one innholder and one alderman were licensed, the latter two individually and the 13 vintners in four partnerships.[30] However the situation had changed dramatically by 1583. By letters patent dated 4 May 1583 Walter Raleigh had been granted the privilege for 21 years to grant wine licences. Raleigh's deputies came to York on 10 August and requested the Mayor to have the vintners and taverners assembled to show by what authority they sold wines and kept taverns. In the event 10 vintners and one innholder in two partnerships were granted licences for their natural lives, and then for those of their wives and children.[31]

Sir Walter Raleigh, a royal patentee, continued to hold the privilege of granting wine licences until 1602. He was one of a number of people who had this right, starting with Edward Horsey in 1570. Licences could also be granted by the crown directly or through agents, which in 1757 was the Stamp Office. The law was changed in 1792 and the issuing of wine licences was transferred to the magistracy, who only had the powers to issue them to persons already licensed as alehouse keepers.[32]

Hostelries and Inns

The main purpose of an inn was to provide lodgings and refreshments for its guests. This refreshment could, of course, include ale which was to bring them within licensing legislation, although they were not included in the first licensing act in 1552. However, for them to fulfil their basic function they had to be readily identifiable in the streets of a town or city. On 20 October 1477 York Corporation required that all men and women keeping a hostelry in the city, its suburbs and precincts, should have a sign over their doors. If they did not they were liable to a fine, without any pardon, of 13s 4d, half of which was to go to Corporation funds and the other half to the sustenance of the pageant performed by the hostellers in the Mistery Play Cycle. To avoid this penalty all hostels without signs had to have them in place by the Feast of the Nativity next (25 December 1477).[33]

A generation later the requirement to have a sign on a hostelry seems to have been forgotten as, on 9 April 1503, the Corporation ordained 'that every person that keeps a hostelry within the city and suburbs must have a sign over their doors before the next feast of Ascension'. If the signs were not in place by the appointed time then a fine of 20s for 20 horses or 10s for 10 horses or under was imposed.[34] The next attempt to control innkeepers came in 1618, not as a result of local concerns, but on a national basis. In that year Sir Giles Mompesson was granted a patent by James I, who took a cut from the revenue received, authorising him and his agents to license inns providing accommodation throughout the country. Mompesson so abused this privilege that he was impeached by Parliament in 1621 who revoked his patent. Many hundreds of inns had been licensed in the three year period but after the revocation any inns which sold ale and beer were required to take out alehouse licences.[35] The York Innholders Ordinary of 23 May 1623 required that the keepers of inns and hostelries should not take any money unless they had a hanging sign at their doors.[36]

After 1828

The 1828 Alehouse Act repealed most of the previous licensing legislation and provided a consolidated basis for granting licences to sell beer, wine and spirits and for regulating all inns and alehouses. Control was, however, considerably jeopardised by the passing in 1830 of the Beerhouse Act, sometimes known as the Duke of Wellington's Beerhouse Act after the Prime Minister at the time. Its ostensible purpose was to discourage people from consuming spirits by making beer more readily available.

The preamble to the Act stated that it was 'for the better supplying of the public with beer in England ... greater facilities for the same thereof than are at present afforded by licences to keepers of inns, alehouses and victualling houses'. For the sum of two guineas any householder living in a house of a rateable value of more than £10 *per annum* could obtain a licence to sell beer, for consumption both on and off the premises, from the Excise, not from the justices. Permitted hours were from 4 am to 10 pm but, as with alehouses, the establishments had to remain closed during Divine Service on Sundays, Christmas Day and Good Friday. There was no test of suitability and the result, in York, was that within eight years of the passing of the Act there were 43 beerhouses in addition to all the other houses with full licences. Throughout the kingdom 23342 beer licences were issued in the first three months of the introduction of the Act.[37]

Having introduced this apparently well-intentioned Act, the Government were soon to regret it. All the old problems of disorderly alehouses that had been eliminated with so much time and effort returned. A special committee reported that 'considerable evils had arisen from the present management and conduct of beerhouses'. Unable to compete with the complete service offered by publicans with full licences, the beer house keepers resorted to adulterating the beer in order to undercut the prices offered elsewhere. To avoid turning away customers every kind of disorderly conduct was permitted on the premises. Worst of all, the opening of the beerhouses had no effect whatsoever on the sale of spirits. In an attempt to rectify the ills of the 1830 Act, a new Act was introduced in 1834 which separated 'off' and 'on' licences. The former were made more easy to obtain, with an annual fee of only one guinea, while on licences were only issued on payment of three guineas and on production of a certificate of good character signed by six rated householders from the parish in which the beer house was situated.[38]

Even these extra measures were not enough. A second amending Act was passed in 1840 to cover further abuses. Houses already licensed were not affected but for any new ones the applicant had to produce certificated proof that he was the real occupier of the house for which either an 'on' or 'off' licence was required. The 1830, 1834 and 1840 Beerhouse Acts were replaced in 1869 by the Wine and Beerhouse Act which now required the magistracy to give a 'certificate of permission' before an Excise licence could be obtained by a beerhouse. By these means the number of new beerhouse licences were limited but those houses already in existence prior to the Act were given protection. The magistrates could not refuse to renew certificates of these houses unless one or more of four provisions were not met: if the applicant failed to produce satisfactory evidence of good conduct, if the applicant's house was of a disorderly character or frequented by thieves and prostitutes, if the applicant had previously forfeited or had been disqualified from receiving a licence, or if he and his house were not qualified as required by the law. The full licences, to distinguish them from beerhouse licences, were now referred to as innkeeper's (later publican's) licences.[39] Three years later a new Intoxicating Liquor (Licensing) Act further consolidated and strengthened the licensing system and brought all drink retailers under the authority of the licensing magistrates.

There were still too many public houses and the licensing bench refused to renew licences whenever it thought it had sufficient grounds. On some occasions this was done without any compensation to the licensee and owner of the premises. To protect them, a new law, the Licensing Act 1904, required that compensation for closure, was to be paid from a levy raised from all licensed houses and breweries in existence in the locality at the time the Act became law, except for misconduct by or unfitness of the licensee and structural unsuitability of the premises. It was not to be levied on new licences.[40] By the time of the 1981 Licensing Act, which empowered the dispersal of the compensation fund, the national fund had accumulated five million pounds from 77 years of continuing levies. Half of this went to the Alcohol Education and Research Council, a quarter to the Licensed Trade Charity Trust, and the remaining quarter was to be distributed, on application, to the lineal successors of the original contributors. In the York area, one of 50 areas from which applications were invited, the possible claimants were a Northern brewery with 16 public houses in York, a national brewery with 35 public houses in the area, and the owner of a free house which had been in existence prior to 1904.[41] Licensing Acts and Acts affecting the sale of intoxicating liquors have continued to appear fairly frequently through the 20th century. The present control of licensing is covered by the Licensing Act 1964, a consolidating rather than an innovative statute, although there have been a number of extending Acts since that date.[42]

Numbers of Licensed Houses

As recently as 1939 the city of Norwich was able to boast
> There is a pub for every day of the year,
> and a church for every Sunday.

But even this was a mere shadow of its former self. In 1870 Norwich had 780 public houses, more than two for every day.[43] Even at its heyday York has never been able to emulate Norwich on either score. Before the reformation it had only 40 churches[44] and the maximum number of public houses, or rather licences issued, was not to exceed the total of 263 achieved in 1663.

Records of licences issued exists in various forms from 1552, the date of the first Act licensing alehouses, but not inns and taverns which may have been included in the totals if they were also beer sellers in addition to their prime function. But even before this date it is possible, from other records, to make an estimate of the number of alehouses, inns and brewers in the city. Of primary importance is the *Register of Freemen of the City of York* which starts in 1272.[45] Coupling this with additional names appearing in other records[46] made between 1297 and 1319 produces 47 brewers and 98 taverners, hostelers and innkeepers, some of whom also appear as brewers. There is no record of any alehouse keepers, but as has already been seen alehouses were low establishments with unsavoury reputations and their transient keepers would not have had the status to appear in documents and records. Thus the figure of 98 is liable to be a considerable underestimation.

From 1552 a *Book of Recognizances entered into by Brewers, Innholders, Tiplers and others* was kept. Three volumes cover the period 1552 to 1605. The first includes an initial listing of 58 licensees in Bootham, 41 in Monk and 92 in Walmgate Wards, a total of 191, but Micklegate Ward, on the west bank of the Ouse, is not included.[47] Allowing a figure of 40 for the missing licensees, the total for the city would be 231. This may well have been due to the first flush of enthusiasm for the new system and included many undesirable alehouse keepers for, ten years later, in 1562, there were only 139 'innholders, brewers and honest citizens' allowed to sell ale in the city, 44 in Bootham, 21 in Micklegate, 24 in Monk and 50 in Walmgate Wards.[48]

In 1596 the licensees were divided into 83 brewers, 103 tiplers (alehouse keepers) and 64 innholders, the latter two categories totalling to 167.[49] After another purge on unofficial establishments in 1608 the 156 alehouse keepers and 38 innholders, a total of 194, were licensed. From 1647 to 1663 a register of alehouse keepers was kept; the peak year was reached in the latter year when 263 were recorded. A gap in the records then occurs until 1754 and continues spasmodically until 1807.[50] Thereafter the granting of licences appear in the Quarter Sessions minutes[51] and later in the century in the Chief Constable's Annual

Reports. The current trend is bottoming out but there may be a reversal of this with the opening of the new style café-bars and large public houses on or near the ringroad.

Figure i - Licences in York

1552 - 231*	1656 - 209	1783 - 183	1838 - 214 (43)	1930 - 186 (25)
1563 - 139	1683 - 263	1787 - 169	1884 - 235 (39)	1941 - 170 (16)
1596 - 167	1754 - 230	1795 - 164	1896 - 243 (39)	1956 - 163 (11)
1608 - 194	1765 - 258	1822 - 173	1910 - 212 (32)	1966 - 155 (0)
1648 - 141	1775 - 222		1920 - 204 (31)	

The figures in brackets are beer house licences included in the total
* - estimated (see above)

While the year scale is not linear and there are several gaps for which information is not known certain trends can be seen in figure i. From 1562 to c.1700 there is a general increase in the number of licence holders followed by a decline to the beginning of the 19th century. The population of the city was to increase during the 19th century and the number of public houses and beer houses increased correspondingly to a peak around 1900. This was followed by a decline during the 20th century. At the first peak in 1700 the population of the city was about 10,000 so there was a drinking establishment at that time for every 39 citizens. The second peak, in 1900, coincides with the great survey of poverty in York made by Seebohm Rowntree. His study included factors which affected the conditions which governed the lives of the working classes in York. One of these factors was, naturally, the availability of alcohol. He found that the population of the city, 77,793 people, was served by 199 fully licensed houses, 37 beer houses and 102 'off' licences, that is one licensed establishment for every 230 persons. York was in an above average position amongst other towns for which Rowntree had obtained information. Heading the table with an outlet for every 167 persons was Northampton. At the other end, surprisingly, was Cardiff where the figure was 458, nearly a hundred more than Leeds at 362.

Rowntree was also concerned with the use of public houses and made a special survey of three public houses. One was an unnamed pub, 'a small dingy looking house in a narrow street in the heart of a slum district'. Behind the bar was a small and somewhat dirty parlour which could accommodate about 10 persons. No music was provided. This pub was watched for 17 consecutive hours on Saturday, 7 July 1900. During the day 550 people entered the pub, 258 men, 179 women and 113 children. Of the men 17 made return visits while 23 women did the same. While morning trade was light, never exceeding 18 people per hour the afternoon and evening saw double the usage with figures between 28 and 44 per hour. The peak usage was reached between 9 and 10 pm with 83 customers, while in the next hour 74 were recorded. Of the adults 278 entered singly, 90 in couples and 69 in parties of three or more. The observers were apparently able to identify all the pub's customers individually and found that of the 258 men entering the house 158 stayed for more than 15 minutes while only 44 of the 179 women remained for the same period.

Rowntree took these figures to indicate that this was a pub in which "social drinking" with an element of treating was carried on. This pub had two entrances, a fact that Rowntree obviously considered significant as he recorded, without giving the reason for his interest, the number of doors each of the 236 licensed houses had:

1 entrance	113 houses
2 entrances	111 houses
3 entrances	11 houses
4 entrances	1 house

Almost all the public houses had one or more parlours behind the bar, reserved for the use of regulars, who would spend the evening there, smoking, chatting, drinking and even placing illegal bets. Some pubs offered their customers the facilities to play dominoes, darts and, in some of the largest, billiards. Casual customers who merely dropped in for a quick glass of beer and the less respectable heavy drinkers were served in the taprooms or bars. Many of the new public houses in the city particularly catered for the dedicated "perpendicular" drinkers by providing no seats in the bar. Only about 12 public houses had music licences but there was music and singing of songs ranging from maudlin sentimentality to unreserved vulgarity, in many others, entertainment particularly enjoyed by young men, including soldiers, and women sitting round the room at small tables. Much public house drinking was by girls and, while this did not lead to much actual drunkenness, Rowntree had no doubt that many girls were there 'with a view to meet men for immoral purposes'. Nevertheless during his round of public houses Rowntree was struck very forcibly by their social attractiveness, their air of jollity and the absence of irksome restraint. This pointed to the need for the establishment of an equally attractive alternative on temperance lines.

Prior to the time of the survey, public houses in York had been largely used as meeting places for Football Clubs, Trade Unions, Friendly Societies, etc. but this function had been taken over by less expensive accommodation in coffee houses and elsewhere which was preferred by the club members. Nevertheless, with demand still in excess of the supply, public houses often had a club or other room available for these meetings.

In essence York was clearly a beer drinking town. In the experience of the police 80% of drunkenness was due entirely to beer. Most of the public houses were to be found in the old streets and crowded districts within the city walls, a fact which Rowntree attributed to York's previous role as a coaching centre. Although the city had in the 19th century expanded with the building of suburbs outside the walls there were comparatively few public houses in these new districts, even in those areas inhabited by the working class. This showed the unwillingness of the licensing magistrates to grant licences beyond the number actually required to supply the needs of the population in these districts.[52] In fact, new licences were rarely granted without the surrender of one or more elsewhere, a policy pursued for most of the 20th century.

Pub Signs and Names

The proverb 'A good wine needs no bush' stems from the ivy and vine leaves symbols of the god Bacchus which were used as the general sign for a tavern. The garland of foliage was attached to a projecting pole, known as an ale–stake, and displayed on the house where the alcoholic beverage was offered for sale. Public houses in earlier times could also be distinguished by lattices, painted red, placed across the glassless windows of the establishment.[53] It may well have been general signs of this sort which were required to be displayed on ale-houses throughout the kingdom by an Act in 1393 and on inns in York by an order of the Corporation in 1477. The more enterprising proprietor, seeking to attract customers from a particular stratum of society or, even, to ensure they could find his house again from a mass of others with no distinguishing features, would put up a sign containing features of particular significance to him or his patrons.

The earliest known sign in York is *The George,* mentioned as *Hospicium Georgii* in a will of 1455. Next is *The Bull,* referred to in a Corporation Ordinance of 27 April 1459 when 'it was ordained that, from this day forward, no aliens coming from foreign parts shall be lodged within the said city, liberties, or suburbs thereof, but only in the Inn of the Mayor and Commonalty, at the sign of *The Bull* in Conyng Street.'[54] *The Bull* gets another mention in the same year in the Ouse Bridge Masters' Accounts.[55] A badge of the Clarence family, it is one of several signs with a Royal or Heraldic origin. Others are *The Crowned Lion* (1483), the royal crest, *the Dragon* (1484), a badge of Edward IV and a Tudor supporter, and *The Boar* (1485), a badge of Richard III, *The Swan* (1487), a badge of Henry IV. These with *The Mitford* (1489), are among the earliest known in York. They are followed later by signs with a religious significance, such as *The Three Kings* (1554) and *The Star* (1580).

As alehouse and inn licences were granted to individuals rather than the house itself, the sign by which the house was known does not appear in the earliest civic records. The first references to pub signs are thus only to be found in passing references in a variety of documents. It is not until 1733 that a list of inns can be found and then only as the places where common carriers could be found. Thomas Gent, the eccentric printer, in his *Ancient and Modern History of Ripon* includes a seven page advertising supplement which contains 'A List of carriers who inn at York'. In this, 20 inns are mentioned of which only three are still in existence today.

The first comprehensive dated list still in existence, giving licensees and signs, was compiled in 1783. An earlier undated list includes four establishments in All Saints, North Street, parish, all called *The Chequer*, a general sign for a public house with no other name. In another contemporary, but again undated listing, three of these houses are included under *The Trellis*,[56] an indication that the two signs were, in fact, the same. The latter could originate in the red lattices displayed in the windows of early houses. *The Chequer* sign, however, was usually painted with a chess board and is said to originate in Pompeii and indicated that a game of draughts could be enjoyed there whilst consuming liquid refreshment. Later establishments without a sign appear under the name of *The Board*. An alternative explanation for *The Chequer* is an adaptation of the arms of the Earls of Warren and Surrey *chequy or and azure*. In 1795 there were still two public houses using the *Trellis* sign, one in Goodramgate and the other in Coffee Yard but all others have signs particular to the house, even if many are duplicated, triplicated or more. There were at this time nine Blue Bells, nine Bay Horses and seven Punch Bowls in the city![57]

Still extant is the Ordinary of the Innholders' Company which includes a list of innkeepers who became free of the company between 1785 and 1824. Against the name of each person is recorded the name of the establishment of which he was landlord so providing another useful record of pubs in the city in this period. Street directories start in 1798 and continue at frequent intervals until 1975 and contain lists of pub names.[58] Licensing court records provide another obvious source, and specially valuable are the registers of alehouse and beer house licences which cover the period from c.1890 to c.1969.[59]

One particularly thorough record is a survey of all publican's and beerhouses' licences which was compiled by the Chief Constable in February 1902 on the instruction of the magistrates who were concerned with the over provision of licensed premises in the city. This was, perhaps coincidentally, just prior to the passing of the Licensing Act 1904 which improved the chances of obtaining closures of public houses by creating a compensation scheme for their owners and licensees. The Chief Constable's survey included the name and address of the owner, the name of the licensee, whether the house was free or tied, the extent of sleeping accommodation for family and travellers, the provision of stabling, the number of public entrances (a statistic which Seebohm Rowntree also considered to be of relevance), the rateable value, the number of times the licence had been transferred in the last five years, and the distances to the two nearest licensed premises. Finally under 'General Remarks' the Chief Constable commented on the suitability or otherwise of the house, the provision of urinal and WC facilities where these were sub-standard, as well as other factors which might influence the decision to oppose the renewal of the licence. He drew special attention to eight ale houses and five beer houses about which he was particularly concerned. Only two of these, *The Beeswing* and *The Minster Inn*, are still in existence today, both, however, in new premises.[60]

Over 1,350 names for inns, taverns, alehouses, beer houses, coffee houses and public houses have been identified over the centuries in York and the villages it has more recently embraced (see the directory which follows) but that is not to imply that this is the number of separate establishments which have existed. Many houses have changed their names for a variety of reasons over the centuries setting the precedent for the present fashion adopted by national chains. This type of change is made, without any reference to local or historical tradition and is made to promote a national image by having standard names wherever in the country they appear. This modern tendency has been named by one writer as the 'Great Pub Name Scandal'. He was of the opinion that:

> Pub names are as intimately woven into the cultural fabric of Britain as the Crown Jewels. Yet every week another ancient inn falls victim to what is surely the naffest and smuttiest of all the Nineties' cultural trends. Can nothing be done to deter the smirking philistines who run their big breweries from their Orwellian mission to erase all traces of local History from the pubs they control?[61]

In York, examples of this are *The Firkin and Phalanx, Edwards* and *Scruffy Murphy's*. On a national scale even such treasures as *The Bat and Ball* at Hambledon, Hampshire, the centre of English cricket in the 18th century, has recently been renamed *Natterjacks*.

Criticism of this practice of rebranding pubs with trendy names which destroyed the establishments links with local history was made by a Government Minister, Chris Smith, the Labour Culture Secretary, in 2000. On the floor of the House of Commons he voiced his fears and hoped that breweries would bear in mind the unique, historic role that public houses have 'and think twice before destroying a link with the past'. He thought that the pub's regulars and the local community should be consulted before any renaming took place. Eighteen months previously a private member's bill had been prepared which would have required both consultation and planning permission.[62] At the same time York Civic Trust was bemoaning the opening in Grape Lane of the *Slug and Lettuce* 'a most unfortunate name. Slugs are hardly the sort of creatures to command admiration'.[63] CAMRA were much more pragmatic about the whole thing. 'If it comes to a pub closing or changing its name to *Rat and Parrot* we would rather the latter. Any pub is better than no pub at all.'[64]

Nearly 300 years ago a previous call had been made by *The Spectator* for the government to appoint an official to control the more absurd naming of pubs. 'Our streets are filled with blue Boars, black Swans and red Lions: not to mention Pigs and Hogs in Armour'.[65] None of these signs are as uncouth as some of today's outlandish coinings and most have good heraldic precedent to support them. If heraldry can admit animals in non-natural colours then why not also as pub names, especially as the heraldic reference would have been a tribute to the owner of the building, the lord of the manor, or some other dignitary of local importance.

So opposition to changing pub names is of long standing as also is the practice of changing names. The earliest known sequence in York starts with *The Bull* in Coney Street, first known in 1459. By 1506 it had become *The Rose.* The need to change names can arise in many ways; historic events, change of licensee, adoption of a nickname as the permanent name, a successful racehorse with local support, an addition of a prefix to an original name to avoid confusion with another nearby establishment, or the need for a change of image, are just a few of the possibilities.

Of historic events success in battle gave rise in York to seven pubs with the name *Lord Nelson* (one sometimes called *Admiral Nelson*). Also during the Napoleonic Wars several pubs took the name *Wellington*, amending it as he rose through the ranks of nobility to *Lord Wellington, Marquis of Wellington*, and finally *Duke of Wellington*. In one case, some years after his death *The Wellington*, in Alma Terrace, displaced another general, *Sir Colin Campbell*, a junior office in the Peninsular War but, significantly, in command of the Highland Brigade at the Battle of the Alma. The *Sun Inn*, in Tanner Row, having changed its name to Admiral *Sir Sidney Smith* by 1818, reverted to its original name, shortly after his death in 1840. The accession of a new monarch gave an opportunity for a display of affection and loyalty to the crown, particularly to Queen Victoria, who eventually had six public houses using her name.

Licensees became attached to a particular name. When Christopher Barthorpe, the City Huntsman and licensee of a pub just outside Monk Bar (later the *Bay Malton, The Bay Horse*, and now, *Corner Stones*) moved to *The Old George* in Pavement he took the name *Hare and Hounds* with him. After he left that pub it reverted to its earlier name. *The Barleycorn* in Walmgate, previously the *Hope and Anchor*, was renamed c.1838 *The Full Moon* by the landlord, Thomas Moon. It was also known more familiarly as *The Moon*. *The Oddfellows Arms* in Hungate had its name changed to *The Whale Fishery* c.1843 when Christopher Bean, who had been a harpooner in the polar regions, became the licensee there. A similar situation occurred in St Sampson's Square when a pub known variously as *The Barrel Churn* (1783), *The Cooper* (1788), *The Barrel* (1818) became *The Mail Coach* (c.1834) when a mail coach guard took over the pub. It had a fifth change of name in 1970 when it finally (?) became *The Roman Bath* after a refurbishment which opened up the remains of the Roman bathhouse in its cellars.

Pubs often have nicknames by which they are familiarly known by their regulars. In time they become adopted as the official name, as in the case of *The Corner Pin*, Tanner Row which, in 1985, formally changed its name from *The Unicorn* to the alternative name by which it had been known since at least 1804, despite a short period between 1838 and 1841 when it was called *The Oddfellows Arms*. On the first Ordnance Survey map of the city made in 1852 there is a pub in Museum Street called *The Gun*. This was in fact its familiar name. Its proper name was *The Cannon* and one can imagine that the sign over the door portrayed just a piece of ordinance without any wording. When the military officer was making his survey he must have asked a passer-by what its name was so that he could include it in his notes for eventual recording on the finished map. Not knowing the importance of accuracy in these matters the passer-by must have answered "*The Gun*, of course", the name he habitually used. The surveyor, with no reason to doubt the accuracy of this information, has chronicled the nickname officially for posterity. One cannot imagine that *The Putrid Arms*, in Skeldergate in an 1818 street directory, was anything other than a nickname, but as there was a large number of pubs in the street at that time it is difficult to work out its real name.

A lucky flutter on a racehorse by the landlord or regulars of a pub must have been another reason for a house to change its name. Before the successes of Mr Orde's bay mare in the Ascot Gold Cup in 1842 and a hat-trick of wins in the Doncaster Gold Cup between 1840 and 1842, *The Beeswing* in Hull Road was called *The Black Swan*. Not all the breweries' sign painters, however, have realised the origin of the name and have featured an insect in their artwork. *The Marcia* in Front Street, Acomb (since 1998 *The Poacher*) was previously called *The Square and Compasses* but got a change of name after the success of Mr Garforth's grey mare, Marcia, in the King's Plate at York in August 1802. In fact, an alternative name for the pub was *The Grey Mare*. It has been suggested that a public house in Lawrence Street, previously *The St Nicholas* and then *The Burns*, got its present name *Tam O'Shanter* after the winner of the Chester Cup in 1876. However, the pub already had this name by 1855 so it is more likely that it refers to the well known poem by Robert Burns. In fact it is listed in the Chief Constable's 1902 report as *Burns' Hotel,* with its more usual name listed as an alternative.

Perhaps the simplest reason for changing a name and the simplest way of achieving it is by the addition of a prefix like 'Old' or 'Original'. In all 21 pubs have names that begin with 'Old' while 'Original' is limited to one, *The Original Duke's Head* in Aldwark. *The Duke of York* opened in or before 1823 and was occasionally known as *The Duke's Head* after the painting on the sign. Sometime after 1830 the landlord, Robert Merrington, moved next door and called his new house *The Old Duke's Head* as another pub had been opened in the original premises with the name *The Duke's Head.* As long as there was this slight difference between the names there was a minimum of confusion but the landlord of the original premises occasionally called his house *The Original Duke's Head* or even *The Old*

Duke's Head on the grounds, presumably, that the house he occupied was, in fact, the original public house with that name even if he was not a lineal successor of the first licensee. Matters were finally resolved when *c*.1860 *The Old Duke's Head* closed enabling the survivor to revert to the simpler form of *The Duke's Head*.

A change of name to get a change of image is perhaps a modern phenomenon. *The Great Northern*, George Hudson Street, originally a hotel, was in 1966 given a make-over and re-opened as *The Pageant* aiming at a young clientele who liked loud music and flashing lights. Disturbances and noise caused the landlord to lose his licence early in 1984. The owners, after another face-lift, re-opened it later in the year under the original historic name with the pledge that it would be no haven for trouble-makers and there would be no juke box or disco. A later change of heart and a new name, *Merlin's*, have restored something of the ambience of *The Pageant* without the troubled reputation that it had then.

There are many other reasons for pubs having changed their names and pubs, of course, will continue to change their names but, it is to be hoped, for reasons other than the promotion of a national brand. Pubs are part of the fabric of a community and their names should reflect their place in that community. If it is necessary to alter their names, careful consideration and consultation should be undertaken before any change is implemented.

NOTES

1. Monckton H.A. *A History of English Ale &Beer* (1966) pp 32-36.
2. Collins F. *Register of the Freemen of the City of York Vol 1* 1272-1558, Surtees Society 94 (1897).
3. Attreed LC *The York House Books 1461-1490* Vol 1 (1991) p. xi.
4. Tringham NJ (ed.) *Charters of the Vicars Choral of York Minster* (1993);
    Yorkshire Archaeological Society Record Series 148, p. 210.
5. Collins *op. cit.* in note 2, p. 3.
6. Prestwich M *York Civic Ordinances 1301* (1976) University of York Borthwick Paper 49 p. 28.
7. Johnson AF & Rogerson M *Records of Early English Drama: York* (1979) pp. 25,26.
8. For instance YCA B20 f 124.
9. Delderfield ER *British Inn Signs and their Stories* (1972) p. 14.
10. 11 Henry VII c2 1495
11. 5/6 Edward VI c.25.
12. YCA B20 f 102.
13. YCA E44 1552-1564.
14. YCA B20 ff 105v, 124.
15. YCA B23 ff 48v, 50v.
16. YCA B24 f 223v.
17. YCA B25 f 5v.
18. YCA B31 ff. 95v, 96.
19. 1 James I c.9.
20. YCA B33 f. 16v.
21. York City Library Ms Y352/EF.
22. YCA B24 f 253.
23. 2 George II c. 28.11;
    Monckton H A *A History of the English Public House* (1969) p 37.
24. 17 George 11 c.17 & 19.
25. 24 George II c.31 s.9; 26 George II c.31.
26. 9 George IV.
27. French R V *Nineteen Centuries of Drink in England: A History (n.d.* but 1884) pp106/7.

28. 7 Edward VI c.5.
29. YCA B21 ff 18/18v.
30. YCA B24 f. 252v.
31. YCA B28 f. 107.
32. Gibson J & Hunter J *Victuallers' Licences* (1997) p. 7.
33. Attreed L A(ed.) *York House Books 1461-1490* (1991) p. 122;
    YCA B f. 68.
34. YCA B9 f. 2.
35. Gibson J & Hunter J *Victuallers' Licences* (1997) p. 6.
36. YCA E55.
37. Peacock AJ *York 1900 to 1914 (n.d.* but c. 1992) p. 26;
    Monckton HA A *History of the English Public House* (1969) p. 79.
38. Monckton HA A *History of the English Public House* (1969) pp. 80/90.
39. Monckton, HA A *History of English Ale and Beer* (1966) p. 178;
    Monckton, HA *A History of the English Public House* (1969) p. 83.
40. Monckton HA *A History of the English Public House* (1969) p. 102.
41. *Yorkshire Evening Press* 20 March 1983.
42. Information from the York Licensing Justices' Clerk.
43. Young JR *The Inns and Taverns of Old Norwich* (1975) p. 7.
44. Hutchinson J & Palliser D *York* (1980) p. 53.
45. Collins F *Register of the Freemen of the City of York Vol 1* Surtees Society 96 (1897).
46. Stell P *Yorkshire Medieval Biographical Data-bank.*
47. YCA E44.
48. YCA B23 f 50v.
49. Cooper TP *Some Old Inns of York* (1929) pp 20-29.
50. YCA K68 & 69.
51. YCA M30/39.
52. Rowntree BS *Poverty, a study of Town Life* (1902) pp. 307-326.
53. Hill B *Inn-signia* (1949) pp. 9/10.
54. Drake F *Eboracum* (1736) p 331.
55. YCA Ouse Bridge Masters Accounts C83 i8 membrane 3 *dorso.*
56. YCA K69.
57. YCA K69.
58. YCA E55.
59. YCA Acc. 189.
60. YCA Acc. 258.
61. *Times 24* August 1996.
62. *Times* 11 July 2000.
63. *York Civic Trust Annual Report* 1997-98 p. 17.
64. *Times* 11 July 2000.
65. *Times* 14 July 2000.

The Directory of York Pubs

The qualification for an appearance in the directory is that the pub concerned has displayed a sign indicating that it, or its proprietor, has or has had at some time, a licence of some sort allowing the sale of intoxicating liquors to members of the public. The pubs are, naturally, listed in alphabetical order but certain conventions have had to be observed to facilitate this.

1. The definite article with which most names start has been omitted, although within the entry itself, if a pub is mentioned, it is included. There is one exception and that is if the pub name has been antiqued by turning 'The' into 'Ye'.

2. Words such as, Inn, Hotel, Tavern etc., although included in the heading in bold type, have been ignored in deciding the alphabetical order of listing. After the pub name the next word in deciding the position of the entry in the list is the street name.

3. Street numbers have, in general, been omitted. Only if there were two pubs with the same name in the same street have numbers been included to distinguish them. In these cases the numbering system in use at the time has been used and might not relate to the present odd/even system that has been gradually adopted over the years to replace the earlier consecutive system.

4. Abbreviations have been alphabeticised as if the abbreviated word is written in full i.e. St Peter's Vaults will appear in the directory before The Snickleway.

Other conventions observed in the compilation of the directory are:

1. The italicising of pub names within an entry. This indicates a cross reference and avoids the tedious repetition of 'q.v.'.

2. Each entry includes previous and later names for a particular house but is mainly concerned with the history of the pub while it had a particular name. Thus to find the full history a number of entries may have to be consulted.

3. In general, ownership of the pub by an individual or a brewery, has not been included as this would have produced, especially in more recent years where some pubs have changed hands many times, longer and more complicated entries.

4. Some pubs in earlier centuries were often identified only by the name of the licensee i.e. Widow Soulsby's or Mother Margaret's, rather than by its sign. In these cases if the sign is not known the pub is not included.

5. References are cited in abbreviated form within the entries i.e. (Davison p. 32). The full detail of the source, if required, can be found at the end of the directory.

6. ¶ after the name of a public house indicates that it is illustrated in the picture section.

7. If an explanation of the choice of sign is offered, it is included under the first reference to the particular name.

18 Cert, Gillygate
Previously *The Bay Horse*. given this name in 2003 at a time when its near neighbour, the former *Waggon and Horses*, also lost its former long-standing identity.

Abbey Park Hotel, Blossom Street
Previously the Park Hotel it was renamed in 1953 (Dir). A residents' licence was granted on 10 May 1953 followed by a full 'on' licence on 25 November 1964 (YCA Acc. 189).

Ackhorne, St Martin's Lane
Previously *The Acorn*, it reverted to its original name when it reopened after refurbishment in 1993 (YEP 29 12 1993).

Acomb Hotel, Green Lane
Opened in 20 June 1940 (YCA Acc. 189), its licence transferred from *St Peter's Vaults,* Walmgate 8 February 1939 (YEP 7 4 1939). The licence of *The King William IV,* Layerthorpe, was also surrendered in consideration of this transfer (YCA Acc. 189).

Acorn, St Martin's Lane ¶
In 1783 a house and yard was purchased by John Hill, owner of *The Golden Ball* in Fetter Lane, who converted it into a public house called *The Ackhorne* (Johnson p. 8.) Later it was given the more conventional spelling of *The Acorn*. In 1902 it had three bedrooms, all occupied by the family, no sleeping accommodation for travellers, a club room upstairs, a smoke room, a dram shop and two kitchens, one private but food could be supplied from the other if requested. There was only a WC used by both the customers and the family (CC). In 1993 it was refurbished and re–opened under its original name (YEP 29 12 1993).

Addison's Hotel, Davygate
Opened as a lodging establishment by James Addison in August 1838 (YG 25 8 1838). Later *St Helen's Hotel* and then *Clarence Hotel.*

Adelphi Hotel, George Hudson Street ¶
A temperance hotel in 1851, it was built on the site of an earlier public house, *The Royal Oak,* by 1647 *The Ship* (Johnson p. 7). It was sold by tender in 1880 and gained its licence soon afterwards (YG 27 3 1880). In 1902 it boasted 23 bedrooms, a coffee room, a commercial room, a billiard room, a smoke room, a bar, a vault, a private room and a kitchen. It was considered to be a good commercial hotel and suitable for the business of a licensed victualler (CC). Renamed *The Railway King* in 1971 (YEP 15 12 1971) and later *Edwards,* then *Reflex.*

Admiral Hawke, Walmgate ¶
Opened by 1795 (YCA K69) and named after Edward Hawke, 1st Lord Hawke, (1705–1781), whose fleet was victorious against the French at Quiberon 1759. He entered the Navy as a volunteer in 1720 and gained the rank of Admiral of the Fleet in 1768. He was First Lord of the Admiralty from 1766 to 1771. In 1902 it had six bedrooms, two of which were not furnished and another two used by travellers, a sitting room, a smoke room, a dram shop and two kitchens, one private but food could be supplied from the other if required (CC). It closed 3 February 1951 (YCA Acc. 189). It was also known as *The Lord Hawke* (YG 8 1 1831) and was mistakenly called *The Admiral Oak* in 1825 (YCA F30A).

Admiral Nelson, Walmgate
See *The Lord Nelson.*

Admiral Oak, Walmgate
A mistake for *The Lord Hawke* in the official licensing records in 1825 (YCA F30A).

Ainsty, Boroughbridge Road
Built by John J. Hunt in the 1930s (CAMRA). First appearance in a street directory 1934. Transferred from the Tadcaster Licensing District 1 April 1937 on the extension of city boundaries (YCA Acc. 189).

Albert Inn, George Street ¶
A beerhouse, only 12 feet wide on the corner of Albert Street, from which it got its name. Opened by 1872 (Dir). In 1902 it had an attic, a bedroom, a sitting room upstairs, a smoke room, a taproom, a serving bar, a cellar and a private kitchen. The smoke room was very small, it was short of room upstairs and there was only one WC for the family and the customers who had to pass through the kitchen to get to it and the urinal (CC). Closed in 1903 (YG 7 3 1903), the renewal of its licence having been refused at the Brewster Sessions that year. An appeal against its closure was dismissed on 9 April 1903 (YCA Acc. 189). Purchased by York Industrial and Equitable Society in 1904 for £470 and converted into a shop. (Co-op p. 178.)

Albert, Skeldergate
Previously *The Bay Horse* but by 1872 had changed to this name (Dir). In 1902 it had four bedrooms all used by the family and could not accommodate travellers. There was a large club room upstairs, a smoke room, a bar, a taproom, a cellar and a private kitchen from which refreshments could be supplied. It was particularly used by carriers especially on Saturdays (CC). It was referred for compensation on 26 February 1937 and closed on 14 July 1938 (YCA Acc. 189).

Albion, Goodramgate
A beer house next to Albion Iron and Brass Factory just inside Monk Bar. Opened by 1857 (Dir) and sold 1859 (YG 17 12 1859).

Albion, Parliament Street
Previously *The Yorkshireman*. Changed to this name by 1841 (Dir). In 1843 it advertised that its beds were 'good and well aired' (Dir 1843 Advt). When it was offered for sale in 1877 there was a brewery attached (YG 1 10 1877). Closed by 1881 (Dir).

Albion, St Andrewgate
Previously *The Brewers Arms* and then *The Anglesey Arms*. Changed to this name by 1867 (Dir), closed by 1872 (Dir).

Alexandra, Market Street
Previously *The Horse and Jockey* and *The Turf Tavern*. Changed to this name by 1876 in honour of Princess Alexandra, wife of Albert Edward, Prince of Wales. In 1902 it had seven large bedrooms, four of which were set apart for travellers, a dining room, a sitting room and kitchen, from which food could be supplied, upstairs a large concert room and a dram shop. The kitchen was, in fact, inconveniently located on the second floor. The whole of the ground floor was devoted to customers (CC). It was closed on 4 June 1937, its licence voluntarily surrendered on the transfer of the licence of *The Bell Hotel*, Micklegate to *The Imperial*, Crichton Avenue (YCA Acc. 189).

Alice Hawthorn, Wheldrake

In 1857 John Boulton, shoemaker and carrier, was selling beer from his premises in the village. He was followed by two other members of the family, William and Alice. By 1896, when William was the proprietor, the establishment had gained a name (Dir). It is generally accepted that the Alice Hawthorn referred to was a bay filly, by Muley-Moloch out of Rebecca. During her racing career of seven seasons she won 52 races out of 71 starts including the Great Ebor Handicap on the Knavesmire in 1844. However Alice Hawthorn was also the pen-name of Septimus Winner (1827-1902), an American songwriter and composer, responsible for such works as *Maryland, My Maryland*. The pub had ceased to exist by September 1999 when it was reported that it had been closed for more than four months (YEP 7 9 1999).

Alma Tavern, Alma Terrace

Opened by 1872 (Dir) and closed by 1885 (Wilson pp. 7/8). The name of a river in the Crimea and the scene of a battle during the Crimean War.

Anchor, First Water Lane (King's Staith)

For sale 1766 (YCo 18 3 1766), mentioned in 1828 (Dir). By 1841 it was called *The Crown and Anchor*.

Anchor, North Street Postern without

Mentioned 1834 (YG 19 4 1834).

Anchor, Low Ousegate (Ouse Bridge)

Previously *The Golden Anchor*, mentioned 1770 (Benson p. 167), 1778 (YCo 25 8 1778), and 1783, 87, 95 (YCA K69, Cooper2 p. 45).

Anchor, Paragon Street

Mentioned 1829 (YG 8 Aug 1829).

Anchor, Queen's Staith ¶

Previously *The Queen's Staith Inn*, it had gained this name by 1885 (Dir). In 1902 it had five bedrooms, three of which were used by lodgers, a smoke room, a dram shop, a cellar, a sitting room and a kitchen from which food could be supplied if desired. It was described as 'a very old property, the dram shop is on a level with Queen's Staith and is never used, and is sometimes flooded. The entrance to the house is by means of a number of steps leading to the second floor. There is only one WC for the use of the customers and family; lodgers taken in' (CC). Closed 10 October 1907 on expiry of licence (YCA Acc. 189), compensation of £425 paid (YG 9 3, 15 6, 20 7 1907). Purchased by the Methodists to use as a Men's Institute and caretaker's house for the Skeldergate Mission (VCH p. 410).

Angel, Coney Street

Mentioned 1697 (Fiennes p. 76).

Angel, Goodramgate

To be let (YCo 24 5 1748). A privileged place [in the Liberty of St Peter] any person may carry on business there without being free of the city (YCo 27 2 1750). Mentioned 1770 (Benson p. 167).

Angel, Walmgate ¶
Earliest mention 1818 (Dir). In 1902 it had three bedrooms, including accommodation for four travellers, a sitting room upstairs, a smoke room, a taproom, a serving bar, a private kitchen, from which food could be supplied, and scullery. It shared its back yard with an adjoining shop (CC). Closed 3 February 1951 after compensation paid (YCA Acc. 189).

Anglers' Arms, Goodramgate ¶
Previously *The Square and Compass*, and *The Board* or *Cooper's Vaults*. Changed to this name by 1896 by Edward Staines who by this time was the owner of *Cooper's Vaults* (Dir). In 1902 it had five bedrooms, all used by the family, a sitting room upstairs, a smoke room, a dram shop, another sitting room and a private kitchen from which food could be supplied. There was a private WC upstairs which was not available for customers (CC). Renamed *The Snickleway Inn* 1994. A Grade II listed building (CAMRA2).

Anglesey Arms, St Andrewgate
Previously *The Brewers Arms*, and later *The Albion*. It was using this name 1846 to 1858 (Dir), public house brewery 1850 (Davison p. 38).

Arrows, Gillygate
The Sign of the Arrows 1843 (YG 10 10 1843). An alternative name for *The Three Arrows*.

Artichoke, Micklegate
Earliest mention in 1783 (YCA K69). Last mention in 1826 (YCA F31). In 1795 it was recorded as *The Harty Chalk* (YCA K69). Later *The Barefoot.*

Bacchus, Bar Lane, Micklegate
A colloquial name for *The Jolly Bacchus.*

Bar 38, Coney Street
A café bar opened 4 August 2000 (YEP 4 8 2000)

Bar Hotel, Micklegate ¶
Building purchased 12 Sept 1861 by James Wake who opened it as a hotel (Johnson p. 10). In 1902 this was considered to be a good suitable house for the business of a licensed victualler. It had 10 bedrooms, five of which were for travellers, three smoke rooms and a bar. Other refreshments besides drink could be supplied if required (CC). By 1996 its name was changed to *Scruffy Murphy's* (Thomson). Later *The Micklegate.*

Barefoot, Micklegate ¶
Previously *The Artichoke*, changed to this name in 1827 (YCA F31). Also known as *The Horse Barefoot* 1841 (Dir). Named after Mr Watt's chestnut colt, Barefoot, by Tramp out of Rosamund, which won the St Leger in 1823. (Fairfax p. 501). A beerhouse in 1861 (Dir) but it had an ale licence by 1902 when all the rooms were described as being very small. They comprised three bedrooms, all used by the family, a bar, a snug, a kitchen, a cellar and a back kitchen. Customers could be supplied with food if they required it (CC). It closed on 30 September 1927 having been referred for compensation on 9 March 1927 (YCA Acc. 189, YEP 16 7 1927). See also *The Bear's Paw.*

4

Barge, Terry Avenue

A former grain barge, laid out as an inn and night club, in existence by 1979 (YEP 24 4 1979). For sale March, sunk August 1984 (YEP 22 3, 6 8 1984). Refloated and towed to Naburn Lock where it was burnt 1985 (YEP 3 10 1985). Replaced by *The Flying Dutchman.*

Barley Sheaf, Nunnery Lane

A beerhouse, previously *The Golden Ball,* it was using this name as an alternative to *The Wheatsheaf* between 1840 when Thomas Procter, its licensee, advertised himself as a wholesale and retail brewer 1840 (YG 29 2 1840), and 1848 (Dir). Next *The Crown* and then *The Wheatsheaf* again.

Barleycorn, Bedern

Earliest mention 1818 (Dir), last mention 1848 (Dir).

Barleycorn, Coppergate

Previously *The Blue Bell,* changed to this name by 1801 (YH 10 10 1801). Closed and purchased by York Corporation 1900 (YG 8 9 1900). The licence had lapsed by September 1901 (YCA Acc. 189).

Barleycorn, Davygate

Mentioned in 1818 (Dir). By 1822 it had become *The Wheatsheaf* (YCA F30A).

Barleycorn, Walmgate

Earliest mention 1795 (YCA K69). Name changed to *The Hope and Anchor* by 1830 (Dir) later *The Full Moon.*

Barrack Tavern, Fulford Road ¶

A public house since 1801 (Wilson p. 3) so named because it was adjacent to the Cavalry Barracks built in 1796. In 1880 the government were considering requisitioning it as a site for an artillery barracks (Avis p. 53). In 1902 it had five bedrooms, occupied by the family, three attics which were not in use, a drawing room , a smoke room, a bar parlour, a bar and a private kitchen from which food could be supplied to customers. Renamed *The Fulford Arms* in 1976 (YEP 9 6 1976).

Barrack Tavern, Lowther Street

Previously called *The Blacksmiths' Arms* but by 1852, when it was offered for sale, it had gained this name because it was near the Militia Stores Depot (YG 24 12 1852, 1852 OS). The property included a brewhouse when offered for sale in 1853 (YG 1 1 1853).

Barrel Inn, Little Blake Street

Mentioned only in 1823 (Dir). TP Cooper suggests this was an earlier name for *The Shakespeare Tavern* (Cooper p. 79) and certainly there are two entries for Robert Smith who is shown as landlord of both establishments. However there is another entry for *The Barrel* showing John Lund as licensee.

Barrel, St Sampson's Square
Previously *The Barrel Churn* and *The Cooper*. It had gained this name by 1818 (Dir). By 1830 it had changed to *The Coach and Horses* (Dir) and later it was renamed *The Mail Coach* and eventually *The Roman Bath*.

Barrel(l), Walmgate
An alternative name for *The Golden Barrel* 1822–28 (YCA F30A, F31), 1902 (CC) and 1935 (YCA Acc. 189).

Barrel Churn, St Sampson's Square
Earliest mention 1785, name changed to *The Cooper* by 1795 (YCA K69). Later *The Coach and Horses, The Mail Coach* and *The Roman Bath.*

Barstow Arms, Askham Bryan
Mentioned 1872, named after the branch of the Barstow family who lived in the village and who had, in 1862, built two almshouses near the church. Still using this name in 1909 but shortly afterwards changed to *The Nag's Head* (Dir).

Bay Horse, Aldwark
Earliest mention 1822 (YCA F30A). Later a beer house, TP Cooper suggests this was the eventual name for a public house previously called *The Leopard* and *The Spotted Dog* (Cooper p. 77). However in 1843 both *The Bay Horse* and *The Leopard* existed in Aldwark with separate licensees while the latter had a continued existence for another 15 years (Dir). Application for a spirit licence made in 1846 but refused (YG 29 8 1846) when it apparently closed.

Bay Horse, Askham Bryan
Listed in Ainsty licensing records from 1822 to 1828 (YCA F30A, F31).

Bay Horse, Blossom Street ¶
The building had become an inn by 1748 (RCHME III p. 65b). It is probably named after Lord Rockingham's bay horse, Bay Malton, which won a Great Subscription Race at York in August 1766. Between 1862 and 1874, was owned by the Institute of the Blessed Virgin Mary (Gregory p. 1). When it was offered for sale in 1863 the premises included a brewhouse (YG 21 2 1863). In 1902 the Chief Constable thought it was a neat clean house, suitable for its purpose. It had four bedrooms, all used by the family, a club room, a small sitting room, two smoke rooms, a bar, a cellar, a small sitting room and a private kitchen (CC). It was restored by John Smith's architects in 1969 (Nuttgens p. 73). A Grade II listed building (CAMRA2).

Bay Horse, Coney Street
Earliest mention 1746 (YCo 18 11 1746). Last mention 1750 (YCo 27 11 1750).

Bay Horse, Elvington
Mentioned in 1823, but by 1840 had become *The Grey Horse* (Dir).

Bay Horse, Gillygate
Earliest mention 1822 (YCA F30A). In 1902 it was described as a market house, suitable for carrying on the business of a licensed victualler. It had four bedrooms, two of which were used for travellers, a smoke room, a kitchen, a bar as well as a 'living' kitchen. Food could be supplied if required (CC). Later *The 18 Cert.*

Bay Horse, Goodramgate
Earliest mention 1818. By 1849 it had become *The Square and Compasses* and by 1851 *The Joiners' Arms* (Dir).

Bay Horse, Hungate
Mentioned 1858 (Dir). An alternative name for *The Cotherstone*.

Bay Horse, Low Jubbergate, [Market Street]
Mentioned in 1784 when John Hardcastle, the landlord, moved to *The White Swan* (YCo 1 6 1784). Last mentioned 1846 (Dir) although it had been offered for sale in 1843 (YG 27 5 1843).

Bay Horse, Low Petergate
Earliest mention 1783 (YCA K69). Closed in 1864 when site acquired by Merriman for a pawnbroker's shop (YEP 2 9 1955).

Bay Horse, Main Street, Fulford ¶
Earliest mention 1825 (Briddon p. 26). Rebuilt before 1930. Completely refurbished 1982 (YEP 20 2 1982). Also known as *The Horse*.

Bay Horse, Main Street, Heslington
Previously *The Robin Hood, The Horse* and *The Chestnut Horse*, gained this name by 1840 (Dir). Later *The Charles XII.*

Bay Horse, Marygate ¶
Sold in 1819 on the bankruptcy of John Kilby. It was then held on a 12 year lease, which had started on 11 October 1809, at a rent of £7 10s 0d a year (YG 25 9 1819). At this time it was located in the gatehouse of St Mary's Abbey (Murray p. 58). In 1839 the lodge was converted into a dwelling for the keeper of the Yorkshire Philosophical Society's Museum. A new public house was built against St Mary's Abbey walls and demolished *c*.1893. Rebuilt to the designs of WG and Arthur Penty, architects, on the opposite side of the road in 1896 (YG 4 7 1896) it had, in 1902, four bedrooms used by the family, a large dining room in which the landlord could cater for large functions, and a bathroom upstairs. On the ground floor were a smoke room, a bar parlour, a bar, a bottle and jug department, private kitchens and a private sitting room (CC). Also known as *The Bay Mare*.

Bay Horse, Mint Yard
While called *The Horse and Groom* in the 1823 street directory (Dir), it was listed in the licensing records with this name in 1822 and then every year until 1828 (YCA F30A, F31). The annual rental paid to the Corporation in 1828 was £28 (YCA E78A). Last mentioned in 1834 (Dir).

Bay Horse, Monkgate ¶
Earliest mention 1761 (YCo 24 2 1761). Described in 1902 as a very good market house, where carriers put up, it had six bedrooms, including nine beds set apart for travellers, a large dining room upstairs, two smoke rooms, a taproom, a market room, two cellars and two private kitchens. Food could be supplied (CC). Also known as *The Bay Malton*. Name changed to *The Keystones* 1995 (YEP 12 12 1995).

Bay Horse, Murton
Previously *The Jerry* and *The Horse and Jockey*, it had been given this name by 1857 (Dir).

Bay Horse, North Street
Mentioned 1795 (YCA K69).

Bay Horse, St Mary Castlegate, parish
Two public houses of this name are mentioned in this parish in 1783 and 1787 (YCA K69, Cooper2 p.42).

Bay Horse, Skeldergate
Earliest mention 1777 (YChr 18 4 1777). Name changed to *The Albert* by 1872 (Dir).

Bay Horse, Skelton
Mentioned 1823, closed between 1935 and 1939 (Dir).

Bay Horse, Swinegate
Earliest mention 1795 (YCA K69). For sale 1820, held on a lease from the Dean and Chapter, 31 years still to run (YG 19 8 1820).

Bay Horse, Tanner Row
Mentioned 1823 (Dir).

Bay Horse, St Sampson's Square
Mentioned 1783 and 1795 (YCA K69).

Bay Horse, Walmgate ¶
Earliest mention 1753 (YCo 30 10 1753). Listed in 1823 under this name and that of *The White Horse* (Dir). For a period between 1876 and 1879, when William Horwell was licencee it was called *The Spotted Dog* (Dir). Newly rebuilt in 1902 it had three bedrooms with sleeping accommodation for eight travellers and a club room upstairs. There were only two rooms on the ground floor, both licensed, a bar and a kitchen from which food could be supplied. The family and the customers shared the only WC in the building (CC). Closed by 1970 (Dir).

Bay Horse Standstill, St Michael le Belfrey parish
Earliest mention 1783, last 1787 (YCA K69, Cooper2 p.42). No trace can be found of a bay horse called Standstill in Orton's *Turf Annals of York and Doncaster*.

Bay Malton, Monkgate
An alternative name for *The Bay Horse* by which it was known between 1794 and 1828 (YCA E55 and F31). Named after Lord Rockingham's bay horse, Bay Malton, which won a Great Subscription Race at York in August 1766.

Bay Mare, Marygate
An alternative name for *The Bay Horse* by which it was known between 1834 and 1841 (Dir).

Baynes' Coffee House, Petergate
Mentioned in 1804 when the Ancient Society of York Florists held a show there (Duthie p. 45). William Baynes, clerk to Robert Sinclair, became free in 1798, macebearer in 1800

and swordbearer in 1810 (Murray4 p. 20). By 1813 it had become *Baynes' Hotel* although still using the former name in 1828 (YG 9 2 1828).

Baynes' Hotel, Petergate

Previously *Baynes' Coffee House*. Earliest mention 1813 (RCHME V p. 196), named after its proprietor, William Baynes (Dir) who is shown as the licensee of *The Grapes* from 1822 to 1827, when he is succeeded by his wife, Ann (YCA F30A). This may have been its name throughout all changes of ownership as it is still shown as *The Grapes* when Elizabeth Tomlinson is the licensee in 1828 (YCA F30A, F31) and later. Next *Tomlinson's Hotel, Jackson's Hotel, Thomas's Hotel,* and then *The Londesborough Arms.*

Beagle, Foxwood Lane

Opened 12 December 1977 (YEP 12 12 1977).

Bear, Coney Street

Mentioned in 1573 (Benson p. 166). A capital messuage was owned, prior to 1596, by John Stephenson. The site had once been occupied by The Bear and afterwards *The Golden Lion.* (Davies pp. 63–64). According to TP Cooper, *The George and Dragon,* later *The George*, was built on this messuage (Cooper2 p. 5, Benson2).

Bear, Fossgate

Mentioned 1753 (YCo 13 11 1753).

Bear's Paw, Micklegate

In 1891 this public house, belonging to Mr Preston of Bootham, was on offer for £2000. He had refused an offer of £2300 twelve years previously. Tadcaster Tower Brewery Co. decided to negotiate (Avis p. 189). Is this *The Barefoot*?

Bedroom, Micklegate

Previously *Harry's Bar* which, after being given a £400,000 overhaul and a new look, opened on 20 December 2002 (YEP 20 12 2002).

Beech Tree, Goodramgate

Known by this name 1848 to 1872 (Dir). Previously and later *The Fox.* Also known as *The Lord Byron* (Cooper p. 49).

Beehive, Peter Lane

Earlier there had been a house on this site called *The Three Tuns.* In 1863 a beerhouse was opened here (Cooper p. 60.) The landlord in 1870 was charged with harbouring prostitutes after 18 were found on the premises (Finnegan p. 151). In 1902 it was recorded as having five bedrooms and a sitting room upstairs. On the ground floor there was a taproom, a bar and two kitchens, one of them private. There was also a cellar (CC). Renewal of the licence was successfully opposed at the 1908 Brewster Sessions on the grounds of the unsuitability of its buildings (Peacock pp. 155/6). Its licence was extinguished on 5 October 1908, having been referred for compensation on 11 March that year (YCA Acc. 189).

Beeswing, Hull Road

Previously *The Black Swan* (Cooper pp. 39/40). By 1846 it was named after Beeswing (Dir), a bay mare by Dr Syntax out of Tomboy's dam, foaled by Mr Orde at Nunnykirk in

1833, winner of 51 of her 64 races including the Gold Cup at Doncaster in 1840-1843 (Fairfax p. 327). The present premises were built in 1902 after the previous building had received a less than glowing report from the Chief Constable. He found it had four bedrooms, two used by the family while the other two had low roofs and were not useable. Travellers could thus not be accommodated. On the ground floor were two smoke rooms, a small kitchen, from which food could be supplied to customers, and below these a cellar. All the rooms were very small with low ceilings. The kitchen was used as a drinking room and the family and customers shared the only urinal which had bad drainage. All in all, the house was not suitable as it was then arranged and the Chief Constable specially noted it for the attention of the Licensing Justices (CC).

Bell Tavern, Feasegate
A colloquial name for *The Blue Bell*, mentioned 1774 (JWK).

Bell, Micklegate
Previously *The Blue Bell* (Cooper p. 72). Gained this name by 1867 (Dir). In 1902 it had upstairs, nine bedrooms of which six were set aside for travellers, a commercial room and a sitting room. On the ground floor were two smokerooms and a serving bar. Below this were a cellar and a cellar kitchen from which food could be supplied if asked for. The sanitary conveniences were in a yard at the rear. (CC). It had closed by 1937 when its licence was transferred to *The Imperial*, Crichton Avenue (YG 6 6 1936) which opened on 4 June 1937 (YCA Acc. 189).

Bell, Thursday Market (St Sampson's Square)
Mentioned in 1639 (Palliser p. 20), possibly the establishment later known as *The Blue Bell*.

Bell, Spurriergate
Mentioned on a trade token in 1668 (Benson3 p. 89).

Bell Inn, Walmgate
Mentioned in 1830 (YG 9 1 1830), a familiar name for *The Blue Bell*.

Beverley Arms, High Petergate
Leased from the Dean and Chapter 1 January 1799 at 8s. a year, one of the lots offered for sale in 1819 on the bankruptcy of John Kilby (YG 28 8 & 25 9 1819). It was closed by 1848 (Dir).

Big Coach, Nessgate
A nickname given to *The Coach and Horses*, Nessgate, to distinguish it from *The Coach and Horses*, Micklegate.

Billiard Table, Stonegate
Mentioned in 1731, 'the Sign of the Billiard Table' (YCo 20 7 1731). Also known as *Keregan's* (Benson p. 166).

Bingley Arms, Grimston
Mentioned in 1867 when John Darby was licensee (Dir).

Bird in Hand, Bootham ¶

The first house of this name, mentioned in 1746 (YCo 15 7 1746), was demolished in 1835 (YCo 16 4 1835) after the barbican of Bootham Bar was pulled down. It was rebuilt on the corner of Bootham and St Leonard's, adjacent to Queen Margaret's Arch. The property included a brewhouse when offered for let in 1851 (YG 30 8 1851). During the tenancy of Ann Morley it was also known as *St Leonard's Hotel*. In 1878 it moved to new premises in Bootham on the creation of Exhibition Square (YG 2 11 1878) and by 1881 became *The Exhibition* (Dir).

Bishop Blase, Coppergate

Mentioned in 1770 (Benson p. 167). Blaise was a bishop of Sebaste in Armenia who was martyred in c.316 when he was barbarously lacerated with wool combs before being beheaded. He was canonised at the Council of Lyons in 1244 and is the patron saint of woollen manufacturing. His feast day, 3 February, was particularly known in York for a few years in the late 15th century and after 1737 as the day when the newly elected City Chamberlains took office.

Bishop Blaze, Bootham

To be sold 1751 (YCo 26 11 1751).

Black Boy, Feasegate

Mentioned from 1824 to 1826 when the licensee was James Turner (YCA F30A; F31). An error for *The Black Dog*.

Black Boy, Fossgate

Mentioned in 1778 (YCo 1 9 1778).

Black Boy, First Water Lane (King Street) ¶

Earliest mention 1783 (YCA K69). In 1852, on building of King Street, its name was changed to *The Grapes* (Johnson p. 27).

Black Boy, George Street

Mentioned in 1841 (Dir, St George Street).

Black Boy, Lendal

Mentioned in 1823 (Dir). TP Cooper says that this was an earlier name for *The Cannon* (Cooper p. 17) but both pubs were in existence in 1823 with different landlords (Dir).

Black Boy, North Street ¶

A gill mug was stolen from the premises in 1750 (YCo 8 5 1750). Offered for sale in 1844 when the property contained a brewhouse (YG 13 1 1844). Demolished c.1849 (YG 27 7 1849) when St John's church school was erected (Cooper p. 41).

Black Bull, Bootham

On 10 January 1495/6 belonged to the Merchant Adventurers' Company. Sold by the Company 1564 (MercAdv pp. 54,140).

Black Bull, Davygate
Mentioned in 1770 (YCo 2 1 1770). Later *The Little Black Bull*.

Black Bull, Hull Road
Mentioned in 1840 (Dir). Bought by Samuel Border, grocer, in 1892 (YG 16 4 1892) and rebuilt as a road house c.1935.

Black Bull, Osbaldwick
Earliest mention 1823 (Dir), name changed to *The Derwent Arms* 1937 (Wilde p. 108).

Black Bull, Petergate
Mentioned 1744 (Benson p. 166).

Black Bull, St Sampson's Square ¶
Mentioned in 1687 in an advertisement about bull baiting, as a meeting place of curriers in 1711 (JohnsonB p. 55), and in 1778 when it was taken by John Bickers who had been servant to the Revd Mr Morley for 20 years (YCo 2 6 1778). A very old jettied timber framed property which included a brewery on the premises in 1858 (YG 18 12 1858). In 1902 it had ten bedrooms, seven of which were used by travellers. There was also a dark and badly lit bar which was sometimes used as a singing room where regular concerts were held, a dressing room for the professional singers, and a kitchen, from which food could be supplied. The urinal in the yard was not properly screened off from cottages overlooking it and there was only one WC for both family and customers to use. The Chief Constable thought that it was worthy of special consideration, with a view to closing it, by the Licensing Justices (CC). Short of room it absorbed the adjacent premises, *The Hand and Heart*, in 1903, after that public house's licence was surrendered (YCA Acc. 189) and closed on 30 September 1932 (YG 11 3 1932, YCA Acc. 189).

Black Bull, Walmgate ¶
For sale by auction 1809 (YCo 20 11 1809). In 1902 it had five bedrooms, two of which were available for travellers, one bar with a corner screened off by a curtain, the only room licensed for public use and a back kitchen from which food could be supplied if asked for. A very small back yard contained poor sanitary arrangements, a single WC for both the family and customers which was also used as a urinal (CC). At the 1906 Brewster Sessions the renewal of its licence was successfully opposed on the grounds of non–necessity. It was said to be one of the worst six houses in York. Compensation of £471 was paid to the lessee, the Tower Brewery Company, and £110 to the tenant. (Peacock p. 92). The licence expired on 16 February 1907 (YCA Acc. 189).

Black Dog, Coppergate
A well accustomed ale house in good repair, to be sold 1765 (YCo 3 9 1765).

Black Dog, Feasegate
Earliest mention 1783 (YCA K69), last mention 1828 (YCA F31). Mistakenly called *The Black Boy* in records between 1824 and 1826 (YCA F30A; F31). Familiarly known as *The Dog*.

Black Dog, Jubbergate
Mentioned 1787 (Cooper2 p. 45).

Black Dog, 5 Low Jubbergate
To be let 1756 (YCo 2 11 1756). Earliest mention at this address 1818 (Dir). In 1830 known as *The Original Black Dog* to avoid confusion with the next (Dir). Last mention 1846 as *The Dog* (Dir).

Black Dog, 59 Low Jubbergate
Previously *The Old Black Dog*. Mentioned under this name between 1822 (YCA F30A) and 1834 (Dir), having apparently dropped the 'Old' although one of the other two Black Dogs originally in the street was still in existence. However the name *The Old Black Dog,* was again used in 1828 (Dir).

Black Dog, High Ousegate
Mentioned in 1770 (Benson p. 167) and 1787 (Cooper2 p. 45).

Black Dog, Thursday Market, St Sampson's Square
To be sold 1810 (YCo 5 11 1810).

Black Dog, St Saviourgate
Mentioned 1849 (Dir).

Black Horse, Black Horse Passage, Fossgate [Tenter's Passage]
Earliest mention 1783 (YCA K69). While an application for a new licence to be granted to this beerhouse was refused in 1846 (YG 29 8 1846), it still appeared in the street directories until 1867 (Dir). A haunt of thieves and prostitutes (Finnegan p. 151).

Black Horse, Blake Street
In 1730 the proprietors of the Assembly Rooms proposed to build rooms for footmen under the portico towards this alehouse. It had been demolished by 1734 when Mr Gibson sold the ground where it had once stood, to the proprietors of the Assembly Rooms [now part of the widened road at the Museum Street end of Blake Street] (YCA M23/1 pp. 14 & 102).

Black Horse, Bootham ¶
Earliest mention 1745 (YCo 7 5 1745) and then in a lease of adjacent property (now No 33 Bootham) in 1746 (YCA E93 p. 195). The property contained a brewhouse in 1851 when offered for sale (YG 20 12 1851). Offered for sale again in 1866 (YG 29 9 1866) and was rebuilt, re–opening as *The Bootham Tavern*, a beerhouse (1867 Dir).

Black Horse, Monkgate ¶
Earliest mention 1822 (YCA F30A). It was rebuilt to the designs of WG Penty, architect, in 1897 (date on building) by JJ Hunt who had become its owner in Acc. 1895 (YCA Acc. 189). In 1902 it was described as a very good market house where travellers put up. Upstairs it had six bedrooms, with nine beds set apart for the travellers, and a large dining room. Below these were two smoke rooms, a taproom, a market room, two cellars and two private kitchens. Food could be supplied for the travellers if they required it (CC). In 1988, after a £100,000 facelift, it was reopened as *The Tap and Spile* (Star 28 7 1988).

Black Horse, Pavement (Also Hosier Lane)
First mentioned in 1743 in Hosier Lane (YCo 22 5 1743). Sold in 1819 on the bankruptcy of John Kilby (YG 25 9 1819). Last mention 1861 in Pavement (Dir).

Black Horse, Walmgate ¶
Earliest mention 1733 as a place where common carriers could be found (Gent). Sold in 1819 on the bankruptcy of John Kilby (YG 26 6 1819). In 1902 it had two bedrooms upstairs, a sitting room and an inconvenient kitchen upstairs. An area on the ground floor was licensed and consisted of a dram shop with a small snug partitioned off and a smoke room. Underneath was a cellar which contained the WC for the family and customers. There was, however, a public urinal opposite. Only drink was supplied, the landlord could not be troubled to provide food (CC). Although renewal of its licence was refused in 1903 it was granted on appeal (Peacock p. 66). However a further attempt to close this house was successful on 26 May 1910, having been referred for compensation in April that year (YCA Acc. 189, YG 28 5 1910).

Black Horse, Wigginton ¶
First mentioned 1840 (Dir).

Black Lion, Jubbergate
On the corner of Feasegate 1752 (YCo 10 10 1752). A canary show was held there 1784 (YCo 19 10 1784).

Black Swan, Askham Richard
Although mentioned with this name in 1823 (Dir) the licensing records from 1822 to 1828 show it as *The Swan* (YCA F30A, F31). By 1857 is has become The Black Swan again (Dir).

Black Swan, Bishopthorpe
Mentioned in 1838 and 1843 (Dir). Possibly the predecessor of *The Woodman* (Brayley p. 10).

Black Swan, Coney Street ¶
Earliest mention, in connection with a marriage, in 1663 (Cook p. 66). Mentioned in 1688 in John Webster's diary (Malden). The stage coach service to the Black Swan, Holborn, London, initiated 1 April 1706 from here taking four days (Cooper p. 11). In 1902 it had sleeping accommodation for 30 travellers and stabling for the same number of horses. It had a smoke room, commercial room, a private bar, private sitting room, kitchens and six stock rooms. It was entirely suitable for its purpose (CC). It closed on 4 April 1939 (YCA Acc. 189) when its sign, a black swan, was given to the Castle Museum (YG 2 6 1939). The building was demolished in 1968 when a shop was built on the site (YG 16/18 11 1968). An unsuccessful attempt had been made on 8 February 1937 to have the licence transferred to a new house in Lendal (YCA Acc. 189).

Black Swan, Front Street, Acomb
On the corner of Cross Street. First mention 1814 when it is described as a newly erected messuage (AMCR 1767–1837, 8 11 1814). After the tragedy in 1830 on the river Ouse near Acomb Landing, when six Rigg children were drowned in a boating accident, the coroner's jury met there (YG 21 8 1830). Last mention 1858 (Dir). Furniture sold 1859 (YG 7 5 1859). Also known as *The Swan*.

Black Swan, Hull Road
A former name for *The Beeswing* (Cooper pp. 39/40).

Black Swan, Lawrence Street
Mentioned in 1838 (Dir) - same premises as previous entry?

Black Swan, Ouse Bridge
To be let 1741 (YCo 16 6 1741).

Black Swan, Peasholme Green ¶
A medieval Grade II* listed building (CAMRA2), it was the former home of York born Sir Martin Bowes, Lord Mayor of London in 1545. Mentioned in 1710 when the Innholders Company held a social gathering there after a court meeting in St Anthony's Hall (BI MTA.17/1 p. 200). To be let 1763 (YCo 3 5 1763). In 1902 it had five bedrooms and sleeping accommodation for 12 travellers, in large bedrooms. There was also a clubroom upstairs. The bar and smoke room were on the ground floor as well as two kitchens from which food could be supplied. The house also had a cellar and stabling for 20 horses (CC). It was remodelled in the 1930s (CAMRA) and given a major overhaul in 1967 (YEP 3 2 1967) after which a Civic Trust plaque was installed on it (YEP 24 10 1968). Occasionally referred to as *The Swan.*

Black Swan, Low Petergate
Previously *The Bricklayers' Arms* and *The Eclipse*, it had gained this name by 1841 (Dir). Last mention 1855 (Dir).

Blackmoor's Head, Colliergate
Mentioned in 1770 (Benson p. 167).

Blackmoor's Head, Low Petergate
Near the corner of Stonegate, opened on 10 December 1755 by Samuel Kesting, formerly tapster at *The George Inn*, Coney Street (YCo 9 12 1755).

Blacksmiths' Arms, Acomb
Sold in 1819 on the bankruptcy of John Kilby (YG 26 6 1819). A very common name in villages where the blacksmith often doubled up as publican.

Blacksmiths' Arms, Askham Richard
Mentioned in 1876 (Dir).

Blacksmiths' Arms, Church Street
Earliest mention 1818. Its name was changed to *The Harcourt Arms* by 1851 (Dir). When it was advertised for sale in 1845 the property included a brewhouse (YG 25 1 1845). Later *The Talbot.*

Blacksmiths' Arms, Dunnington
First mentioned in 1840 as *The Smiths' Arms* but by 1849 was using this fuller name. For a short period before 1872 and after 1876 it was known as *The Horseshoe*. Closed between 1909 and 1921 (Dir).

Blacksmiths' Arms, over Foss Bridge
Mentioned 1806 (YCo 14 7 1806).

Blacksmiths' Arms, Huntington ¶
First mentioned 1823 when the victualler was John Varey, the blacksmith. Between 1872 and 1876 it was called *The Hammer and Pincers* (Dir).

Blacksmiths' Arms, Lowther Street
By 1852 when it was offered for sale it had become *The Barrack Tavern* but had been known previously by this name. The premises included a brewhouse (YG 24 12 1852).

Blacksmiths' Arms, Main Street, Fulford
In 1815 a deed shows it as a public house called *The Saddle* (now The White House, 14 Main Street, on the opposite side of the road to the present public house of this name) and known formerly by the sign of *The Blacksmiths' Arms* (Briddon pp. 48/9).

Blacksmiths' Arms, Naburn
Previously *The Horseshoe*, by 1857 it was using this name (Dir).

Blacksmiths' Arms, Osbaldwick
Earliest mention 1807 (Wilde p. 109), alternatively known as *The Horseshoe Inn* but from 1893 this latter name was in exclusive use.

Blacksmiths' Arms, Rufforth
Previously *The Buck*, it had gained this name by 1857 (Dir). It reverted to its former name by 1876 and then in its death throes in 1995 became *The Blacksmiths' Arms* again after a make-over. Nevertheless it finally succumbed 1999 (Thomson) when its site was sold for housing.

Blacksmiths' Arms, Skelton
Earliest mention 1823 (Dir).

Blacksmiths' Arms, Wheldrake
Mentioned in 1823 (Dir), rebuilt and renamed *The Wenlock Arms* in 1856.

Blackwell Ox, Grimston
Mentioned 1823 when Robert Summers was licensee (Dir).

Bloomsbury, Grape Lane
Earliest mention 1841 (Dir). Named after Mr W. Ridsdale's bay colt, Bloomsbury, by Mulatto out of Arcot Lass, winner of the Derby 1839 (Orton p. 743). Called *The Horse Bloomsbury* in 1848 (Dir) and *The Flying Dutchman* by 1855 (Dir).

Blue Anchor, First Water Lane
Mentioned in 1787 (Cooper2 p. 45) and 1795 (YCA K69).

Blue Anchor, Low Ousegate
Mentioned 1767 (YCo 2 6 1767), on Dr White's map 1782. Last mention 1795 (YCA K69).

Blue Ball, Holgate
Was located opposite *The Fox*. Licensees listed continuously from 1754 to 1811 (YCA K68). Sold to Hewley Graham in 1823 who demolished it soon afterwards (AMCR 1767–1837). In 1822 it is referred to as *The Blue Bell* (YCA F30A).

Blue Ball, First Water Lane
Mentioned in 1781 (YCo 5 6 1781) and 1783 (YCA K69).

Blue Bell

Mentioned in 1715 as a meeting place of curriers (JohnsonB p. 55).

Blue Bell, Bootham

Mentioned in 1761 (YCo 13 10 1761), 1772 (Pace p. 242) and 1787 (Cooper2 p. 43).

Blue Bell, Coppergate

An alehouse, on Dr White's Map in 1782. Mentioned in 1783 (YCA K69) and 1796, when it was for sale (YH 6 2 1796). By 1801 called *The Barleycorn* (YH 10 10 1801).

Blue Bell, Feasegate

Mentioned 1751 (YCo 22 10 1751) and 1795 (YCA K69). Also locally known as *The Bell* 1774 (JWK).

Blue Bell, Fossgate ¶

Two hundredth anniversary 1998 (YEP 27 7 1998). In 1902 it had three bedrooms, two attics and a sitting room. Accommodation for one or two travellers could be provided. It was a very poor house, not suitable for the licensed trade as it was then arranged, with only two rooms on the ground floor, a bar and a taproom, one of which was used as a kitchen where the family prepared and ate their food. Food could be supplied from here for customers if asked for. There was a cellar and only one WC for both family and customers. In spite of all these defects the Chief Constable did not make any special mention of it to the Licensing Justices (CC). At the Brewster Sessions in 1903 the renewal of its licence was opposed as it was 'neither suitable or necessary' as there were 34 licensed premises between Pavement and Walmgate Bar. This application was refused. George Edwin Robinson who had become the new landlord on 8 January 1903 (licence 23 March 1903) must have made the required improvements. When he died in 1948 his widow, Annie, took over the licence (licence 6 September 1948). After she died in 1963 it passed to her daughter, Edith Pinder (licence 12 February 1964), who retired in 1992, the licence having remained in one family for 89 years. (YEP 24 8 1991, 14 10 1992). A Grade II* listed building (CAMRA2).

Blue Ball, Holgate

Mentioned in 1822 (YCA F30A), in error for *The Blue Ball*.

Blue Bell, Micklegate

Mentioned in 1795 (YCA K69). Sold in 1819 on the bankruptcy of John Kilby. (YG 25 Sept 1819). It had become known as *The Bell* by 1867 (Dir).

Blue Bell, North Street

Mentioned in 1839 (YG 23 12 1839) and 1855 (Dir).

Blue Bell, Pavement

On corner of Hosier Lane (Pavement) and Fossgate, mentioned in 1769 (YCo 20 6 1769), on Dr White's map 1782 and still in existence in 1787 (Cooper2 p. 45).

Blue Bell, Skeldergate

To be let 1781 (YCo 29 5 1781), opposite the Old Crane, for sale 1795 (YH 14 11 1795).

Blue Bell, St Mary, Castlegate, parish

Mentioned in 1783 (YCA K69) and 1787 (Cooper2 p. 45).

Blue Bell, St Sampson's Square
To be let 1750 (YCo 2 1 1750), mentioned in 1834 (Dir), but see also *The Bell*, St Sampson's Square which may be the same establishment.

Blue Bell, Walmgate ¶
Earliest mention 1795 (YCA K69). In 1902 it was described as neat and clean. It had five bedrooms of which two or three could be used for travellers. There was a smoke room and bar. Refreshments such as food, could be supplied if the customers wanted it. Some members of the landlord's family slept on the premises but he slept in a cottage in the yard behind where he also had his private kitchen (CC). It closed on 28 October 1958 and the licence was surrendered in consideration of the granting of a licence for a new house, *The King William*, Barkston Grove (YCA Acc. 189).

Blue Boar, Castlegate
Previously *The Boar*. Bargain and sale of a messuage in Castlegate called the 'Blew Bore' 3 July 1579 (YCA Z506). Mentioned in September 1640 in connection with a brawl there (Benson2). After the execution of Dick Turpin on 7 April 1739 his body rested overnight in the premises (Ash p. 134). Rebuilt on a larger scale 1754 (YCo 14 5 1754). Probably closed in 1775 when William Ellis announced that he had given up public business (YCh 19 5 1775). Not on Dr White's Map 1782.

Blue Boar, Goodramgate 1
Earliest mention 1772 (YCo 15 9 1772). Sold in 1819 on bankruptcy of John Kilby (YG 28 8 1819) and bought by Thomas Belt (Johnson p. 41). When he left in 1825 it became *The Royal Oak* (YCA F30A). Also known as *The Blue Pig*.

Blue Boar, Goodramgate 2
Mentioned in 1795 (YCA K69).

Blue Boar, Thursday Market (St Sampson's Square)
Mentioned 1773 and 1777 (YCo 29 6 1773, YCh 28 2 1777).

Blue Fly, New Street
Previously *The Pavement Café Bar*, it was given this name in 2002 (YEP 4 11 2002).

Blue Pig(g), Goodramgate
A familiar name for *The Blue Boar*, mentioned in 1783, 85 and 87 (YCA K69, Cooper2 p. 44).

Bluitt's Inn, Museum Street ¶
A coaching house, formerly *Gibson's*, later *Ringrose's, Etridge's Royal Hotel*. William Bluitt, once servant to John Boynton Adams of Camblesford, moved in 1867 from *The Black Dog*, Jubbergate, to take over the Inn in Lendal (YCo 7 4 1767). Shortly after his arrival Christian IV, King of Denmark stayed in the hotel (YCo 6 9 1768). In 1785 it became *Ringrose's* when Bluitt was succeeded by John Ringrose who had been a waiter with him for 12 years (YCo 29 3 1785). Bluitt died in 1798 (YH 7 4 1798). Still called *Bluitt's* in 1798 (Dir). John Ringrose was succeeded by Thomas Etridge in 1803 (YCo 5 12 1803).

Adelphi Hotel, George Hudson Street, 1900

Acorn, St Martin's Lane, 1983

Admiral Hawke, Walmgate, 1906

Albert Inn, George Street, 1902

Anchor, Queen's Staith, 1930

Angel, Walmgate, 1909

Anglers' Arms, Goodramgate, 1947

Bar Hotel, Micklegate, 1893

Barefoot, Micklegate (with lamp over door), 1900

Bar Hotel, Micklegate, 1980

Barrack Tavern, Fulford Road, 1881

Barrack Tavern, Fulford Road, 1906

Bay Horse, Blossom Street, 1935

Bay Horse, Main Street, Fulford, 1935

Bay Horse, Marygate, 1890

Bay Horse, Marygate, 1935

Bay Horse, Monkgate, 1909

Bay Horse, Walmgate, 1909

Bird in Hand, Bootham, 1805

25

Black Boy, First Water Lane, 1815, drawn by Henry Cave

Black Boy, North Street, 1830

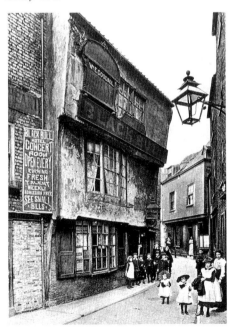

Black Bull, St Sampson's Square, 1909

Black Bull, Walmgate, 1906

Black Horse, Bootham, by Thomas Shotter Boys, 1840

Black Horse, Monkgate, 1925

Black Horse, Wigginton, 1906

Black Horse, Walmgate, a later occupant in 1983

Black Swan, Coney Street, 1919

Black Swan, Peasholme Green, 1895

Blacksmiths' Arms, Huntington, 1906

Blue Bell, Walmgate, 1906

Blue Bell, Fossgate, 1935

Blue Bell, Walmgate, 1950

Bluitt's Inn, Museum Street, 1860

Board Inn, Fossgate, 1950

Bootham Tavern, Bootham, 1935

Bowling Green Inn, Bowling Green Lane, 1906

*Bricklayers' Arms,
Palmer Lane, 1935*

Bridge Inn, Layerthorpe, 1925

Britannia Inn, Heworth Village, 1910

Britannia Inn, Nunnery Lane, 1925

Brown Cow, Hope Street, 1974

Buck, Rufforth, 1900

Boar, Blossom Street
Nearly opposite the entrance to Holgate Road, later *The Sun* (Knight p, 350, Cooper2 p. 6). It is probable, however, that The Boar, mentioned in 1485 and 1487, was not this one but another in Castlegate (see below).

Boar, Castlegate
On 24 August 1485 Sir Roger Cotam met the Lord Mayor and his brethren at 'the sign of the boore' as he feared for his life if he came through the city to proclaim Henry VII monarch in succession to Richard III, slain at the battle of Bosworth. In 1547, a meeting place for merchants, John Hoton was the 'hostler' (Attreed pp. 542 & 734). Although in neither case is the street mentioned, Raine is positive that it stood on the north side of the street just beyond St Mary, Castlegate where a house, containing the remains of an inn was fairly recently demolished (Raine p. 193). Here, within the liberty of York Castle, it would have been a safe haven for Sir Roger Cotam. Next, possibly, *The Blue Boar*.

Board, Bishophill Senior
Mentioned 1858 (Dir).

Board, 5 Bridge Street
Earliest mention 1822 without a name (YCA F30A) then in 1823 as *Rooke's Dram Shop* (Dir). Also known as *New Bridge Street Hotel*. A Beerhouse with a six day licence (YCA Acc. 189), it had gained the alternative name of *The Board* by 1830. By 1902 it was more generally called *Ye Olde No 5.*

Board, Coppergate
Mentioned in 1828 with Henry Donkin Maltby as licensee (Dir). However in the licensing records his pub is shown as *The Three Tuns* (YCA F30A).

Board Inn, Fossgate ¶
Also known as *Seller's Vaults* or *Seller's Dram Shop.* Earliest mention 1822 (YCA F30A) and not mentioned again until 1858 (Dir). In 1902 it had three bedrooms, two sitting rooms and a kitchen, all private and used by the manager who lived on the premises. While the major business was bottling beer, which was stored in two warehouses, there was a long stand–up bar where customers could drink. There were no back yard sanitary conveniences (CC). Demolished in 1956 in connection with creation of Stonebow. which was built and opened in 1957.

Board, Goodramgate
Previously *The Square and Compass*, later *The Anglers' Arms* and *The Snickleway.* Mentioned 1852 to 1891 (OS). Also known as *Cooper's Vaults* 1887 (Dir).

Board, Goodramgate
Opened in 1895 to serve as a shop for WH Thackwray who had taken over John March's brewery behind it in Ogleforth in November 1880 (Davison pp. 42, 49). In seeking a spirits 'off' licence the magistrates required that the beer licence of *The Fox*, Goodramgate, had to be surrendered (YG 7 9 1895). In 1902 there was, as well as the shop, an office and warehouse on the ground floor and store–rooms above. While it had a six day ale licence for consumption on the premises, its main business was off sales, including wines and spirits (CC). It became an 'off' licence on 6 November 1961 (YCA Acc. 189). Also known as *Thackwray's.*

Board, High Ousegate
Mention 1830 (Dir).

Board, 94 High Petergate
Previously *Carr's Coffee House*, *The Chapter Coffee House*, *The Eclipse*, it had gained this name by 1838 (Dir). Rebuilt to the designs of JP Pritchett in 1838 (RCHME V p. 181b). Later *The Chapter Coffee House* again and, finally, *The York Arms*.

Board, 106 High Petergate
Opened as *Wolstenholme's Dram Shop* c.1869, by 1887 it had become *Haigh's Vaults*, by 1902 *Petergate Wine and Spirit Stores and Bar* and gained this name by 1949 (Dir). Full 'on' licence granted 14 February 1961 (YCA Acc. 189). Closed in 1978 because of structural faults (YEP 22 6 1979) and re–opened on 9 December 1981 after repairs as *The Hole in the Wall* (YEP 8 12 1981).

Board, Jubbergate
Mentioned in 1823 (Dir).

Board, 5 Low Ousegate
First mentioned as a wine and spirit merchants in 1823 (Dir). Last mention 1867 by which time it has gained this name and is listed in the street directory under Hotels, Inns and Taverns (Dir).

Board, 9 Low Ousegate
A beerhouse with a six day licence, also known as *McGregor's House*. Earliest mention 1849 (YG 4 8 1849). Referred for compensation 12 March and closed 1 October 1923 (YG 17 3 1923, YCA Acc. 189).

Board, 16 Low Ousegate
In 1838 the premises were occupied by John Bacon, a wine and spirit merchant (Dir). By 1843 he was succeeded by Joseph Hillyard (Dir) and members of his family held a licence until 1933 when Walter Hillyard transferred it to Herbert Outhwaite (YG 6 1 1933). In 1902 the ground floor, over cellars, comprised of a shop, an office, a bottling room, a sample room, a washing room and a packing room. In the upper floors was a private house entirely cut off from the licensed premises. These lock–up premises were almost entirely used for retail trade in bottles as well as wholesale trade (CC). On 14 February 1962 the six day licence was upgraded to a full licence (YCA Acc. 189). At this time its name had been changed to *Hillyard's Wine Lodge*, later *The Lodge, Yates' Wine Lodge, Dukes of York, O'Neills*.

Board, Low Petergate
An earlier name for *Gibson's Vaults* (Cooper p. 78).

Board, Marygate
Mentioned in 1823 (Dir).

Board, Micklegate
By 1872 the premises of Manstead and Wood (Dir), later Walker and Scott, wine and spirit merchants. In 1902 it had, on the ground floor above extensive cellars, two offices, vaults and a warehouse. Above was a house, the private residence of the proprietor. While it had

a six day ale licence for consumption on the premises, its main business was both retail and wholesale off sales, including wines and spirits. It had no urinal or WC for the use of the public or customers (CC). Last appearance in directory 1970 (Dir). Re–opened as *Walker's Bar* 1973.

Board, Museum Street
An alternative name for *Thomas's* (YCA Acc. 189).

Board, Middlethorpe
Mentioned in 1823 (Dir) although it appears in the licensing records from 1822 to 1825 as a house without a name (YCA F30A). Later *The Horse* and *The Horseshoe.*

Board, North Street
A beerhouse, mentioned from 1834 to 1843 (Dir).

Board, Pavement
In the 1880s JJ Hunt, the brewer, acquired the business and premises of William Cooper, wine and spirit merchants, in Pavement. By 1887 it was trading under the name of The Board Inn (Dir). The 'unsightly old property' was replaced by 1893 by a new building in a medieval jettied and pargeted style. The entrance hall was lined with Burmantoft ware and the external decoration was undertaken by the sculptor, GW Milburn (YI). In 1902 the retail portion was described as a lock–up property with two smoke rooms and a dram shop. The room above was used for the storage of spirits while the attics were not used. The remainder of the building was used for the wholesale trade (CC). By 1949 it was also known as *The Pavement Vaults.* It ceased trading on 27 January and the licence was surrendered on 13 February 1963 (YCA Acc. 189).

Board, Spurriergate
The retail outlet for Brett Brother's City Brewery established in Church Lane in 1858. It was located next door to *The Greyhound* and was established by 1872 (Dir). It was continued by JJ Hunt after his purchase of Brett's business in 1897. The licence was surrendered on 16 March and the premises closed on 31 March 1958, at the same time as *The Greyhound* (YCA Acc. 189).

Board, Trinity Lane 1
Mentioned in 1857 (Dir).

Board, Trinity Lane 2
An alternative name for *The Trinity House Hotel*, mentioned in 1902 (CC).

Bonding Warehouse, Skeldergate
The old bonding warehouse, built in 1874 for the storage of goods on which duty had yet to be paid, was converted into a pub and steak bar which opened in June 1981 (YEP 9 10 1980). It was closed after inundation by flood water in November 2000 and did not reopen (YEP 29 10 2001). A Grade II listed building (CAMRA2).

Boot and Shoe, Dunnington
A beerhouse, mentioned in 1857, closed between 1909 and 1921 (Dir).

Boot and Shoe, Friargate
According to TP Cooper a former name for *The Slipper* (Cooper p. 79).

Boot and Shoe, Upper Poppleton
Previously *The Brickmakers' Arms* but known by this name by 1857. Last recorded mention in 1895 (Dir). The building, alongside the A59, was demolished in 1921 (Davies2 p. 46).

Boot and Shoe, Walmgate
Mentioned in 1783 (YCA K69) and 1807 (YCo 23 11 1807).

Boot and Slipper, Bedern
Mentioned 1818 to 1841 (Dir).

Bootham Tavern, Bootham ¶
After the sale of *The Black Horse* (YG 29 9 1866) it was rebuilt and re–opened as a beerhouse (Dir). A full 'on' licence was granted on 14 February 1961 (YCA Acc. 189).

Boulevard, Fossgate
Previously *The Stonebow*. Refurbished and re–opened under this name 1986 (YEP 2 12 1986). Renamed *The Northern Wall* 1993 (YEP 10 12 1993).

Bowling Green, Bowling Green Lane ¶
Earliest mention 1818 (Dir). 'Off' licence from 6 November 1961, trading ceased 31 October 1966 (YCA Acc. 189). Application made to build 12 one–bed flats and six garages on the site (YEP 19 5 1967).

Boy and Barrel, Bar Lane
A nickname for *The Jolly Bacchus* (Larwood p. 31) from the practice of showing on the sign a fat infant sitting on a barrel (Dunkling p. 13).

Bradford Arms, St Sampson's Square
Originally *The Greyhound* and then *The Reindeer* (or *The Stag*). Next and later *The Hand and Heart* (Dir). One of 54 licensed houses belonging to the family brewing firm, Hotham & Co., which were sold to a consortium of local businessmen [Tadcaster Tower Brewery Co. from November 1882] in January 1875 (Davison pp. 40 & 42). Mentioned in 1876 (Dir).

Brewers Arms, St Andrewgate
Mentioned in 1841 and 1843 (Dir). Next *The Anglesey Arms* and then *The Albion* (Dir).

Brewers Arms, Tanner Row
Mentioned 1843 (Dir). The property included a brewhouse when offered for sale in 1864 (YG 28 5 1864). When Tetley's bought the house in 1899 their surveyor reported that its business was mainly 'pint pot trade' (Johnson p. 13). Renamed *Flares* March 2002 (YEP 26 10 2002).

Brewers Arms, Walmgate
Earliest mention 1841 (Dir). In 1902 it had two bedrooms and a sitting room upstairs, with a small and badly lighted snug, a bar, a tap–room and a private kitchen on the ground floor from which food could be supplied to customers (CC). Four years later the Chief Constable claimed it was one of the six worst hostelries in York. While the tenant made 35s 0d profit in a good week and paid £3 to the compensation fund there were six other pubs within 100 yds of it (Peacock 92). As the magistrates considered it was not necessary, its licence was not renewed and expired on 16 February 1907 (YCA Acc. 189). Compensation of £519 was paid to the lessee and £75 to the tenant (Benson2).

Bricklayers' Arms, Palmer Lane ¶
Mentioned 1838 (Dir). A popular venue for linnet singing competitions 1871 to 1915 (Poole p. 5). In 1902 it had a large club room upstairs as well as two bedrooms but sleeping accommodation had never been asked for. On the ground floor were a smoke room, a dram shop, and a private kitchen from which food could be supplied. There was a cellar below. The Chief Constable considered it a fairly good house, suitable for the district (CC). Although the renewal of its licence was objected to in 1903 and 1911 (Peacock pp. 65, 205, 247) it was not until 5 February 1937 that it was closed and its licence transferred to *The Corner House*, Burton Stone Lane (YCA Acc. 189).

Bricklayers' Arms, Peasholme Green
For sale 1852 (YCo 1 9 1752).

Bricklayers' Arms, Peter Lane
Mentioned 1809 and 1811 (YCo 20 9 1809, 28 1 1911).

Bricklayers' Arms, Low Petergate
Beerhouse, licence granted 1837 (YG 16 9 1837). By 1841 it was called *The Black Swan.*

Bricklayers' Arms, Walmgate
Previously *The Malt Shovel* and *The Old Malt Shovel*. Mentioned from 1851 to 1861 (Dir). Later *The Spread Eagle*.

Brickmakers' Arms, Upper Poppleton
Shown by this name on early maps. At the 1841 census the publican was William Baines, a brick and tile maker. He was still there in 1851 (Davies2 p. 48). By 1857 the pub was recorded under the name of *The Boot and Shoe* (Dir).

Bridge Hotel, Bridge Street
Mr Rooke's house 1829 (YG 18 4 1829). Also known as *New Bridge Street Hotel, Rooke's Dram Shop, The Board* and *Ye Olde No 5.*

Bridge Hotel, Huntington Road
Built on land opposite the Corporation Housing Estate on Bell Farm it was granted a full seven day licence on the removal of the licence from *The Full Moon*, Walmgate, 22 May 1939. The licence of *The Garrick Head*, Petergate, was voluntarily surrendered at the same time (YCA Acc. 189). Name changed to *The Fossway* by 1993 (Thomson).

Bridge, Middle Water Lane, King's Staith
A familiar name for *The New Bridge Inn.* Mentioned 1822 (YCA F30A) and 1826 (YG 25 2 & 9 7 1826).

Bridge Inn, Layerthorpe ¶
A beerhouse, mentioned 1867 (Dir). In 1902 it had two bedrooms and a sitting room upstairs. Downstairs, above the cellar, was a small snug, a taproom, a dram shop and although there was a kitchen, food had to be cooked in the taproom. The family and the customers shared the only WC (CC). Referred for compensation and closed 7 October 1921 (YCA Acc. 189).

Brigadier Gerard, Monkgate

An existing private house, once the Gas Works Social Club, was extended to make this pub which opened on 28 June 1984 (YEP 29 6 1984). It is named after a very successful race horse, which included the 2000 Guineas of 1971 (Pepper p. 145) among its 17 triumphs out of 18 starts. His only defeat occurred on 16 August 1972 on the Knavesmire (YEP 29 6 1984). The horse was in turn named after Brigadier Etienne Gerard, the hero of Conan Doyle's *The Exploits of Brigadier Gerard*. It was retired to stud in 1973 (Dunkling p. 35).

Briggs' Coffee House, Stonegate

Mentioned 1798–9, kept by Thomas Briggs (YGS 1953–4). By 1809 it had become *The Saracen's Head Coffee House* (YCo 3 4 1809), later *The Saracen's Head*.

Britannia, Church Hill, Acomb

Earliest mention 1822 (YCA F30A). Alterations, probably including a refronting, were made in 1921 (PCM 28 Feb 1921). Transferred from Tadcaster District of the West Riding County Council on 1 April 1937 on the inclusion of Acomb into the City (YCA Acc. 189).

Britannia Inn, Heworth Village ¶

First licensed 1806 (Appleton p.25). In 1902 it was described as an old property, fairly suitable for the trade. It had upstairs a sitting room and three bedrooms, none of them available to travellers. On the ground floor were two smoke rooms, a bar and private kitchen. Closed 19 July 1967 and its licence transferred to *The Walnut Tree* opposite (YEP 19 7 1967, YCA Acc. 189).

Britannia, Nunnery Lane ¶

Earliest mention 1837 (YG 11 3 1837). In 1902 it was described as just recently constructed. It had upstairs three bedrooms, all occupied by the family, and a clubroom. On the ground floor there was a smoke room, a bar, a bottle and jug department, a private sitting room and kitchen from which food could be supplied to customers if required (CC).

Britannia, Walmgate

Earliest mention 1818 (Dir) Called *The Britannia Coffee House* in 1820 (YG 31 10 1820). Renewal of licence refused at the Brewster Sessions 1900 (YCA Acc. 189) and house closed at the expiry of the old licence in 1901 (Dir).

British Tar, North Street

Mentioned 1843 (Dir). In 1902 it had four bedrooms, all used by the family. On the ground floor there were only two rooms, both licensed, the bar and the kitchen. The family and the customers both shared the WC. It was considered to be a clean and tidy house (CC). At the Brewster Sessions in 1907 the renewal of its licence was successfully opposed (YG 9 3 1907), compensation of £220 was paid (Peacock p.115) and it closed on 10 October 1907 (YCA Acc.189). It was also known as *The Fortunate Tar* (Dir 1879).

Brown Cow, Bishopthorpe

Mentioned from 1822 (YCA F30A) to 1876. By 1881 it had been renamed *The Ebor* (Dir).

Brown Cow, Hope Street ¶

Originally a beerhouse, first mentioned in 1834 without a name but in 1835 it was called *The Red Cow* (YG 26 9 1835). Then by 1838, when it appears to have a full licence, it had become *The Brown Cow*. Also known in 1843 as *The Cow* and in 1849 as *The Dun Cow*

(Dir). It had entrances in both Hope Street and Long Close Lane. In 1902 it was basically a four roomed cottage with only two bedrooms above a smoke–room and kitchen. There was no pantry. The family's food was kept in the cellar. Food was never asked for and not even a biscuit was available for customers. The family and customers shared a single WC. The Chief Constable thought it too small for a full licensed house but, nevertheless, it was kept very clean (CC). Plans were submitted for a larger scale establishment in 1903 (S&B 26 5 1903) and the new pub opened in 1906 (ER). In 1939 it was the scene of half a darts match. The other half was held in The Ark, Maidenhead, the two establishments linked by radio (YEP 14 4 1939).

Brown Cow, Marygate
This pub was housed in the gatehouse of St Mary's Abbey. Earliest mention 1818 (Dir). It was closed in 1840 to allow the gatehouse to be converted into a private house for the curator of the museum of the Yorkshire Philosophical Society.

Brown Cow, Minster Gates
Mentioned 1770 (Benson p. 167).

Brown Cow, Paragon Street
Earliest mention 1787 (Cooper2 p. 46). Last mention 1829 (YG 8 8 1829).

Brown Cow, Petergate
Mentioned 1767 (YCo 31 3 1767).

Brown Cow, St Lawrence parish
Mentioned 1787 (Cooper2 p. 46) and 1795 (YCA K69).

Brubakers, Blossom Street
Licence for a café–bar in the premises formerly Forsselius' Garage, granted in 1993 (YEP 12 8 1993). Closed 20 1 2001 (YEP 6 1 2001).

Brunswick, Fishergate
A beerhouse, previously *The Fishergate Tavern*, it had gained this name by 1902 when it had four bedrooms and an attic above the ground floor where there was a smoke room, a bar parlour, a serving bar and a kitchen. It also had a cellar. The family and customers shared a privy in the back yard (CC). It was referred for compensation on 7 February. This was confirmed on 4 March and the premises closed on 8 November 1947.

Brunswick, Parliament Street
First mention 1851 and then in 1855 as *The Brunswick Vaults,* but its brewing plant, bar fittings and furniture were offered for sale in 1852 (YG 26 6 1852).

Buck, Colliergate
In 1762 John Mowlam moved here from *The Old Sandhill* and renamed it *The Buck and Sandhill* (YCo 28 12 1762).

Buck, Minster Close (Yard)
In existence at the beginning of the 19th century, previously known as *The Horse and Groom* (Cooper p. 21).

Buck, North Street
Mentioned in 1795 (YCA K69).

Buck, Rufforth ¶
Mentioned in 1823. By 1857 it had become *The Blacksmiths' Arms*, a name which lasted until 1876, when it reverted to its former name (Dir). After a refurbishment, an attempt to revive its flagging fortunes, it reopened in 1995 as *The Blacksmiths' Arms* once again (Thomson). Also known occasionally as *The Stag.*

Buck, St John del Pike parish
Mentioned in 1783 and 1785 (YCA K69).

Buck and Sandhill, Colliergate
Given this name by John Mowlam after his removal from *The Old Sandhill* in 1762 (YCo 28 12 1762). The house was presumably previously called *The Buck*. Mentioned in 1764 (YCo 10 1 1764).

Buckles, Tadcaster Road, Askham Richard
Previously *The New Inn.* A new road house was built behind the old premises in 1938 and was given this name to commemorate a dynasty of Buckles who had opened and then run the original pub for at least 35 years.

Bull, Coney Street
Earliest mention 27 April 1459 when an order was made by the Council that aliens coming to York were to stay at the Sign of the Bull in Coney Street (SS125 p. 203). In the same year it was mentioned in the Ouse Bridge Masters' Accounts (YCA C83i8 membrane 3 dorso). On 6 August 1476 John Waterhouse leased The Bull from the Council for seven years at 46s 8d a year. He was to build at his own cost a room or charcoal stove at the inn (Attreed p. 53). Unoccupied in September 1505 (YCA B9 f. 27), by 1506 its name had been changed to *The Rose*. Despite this change the Chamberlains' Account until 1643 show an annual payment of 10s 0d to the Vicars Choral as rent for The Bull (YCA C2–23).

Bumper Castle, Wigginton Road
Built by William Johnson, previously landlord of *The Three Cranes* c1837–1846, in 1846. He died c.1879 and the business was continued by his widow until her death in 1907 at the age of 102, the oldest licence holder in the UK (Benson2). It was rebuilt early in the 20th century after Mrs Johnson's death.

Burland's Coffee House, Micklegate
Opened October 1824 in premises previously known as *The Crown, The Grapes* and then *The Golden Cup* (YG 23 10 1824). Named after its proprietor, William Burland, innkeeper of Micklegate who died in December 1848 (YG 23 12 1848). During Burland's occupancy it was also known as *The Cup,* 1824–28 (YCA F30A, F31) and 1843 (Dir), *The Grapes,* 1830, 1838 (Dir), and *Burland's Hotel,* 1846 (Dir). Later *The Crown* once again.

Burland's Hotel, Micklegate
Mentioned 1846 (Dir). See above.

Burns' Hotel, Lawrence Street
Previously *The St Nicholas* it became *The Tam O'Shanter* by 1854 (YG 1 4 1854) and was alternatively known by this name (CC).

Burns' Coffee House, Burns' Hotel, Market Street
Earliest mention in 1843 when William McLaren was its licensee and had been for five years (Dir 1843 Advt). Known both as *Burns' Hotel* and *Burns' Coffee House* (YG 16 5 & 3 10 1846). Name possibly chosen by its Scottish landlord to commemorate the national poet of his native country. The property contained a brewhouse when it was offered for sale in 1882 (YG 1 4 1882). In 1902 it had six bedrooms, two of which were set aside for travellers, and a kitchen upstairs. On the ground floor were a smoke room, a taproom and a bar. Food could be supplied if required (CC). Renamed *The Hansom Cab* when its frontage was rebuilt in 1975 (YEP 12 3 1975).

Burns' Coffee House, Tanner Row
A beerhouse, next door to the *Great Northern Hotel* mentioned from 1857 to 1861. By 1867 it had become a temperance hotel (Dir).

Burton Stone Inn, Clifton ¶
Previously *The Plough*. Gained this name by 1846 (Dir) from the Boundary Cross base, the Burton Stone, which once stood on the pavement edge. Rebuilt to the designs of Walter Brierley in 1896. During the building work the Burton Stone was resited into an alcove in the new boundary wall. York City Council agreed on 17 March 1899 to pay the owners, the Tadcaster Tower Brewery, 1d a year rent as long as it remained on the brewery property (YCA S&B Ctte minutes). In 1902 it was described as a suitable house, nearly new. It had three bedrooms, all used by the family, with two small attics above. There was no accommodation for travellers. On the ground floor were a club room, a smoke room, a taproom, a bar, a kitchen and a scullery (CC). A Grade II listed building (CAMRA2).

Butchers' Arms, Shambles
Mentioned in 1822 to 1827 (YCA F30A; F31). Also known as *The Neptune* (YG 3 7 1824), which by 1828 had become its official name.

Canteen, The Barracks, Fulford Road
A beer house, mentioned 1823 to 1867 (Dir).

Cannon, Museum Street (previously part of Lendal)
Mentioned 1783 (YCA K69). According to TP Cooper, previously known as *The Black Boy* (Cooper p. 17) but both pubs existed as separate establishments in 1823 (Dir). On 5 April 1809 John Kilby commenced paying an annual rental of £22 to the Corporation. This had risen to £18 when Mrs Chipstead took over in 1828 (YCA E78A). Built into the city walls, it was pulled down early in 1863 when the ramparts were cleared as part of the approaches to the newly opened Lendal Bridge. Familiarly known as *The Gun*.

Carlton, Acomb Road
Previously Disraeli's Hotel, reopened as a public house 1993 (YEP 28 7 1993).

Carr's Coffee House, Minster Yard
Mentioned in 1733 and 1742 (YCo 27 2 1732/3, 27 4 1742). By 1789 *Chapter Coffee House* when it was taken by John Bletsoe, late waiter at *Bluitt's* (YCo 17 8 1789). Later *The Eclipse, The Board, The Chapter Coffee House* again and, finally, *The York Arms*.

Casa, Low Ousegate
A Mediterranean style café bar on the corner of the steps leading down to King's Staith opened in 2001 (YEP 11 8 2001).

Castle Hotel, Castlegate / Clifford Street ¶
Previously *The Wheatsheaf*, it gained this name after 1851 and before 1855 (Dir). On the creation of Clifford Street in 1881 it gained an entrance into that street. In 1902 it was considered suitable for the trade of licensed victualler. Upstairs it had a dining room and six bedrooms and, although one was spare, travellers were not accommodated. On the ground floor, above the cellar, were a smoke room, a bar, a billiard room and a private kitchen from which food could be supplied (CC). It closed in 1969 and was demolished in 1971 (YEP 14 10 1969, 9 12 1971).

Castle Tavern, Castlegate Postern
Mentioned on a trade token 1668 (Benson3 p. 86).

Castle Howard Ox, Nessgate
Mentioned in 1838 (Dir). Presumably named after a prize winner in a local cattle show. Possibly also known as *The Fat Ox*.

Castle Howard Ox, Townend Street ¶
In 1836 William Lund, a cattle dealer, obtained an innkeeper's licence and opened a public house on Bootham Stray (YG 8 10 1836). Bootham Stray begins at Townend Street. In 1902 the Chief Constable reported that it had only two rooms on the ground floor above the cellar, both licensed, a smoke room and a bar. On the upper floor, however, there were five bedrooms, all occupied by the family, and a kitchen. Generally he thought it was an untidy house (CC).

Cattle Market Inn, Cattle Market, Fawcett Street / Paragon Street ¶
Previously *The Paragon Inn*, it gained this name by 1872 (Dir). In 1902 it had four bedrooms, two of which were set apart for travellers, and a club room upstairs. On the ground floor were a smoke room, a taproom in which there was a small partitioned off dram shop and a very small kitchen. The only WC was shared by family and customers (CC). It was renovated in 1980 but closed in October 1983 (YEP 22 10 1983).

Cattle Market Tavern, Heslington Road
Mentioned in 1858 (Dir).

Cattle Market Inn, St Dennis Street
Mentioned in 1843 but this would seem to be an error. Thomas Stephenson is shown as the licensee but he was located at *The City Arms* at the Cattle Market (Dir).

Chapter Coffee House, High Petergate
Previously *Carr's Coffee House*. Using this name in August 1789 (YCo 17 8 1789). Sold in 1819 on the bankruptcy of John Kilby – held on yearly lease from Dean and Chapter of York for 40 years starting February 1788 at a yearly rent of £1 4s 0d (YG 28 8, 25 9 1819). Later known as *The Eclipse*, *The Board*, by 1848 *The Chapter Coffee House* again and, by 1861, *The York Arms* (Dir).

Charles XII, Main Street, Heslington
Previously called *The Robin Hood, The Horse, The Chestnut Horse* and *The Bay Horse*. Changed to this name after the horse Charles XII by Voltaire out of Wagtail, belonging to Major Yarburgh of Heslington Hall, which won the St Leger in 1839 in a re–run after a dead heat (Fairfax p. 330). Earliest mention under new name 1843 (YG 16 12 1843).

Chase Hotel, Tadcaster Road, Dringhouses
Previously *Harker's Hotel*, given this name in 1946 by the then owner, RG Hodgson (YCA Acc. 189). Purchased by Swallow Hotels 1987 (YEP 7 4 1987).

Checker, North Street
Mentioned in 1783, by 1787 it was called *The Sun*. (YCA K69, Cooper2 p.42).

Chequer, Coffee Yard
Mentioned in a lease, dated 24 June 1777, a messuage in Coffee Yard known as the sign of the Chequer (document in possession of Jill Murray). Perhaps the same house that was called *The Trellis* in 1795.

Chequers, Micklegate
Mentioned in 1733 as a place where common carriers could be found (Gent).

Chestnut Horse, The Beckett, Heslington
Previously *The Robin Hood* and *The Horse*, gained this name by 1834 (Dir). Later *The Bay Horse* and *The Charles XII.*

Church Yard, All Saints North Street parish
Mentioned in 1787 and 1795 (Cooper2 p. 42, YCA K69). Probably *The [St] Crispin's Arms,* a name first appearing in 1818 (Dir), located in Church Lane opposite the graveyard of All Saints Church, where a church yard cross now stands.

Churchill's Hotel, Bootham
Previously called *The Bird in Hand*, it had been renamed *The Exhibition* by 1885 and gained this name after its new proprietor, Henry Churchill (Dir). It was purchased by John Smith's Brewery in 1892 when it became *The Exhibition* once again (YEP 13 12 1980).

City Arms Hotel, Fawcett Street ¶
Shortly after the opening of the new cattle market outside the walls on 4 October 1827 the Corporation commenced building a new hotel to serve the needs of those attending the market. It opened in November 1829 (YG 14 11 1829) leased to HR Sanderson (Dir) whose lease, at £90 a year, had commenced in 1828 (VCH p. 489). In 1902 the Chief Constable, who thought it a very good house, found that it had sleeping accommodation for 45 persons, a dining room, a bar, two smoke rooms and two kitchens. These latter two facilities were essential as large formal dinners were held at the hotel. (CC) In 1969 John Smith's Brewery, who had held the licence for 21 years, allowed it to lapse (YEP 19 10 1969). In 1977 eight years after closure it opened as a social club for sportsmen. Also known as *The New Market Hotel* (Dir 1838).

City Arms, 12 Walmgate
Earliest mention 1702 (Johnson p. 20). Still using this name on 11 November 1805 when the licensee, John Taylor, became a freeman of the Innholders' Company (YCA E55). By 1818 it had become *The Five Lions* (Dir).

City Arms, 174 Walmgate
Earliest mention 1843 (Dir). In 1902 it was described as a very old property. It had two bedrooms, none available for travellers, a sitting room and a kitchen upstairs from which food could be supplied if required by the customers. On the ground floor were a smoke room, a taproom and a very small bar, while in the back yard was a clubroom also used as a brassroom. The WC in the yard was shared with the shop next door. It also had a cellar (CC). An unsuccessful attempt was made to oppose the renewal of the licence in 1903 (Peacock p. 65) but it was not until 1925 when this objective was achieved. It was referred for compensation on 10 March and, after confirmation of this on 21 May 1925, the pub was finally closed (YCA Acc. 189).

Clarence Hotel, Davygate
Previously *Addison's Hotel* then *St Helen's Hotel*. It had gained this name by 1851 (Dir). In 1902, when it belonged to Allsopp & Sons of Burton on Trent, it had sleeping accommodation for 18 travellers, a smoke room, a billiard room, a coffee room, a commercial room, a drawing room and a private kitchen (CC). Allsopp's sold it to JF Nutbrown in 1907 (YG 20 7 1907). Although he made some internal alterations in 1909 (YG 9 1 1909) its licence was allowed to lapse in April 1910 (YCA Acc. 189).

Clifford's Tower, Peasholme Green (after 1827 Haymarket)
Mentioned 1783, 85, 87 and 95 (YCA K69, Cooper2 p. 44). Alternatively known as *The Tower*. By 1827 *The Leeds Arms* (YCA F31).

Clifton, Water Lane, Clifton
Earliest mention 1939 (Dir).

Clock Inn, Parliament Street ¶
Previously *The Eagle*. Gained this name by 1867 (Dir). In 1902 it had five bedrooms, one of which was set aside for travellers, and a sitting room upstairs. On the ground floor were a smoke room, a dram shop and a private sitting room. The cellar below also contained a kitchen from which customers could be supplied with food. The family shared the WC with the customers. It had no backyard, only a passage onto which its back door and those of two adjacent houses opened (CC). Closed on 17 4 1966 (YEP 11 4 1966). Also known as *The Clock and Eagle* (Dir 1858).

Clock Inn, Walmgate ¶
Earliest mention 1841 (Dir). In 1845 two persons were convicted of being drunk and creating a disturbance at this pub. The police were instructed to watch it very carefully thereafter (YG 23 8 1845). Nevertheless in 1846 the licence granted to James Gibson was not renewed owing to the generally bad state of the house. It was conditionally transferred to Mr Dickinson of Parliament Street (YG 29 8 1846). When the property was offered for sale in January 1874 it contained a warehouse 'still adapted for a brewhouse' (YG 17 1 1874). In 1902 while it had six bedrooms it did not take in travellers. It also had a sitting room, a small smoke room, a dram shop, a kitchen from which food could be supplied to customers, and a cellar. The family and customers shared the only WC (CC). It closed on 3 June 1957 when the licence was transferred to new premises, *The White Rose*, Cornlands Road, Acomb. (YCA Acc. 189, YEP 24 4 1957).

Clock and Eagle, Parliament Street
A transitional name for *The Eagle*, later *The Clock*, in use in 1858 (Dir).

Coach, Micklegate ¶
A 1980s name for *The Coach and Horses* deriving from a familiar usage.

Coach and Horses, Jubbergate ¶
Previously *The Waggon and Horses*, it had gained this name by 1828 (Dir). In 1902 it had three bedrooms, all occupied by the family, and a clubroom upstairs. On the ground floor, over the cellar were two smoke rooms, a dram shop, a kitchen and a living room. All the rooms were small and badly lit. The family and customers had to share the only WC (CC). At the Brewster Sessions on 9 February 1966 the licence was not renewed, the building having been sold by Charrington's with outline planning permission for shops the previous year. At this time it was described as having only three rooms and a bar, all amounting to 185 square yards (YEP 15 6 1965).

Coach and Horses, King Street
Mentioned 1879 (Dir).

Coach and Horses, Kexby Bridge
Mentioned 1823 to 1881 (Dir).

Coach and Horses, Little Stonegate
The street, now known as Back Swinegate, was once considered to be an extension of Little Stonegate. This pub, on the corner of Swinegate/Little Stonegate (Back Swinegate) appears in the street directories between 1828 to 1867 under Little Stonegate but at other times in Swinegate - see entry under that location (Dir).

Coach and Horses, Low Ousegate ¶
Previously *Harrison's Coffee House, The Coffee House* it had gained this name by 1812 (YCo 31 8 1812) but became *The Commercial Coffee House* by 1824 and *Ellis's Hotel* by 1841 only to change back again by 1843 (Dir). The licensee in 1853 advertised for a brewer (YG 8 10 1853). In 1902 it had nine bedrooms, three of which were let off to travellers, a club room, a private sitting room and a dining room upstairs. Below were two bars, a smoke room and a kitchen from which food was supplied to the travellers. There was also a licensed bar and dance room in King Street connecting with this pub (CC). It was demolished in 1904 together with *The Star and Garter* to allow Nessgate to be widened for the passage of electric trams (YCA Acc. 189, YG 3 6 1905). A new pub, with the same name was built, in two stages, on the new building line extending from Low Ousegate to King Street. The first half was completed in 1908 (YEP 6 7 1981). In 1977 planning permission for a change of use to offices and retail premises was sought (YEP 2 11 1977) and it was sold, as Ousegate House, for its new use in 1978 (YEP 22 2 1978). It was familiarly known as *The Big Coach* to distinguish from *The Little Coach* in Micklegate.

Coach and Horses, Micklegate ¶
Earliest mention 1818 (Dir). When offered to let in 1843 the property contained a brewhouse (YG 25 2 1843). In 1902 there was an unused attic above the only two bedrooms in the house. On the ground floor, over the cellar, there was a bar–parlour, a taproom, a serving bar and a private kitchen from which food could be supplied if customers required it. The major problem with this house was the sanitary arrangements. The urinal, apparently a somewhat makeshift affair, was in a narrow passage leading to a

privy, which was shared by the family and the customers. A proper urinal was required (CC). In 1945 Joshua Tetley acquired the pub at an auction and the next year purchased the building on its north side (Johnson p. 15) The premises were extended into this building in 1972 (YEP 1 9 1972). Usually known as *The Little Coach*, to distinguish it from *The Big Coach* in Nessgate by 1989 it had officially changed its name to *The Coach*, the familiar name which its regulars used. A further change of name came on 17 October 1996 when it became *The Phalanx and Firkin* (YEP 15 10 1996) followed by yet another in March 2003 when it became *The Priory* (YEP 29 3 2003).

Coach and Horses, Mint Yard
Mentioned in 1770 (Benson p. 167), 1787/1795 (YCA K69). On 25 March 1812 John Kilby paid the Corporation £44 for a lease lasting until 5 April 1818 (YCA E8A).

Coach and Horses, Nessgate
See *Coach and Horses,* Low Ousegate.

Coach and Horses, Newgate
Mentioned 1838 (Dir).

Coach and Horses, St Sampson's Square
Previously *The Barrel Churn, The Cooper* and *The Barrel* it had gained this name by 1830 (Dir) during the occupancy of George Pennack who had been a mail coach driver (Cooper p. 54 in reference to The Mail Coach). It had become *The Mail Coach* by 1834 (Dir) although it was again mentioned by this name in 1843 (YG 21 10 1843). Later *The Roman Bath.*

Coach and Horses, Swinegate ¶
Earliest mention 1740 when James Calton, coach master of the York to Scarborough coach, became licensee (YCo 15 7 1740) and probably gave it this name. In 1902 it was described as being nearly new. It had an attic, below which there were two bedrooms used by the family and a living kitchen from which food could be supplied for customers. On the ground floor were a smoke room and bar above the cellar. The family shared its WC with customers (CC). On 27 October 1958 the Licensing Justices made an order for the removal of its licence to new premises, *The Green Tree*, to be opened in Beckfield Lane. At the same time the licence of *The Green Tree*, Barbican Road, was to be surrendered. Both pubs closed on 11 December 1958 (YCA Acc. 189).
See also *Coach and Horses*, Little Stonegate.

Coach and Horses, Walmgate
Mentioned 1749 (YCo 28 2 1749).

Coachmakers' Arms, Little Stonegate
Mentioned in 1818 (Dir).

Cock, Walmgate
Mentioned 1787 and 1795 (Cooper2 p. 46, YCA K69).

Cock and Bottle, Skeldergate
The Plumbers' Arms, a beer house, closed on 1 January 1964 and, after demolition, was rebuilt. The new renamed and upgraded house was granted a full 'on' licence and opened

on 19 May 1965 (YCA Acc. 189). It was later renamed *The Villiers* and, closing after being inundated by floods in January 2001, re-opened under its previous name on 6 April that year (YEP 10 3 2001).

Cock and Crown Inn, Castlegate
Mentioned in 1733 (Benson p. 166) and 1742 (YCo 16 4 1742).

Cock and Crown, Skeldergate
Mentioned 1743 (YCo 6 9 1743).

Coffee House, Davygate
Mentioned in 1824 and 1826 (YCA F30A; F31). See *The Turf Coffee House.*

Coffee House, Lendal
Mentioned in 1812 to 1824 (YCo 19 10 1912, YG 28 2 1824). Also known as *The Grid Iron* (YCA F30A).

Coffee House, Low Ousegate
Previously *Harrison's Coffee House.* Mentioned in 1787 (Cooper2 p. 45). Next *The Coach and Horses, Ellis's Hotel* and *The Commercial Coffee House* and *The Coach and Horses* again.

Coffee House, Micklegate
Mentioned from 1824 to 1828 (YCA F30A; F31). See *Minster Coffee House.*

Coffee House, Nessgate
On corner of Low Ousegate, mentioned in 1795 (YCA K69) and 1824 (YCA F30A). See *Coffee House*, Low Ousegate.

Coffee House, Stonegate
Mentioned in 1783 and 1795 (YCA K69). Possibly *Brigg's Coffee House.* A coffee house in Stonegate, adjoining Coffee Yard, was for sale in 1795 (YH 24 1 1795).

Commercial Coffee House, Low Ousegate
Previously *Harrison's Coffee House, The Coffee House* and *The Coach and Horses.* It was given this name by Thomas Waite in 1824 (YG 28 2 1824). Mentioned in 1828 (YG 1 11 1828). Next *Ellis's Hotel* and *The Coach and Horses* again.

Commercial Hotel, Tanner Row ¶
An unlicensed boarding house in 1872 and then by 1893 a temperance hotel, it had been granted a beer licence by 1895 (Dir). In 1902 the Chief Constable said it was used mainly by commercial travellers but also described it as an eating house. Of its nine bedrooms seven were used by the travellers. It also had a commercial room, a front shop, a private room and cellar kitchens (CC). Its licence was not renewed at the Brewster Sessions 1907 (YCA Acc. 189) and it was demolished shortly afterwards to facilitate the laying of tram lines between Railway Street (George Hudson Street) and Rougier Street.

Compass, Middle Water Lane
Mentioned 1822 to 1824 (YCA F30A). Next *The Square and Compass.*

Cooper, St Sampson's Square

Previously *The Barrel Churn* it had gained this name by 1795 (YCA K69). It was renamed *The Barrel* by 1818 (Dir). Later *The Coach and Horses*, *The Mail Coach*, and *The Roman Bath*.

Cooper's Vaults, Goodramgate

Previously *The Square and Compass* then *The Board* for which this was an alternative name. It had been taken over by W Cooper, a wine and spirit merchant after 1851. He was succeeded by 1872 by Robert Wood who was followed by Edward Staines by 1889 (Dir). Mentioned in 1887 (Dir). Later *The Anglers' Arms* and *The Snickleway*.

Corner House, Burton Stone Lane

Opened in 1837, its licence specially created by the removal of the licence from *The Bricklayers' Arms*, Palmer Lane 6 February 1837 (YCA Acc. 189).

Corner Pin, Tanner Row

Originally a familiar name for *The Unicorn*, its name was formally changed to this in 1985 (YEP 28 10 1987).

Corporation Inn, Friargate

Mentioned 1879 (Dir). Demolished when Clifford Street was formed in 1881 (Cooper p. 53).

Cotherstone, Hungate

Situated on the corner of Carmelite Street and sometimes referred to under that street, it was previously *The Whale Fishery*. Mentioned between 1846 and 1867 (Dir). Named after Mr Baines' bay colt, Cotherstone, by Touchstone out of Emma, which won the Derby and was placed second in the St Leger in 1843 (Orton pp. 710 & 716). Alternatively called *The Horse Cotherstone* (1848, 1855 Dir) and *The Bay Horse* (1851 OS, 1858 Dir). The landlord in 1846, Reuben Dunn, was refused renewal of his licence as the house had been very disorderly during the previous year (YG 29 8 1846).

Cottage Inn, Front Street, Haxby

A new purpose built public house opened in 1980 (YEP 15 4 1980).

Cow, Hope Street

A familiar name for *The Brown Cow* (Dir 1843).

Cowper, Micklegate

Mentioned in 1569 as a place at which the Corpus Christi plays were to be performed (YCA B24 f. 140v).

Craven Ox, George Street

See next.

Craven Ox Head, George Street

Earliest mention 1840 (YG 18 1 1840). *The Craven Ox* in 1846, 1858 (Dir). Name changed to *The Newcastle Arms* by 1867 (Dir).

Cressand, Micklegate

Mentioned in a lease in 1550, in the parish of St Martin cum Gregory (YCA E23 f. 93).

Burton Stone Inn, Clifton, 1895

Castle Hotel, Castlegate / Clifford Street, 1906

Castle Howard Ox,
Townend Street, 1906

Castle Howard Ox,
Townend Street, 1921

Cattle Market
Inn, Cattle
Market, Fawcett
Street / Paragon
Street, 1924

City Arms Hotel, Fawcett Street, 1919

Clock Inn, Parliament Street, 1896

Clock Inn, Walmgate, 1935

Coach, Micklegate, 1985

Coach and Horses, Jubbergate, 1906

Coach and Horses, Low Ousegate, 1905   *Coach and Horses, Micklegate, 1935*

Coach and Horses, Micklegate, 1974

Coach and Horses, Swinegate, 1912

Commercial Hotel, Tanner Row, 1907

Cricketers' Arms, Tanner Row, 1906

Cross Keys, Dunnington, 1906

Cross Keys, Goodramgate, 1900

Cross Keys, Penley's Grove Street, 1950

Crown Hotel, Micklegate, 1927

Crown and Anchor, King's Staith, by J. England Jefferson, 1880

Crown and Harp, Mount Ephraim, 1912

Crystal Palace Hotel, Holgate Road, 1906

Cygnet Inn, Price Street, 1935

Dove Inn, Jackson Street, 1935

Dyson's Family and Commercial Hotel, Bootham, 1910

Eagle and Child, 15 (Great) Shambles, 1906

Ebor Tavern, Inn or Vaults, Aldwark, 1970

Ebor Vaults, Church Street, 1906

Edinboro Arms, Fishergate, 1976

Elephant and Castle, Skeldergate, 1935

Exchange Hotel, St Sampson's Square, 1935

61

Exhibition, Bootham, 1935

Falcon, Micklegate, 1935

Fisherman's Arms, Acaster Malbis, 1870 after the pub had closed

62

Five Lions, Walmgate, 1906

Flying Dutchman, Terry Avenue, 1985

Fox Inn, Holgate Road, 1905

Fox, Nether Poppleton, 1905

Fox, Petergate, 1930

Friendly Tavern, Dennis Street, Piccadilly, 1913

Frog Hall Tavern, Layerthorpe, 1906

Full Moon, Walmgate, 1902

Garden Gate, Carmelite Street, 1935

Garrick's Head, Petergate, 1919

Cricket Ground, Trinity Lane
Previously *The Square and Compass* and *The Cup and Compass* it had become *The Cricketers' Arms* by 1834 (Dir). In 1835 it was noted that it was formerly called by this name (YG 21 2 1835). Next *The Seven Stars* and *The Half Moon*.

Cricketers' Arms, Davygate
Previously *The Turf Coffee House,* it had been given this name by 1867 (Dir). Renamed *The London Hotel* in 1890 after being rebuilt. Also known in 1865 and 1879 as *The Cricketers' Resort.*

Cricketers' Arms, Gillygate
Previously *The Three Arrows* and *The Earl of Dublin,* it had gained this name by 1867 (Dir). The licence was forfeited on 27 October 1888 as the licensee, Joseph William Harper, had allowed the premises to be used as a brothel (YCA Acc. 189).

Cricketers' Arms, Tanner Row ¶
Earliest mention 1846 when Richard Letby was the licensee (Dir). He was a celebrated local cricketer and captain of the old York Cricket Club. The licensee from 1885 to the early 1900s, Harry Dewse was also a well known Yorkshire cricketer and captained York for 18 years. Until 1871 the cricket ground was in Leeman Road when it was vacated to build engine sheds (Cooper pp. 42, 43). The licensee prior to Dewse, William C Herbert, was charged on one occasion with having prostitutes on the premises (Finnegan p. 112). In 1902 it had five bedrooms, two of which were set aside for travellers. On the ground floor were a smoke room, a bar, a store room, a private room and a kitchen from which food was supplied if the customers asked for it. They had to share the only WC with the family (CC). It closed on 31 January 1839 (YCA Acc. 189).

Cricketers' Arms, Trinity Lane
Previously *The Square and Compass* and *The Cup and Compass* and *The Cricket Ground,* it had gained this name by 1834. Last mention 1846 (Dir) but later *The Seven Stars* and *The Half Moon.*

Cricketers' Resort, Davygate
An alternative name in use for *The Cricketers' Arms* in 1865 when the brewhouse was offered for sale (YG 9 12 1865) and also in 1879 (Dir).

Crispin, Hungate
A beerhouse, mentioned between 1843 and 1855 (Dir).

Crispin's Arms, Church Lane, North Street
Probably previously *The Church Yard* it was given this name by 1818 (Dir). Also known in 1846 as *The St Crispin's Arms* (Dir). The licence was forfeited on 10 December 1888 as Thomas Kitchin, the licensee, had allowed the premises to be used as a brothel (Avis pp. 144, 146, YCA Acc. 189). The house was demolished by 1897 (Cooper p. 42) and an open space, on the opposite side of Church Lane from All Saints Church was created with a graveyard cross erected in it.

Cross Guns, Minster Yard (west end)
Mentioned in 1742 and 1783 (YCo 19 10 1742, YCA K69).

Cross Keys, Bedern
Mentioned 1834 when Jane Broadmead was the licensee. In 1830 she had been the licensee of *The Cross Keys*, Goodramgate. It appears she had moved to Bedern taking the name with her. Last mention 1848 (Dir).

Cross Keys, Dunnington ¶
First mentioned 1823.

Cross Keys, Goodramgate ¶
Earliest mention 1783 (YCA K69). It was conveyed to James Melrose of Clifton Croft for £850 in 1888 by an indenture between him, the Dean and Chapter of York, and the Ecclesiastical Commissioners (YML WP pp 158/9). In 1902 it had five bedrooms, all occupied by the family, and a sitting room upstairs. Below was a smoke room, a taproom, a bar, a very small dram shop and a kitchen from which customers could be served with food. The house was not kept in a clean and tidy state. There was a urinal which the customers were not allowed to use. Instead they had to use the wall round the yard. The sole WC, shared by family and customers was in a very dirty condition (CC). It must have come as a relief to all when it was demolished the next year in connection with the creation of Deangate, a new road necessary to solve the congestion caused by the press of two–way horse drawn vehicle traffic through the narrow arch of the gate into the Minster Close at the end of College Street. On 27 October 1903 the plans of CJ Melrose and Co. for a new building were approved (YCA S&B Committee) and, according to the date on it, this was completed in 1904. In 1986 all the small bars were converted into a single room resulting in the house being described as sterile and intimidating, a big brewery outlet with bouncers (YEP 20 11 1986).

Cross Keys, Holgate
Earliest mention 1741 (YCo 24 3 1741), it was built on land which was once part of the estate of the Archbishops of York (YEP 10 2 1986), hence this name based on the attribute of St Peter. It was renamed *The Fox* shortly prior to 1841 (Dir).

Cross Keys, Jubbergate
Earliest mention in 1783 (YCA K69), last mention 1848 (Dir).

Cross Keys, Nether Poppleton
Mentioned in 1857 when Elizabeth Atkinson and in 1872 when John Atkinson were the licensees (Dir). As there was an Elizabeth Atkinson recorded at *The Fox* between 1822 (YCA F30A) and 1838 (Dir) and a John Atkinson in 1871 (Census) it would appear that this was an alternative name for that house.

Cross Keys, North Street
Earliest mention in 1783 (YCA K69), last mention 1867 (Dir). See *The Cross Keys*, St John's, Ousebridge parish.

Cross Keys, Penley's Grove Street ¶
In 1851 it was a beerhouse (Dir) but in October 1852 Thomas Wood, the licensee, was granted a spirit licence (YG 23 10 1852), which may have contributed to his fine the next year for keeping a disorderly house (YG 9 7 1853). When purchased by Brett Brothers in 1893 the property contained a brewhouse. In 1902 it had upstairs a small attic and three

bedrooms, one of which was available for travellers if required. Below was a bar, a smoke room, two small private kitchens but food could be supplied if requested. It also had a cellar. The only WC was shared by family and customers (CC). Its licence was placed in suspense on 19 November 1960, the house having closed as part of the Groves clearance scheme. It was transferred to *The Dick Turpin*, Moorcroft Lane on 19 May 1965 (YCA Acc. 189).

Cross Keys, Shambles
To let in 1745 (YCo 3 12 1745) and still advertising in 1822 (YG 6 7 1822). Mentioned in 1823 (YCA F30A). Using *The Globe* as an alternative or familiar name between 1818 and 1823 (Dir).

Cross Keys, St Helen's Square
Built as a chapel for St Christopher's Guild at the entrance to the Guildhall in 1445 (RCHME V p. xxxix) Earliest mention as a pub in John Webster's diary in 1688 (Malden). The tenant was given notice to quit in January 1724 (YCA E101 p. 89) and shortly afterwards, the building, together with other tenements in front of the Guildhall, was demolished to clear the site for the building of the new Mansion House.

Cross Keys, St John's, Ousebridge, parish
Mentioned in 1787 (Cooper2 p. 42). This may be the pub, with the same name, described as The Cross Keys, North Street. Certainly two pubs with the same name existed at this time in adjacent parishes, both of which contained part of North Street.

Cross Keys, St Peter the Little parish
Mentioned in 1787 (Cooper2 p. 45).

Cross Keys, Tadcaster Road, Dringhouses
Earliest mention 1768 when a new licensee took over (YCo 18 10 1768). Bought by JJ Hunt from the Masters in Lunacy on 21 November 1899 on behalf of Robert Danby who had taken it over on 20 July 1879 (Pocock p. 25). On 1 April 1937 it was transferred from the Tadcaster Division of the West Riding County Council on the extension of York boundaries (YCA Acc. 189). A Grade II listed building (CAMRA2).

Cross Keys, Tanner Row
Mentioned 1787 (Cooper2 p. 42) and 1795 (YCA K69).

Cross Keys, near Walmgate Bar
Mentioned 1762 (YCo 7 9 1762).

Cross Pipes, Skeldergate
To be let 1781 (YCo 4 12 1781). Mentioned in 1783 (YCA K69).

Crow's Coffee House, Coney Street
An exhibition from the Yorkshire Mechanical Museum held here in 1811 (YCo 28 1 1811). Also known as *The White Horse*.

Crown Inn, Castlegate
To be let 1728 – advertisement sheet published by T Gent (JWK p. 346).

Crown Inn, Holgate Road

A pre–1869 beer house (YCA Acc. 189), earliest appearance in a street directory 1872 (Dir). In 1902 it had five bedrooms and a sitting room upstairs. On the ground floor were a smoke room, a taproom, a serving bar and a private kitchen. It also had a cellar. There was only one WC shared between the family and customers. Nevertheless the Chief Constable thought it a very clean house (CC). It was referred for compensation on 10 February and 10 May 1958, closing shortly afterwards (YCA Acc. 189).

Crown, Hungate

A beerhouse mentioned in 1834. It seems to have gained a full licence by 1838 and last appeared in 1885 (Dir).

Crown Inn, Lawrence Street

Mentioned in 1783 (YCA K69) and 1881 (Dir). Almost certainly *The Rose and Crown*.

Crown Hotel, Micklegate ¶

Originally *The Rose and Crown* (Cooper p. 41) but earliest mention in 1733 as *The Crown*, a place where common carriers could be found (Gent). By 1818 its name had changed to *The Grapes*, then *The Golden Cup* followed by *Burland's Coffee House*, *The Grapes* again simultaneously with the previous name, *The Cup* and *Burland's Hotel*. Reverted to its original name by 1851 (Dir). In 1902 it had ten bedrooms, six of which could be let out to travellers if required. Downstairs there were two smoke rooms, a billiard room, a vault and private kitchens. Food could be supplied if required (CC). It was closed in July 1981 after serious structural faults were found. After repairs it was reopened as a furniture shop (YEP 23 9 1982).

Crown, North Street

Previously *The Tiger* or *The Leopard*, by 1848 it had become *The Crown and Cushion* but was usually referred to by the more familiar and unofficial name of *The Crown* (Dir). The Chief Constable, however, referred to it by its official name in his 1902 report when he found that it had an uninhabitable attic and two bedrooms upstairs. On the ground floor there were also only two rooms, a kitchen, from which customers could be supplied with food, and a dram shop out of which a small and dark snug had been partitioned off. A small bottle and jug window was screened off from the dram shop which made the latter exceedingly dark. Because there was no separate kitchen the family had to cook and eat their food amongst the customers. There was both a WC and urinal used by both family and customers but they were some distance from the house. All in all it was a very poor house and it was specially drawn to the attention of the Licensing Justices (CC). The pub had been purchased by JJ Hunt in 1899 for £1650, from which they took an annual rent of £22 (Peacock p. 64) but obviously from the previous description no improvements had been made by the new owner. At the Brewster Sessions in 1903 the renewal of the licence was opposed (Peacock p. 66), unsuccessfully, and the pub continued to trade for another 28 years. It was made redundant in May 1931 (YG 15 5 1931) and closed on 7 October 1931 under its shortened name (YCA Acc. 189).

Crown, Nunnery Lane

Previously *The Golden Ball, The Wheatsheaf* or *The Barley Sheaf*. Mentioned in 1851 and 1855 (Dir). Next *The Wheatsheaf* again.

Crown Inn, Parliament Street

Licence transferred from *The Crown*, St Sampson's Square, 1835 (YG 24 1 1835). When it was advertised to let in 1855 the premises contained a brewery (YG 20 1 1855). Closed in 1871 when the brewing plant was offered for sale (YG 11 2 1871).

Crown, St Helen's on the Wall parish

Mentioned in 1783, 1785 and 1787 (YCA. K69, Cooper2 p. 44). Probably *The Rose and Crown* in Aldwark.

Crown, St Lawrence parish

Mentioned 1783 (YCA K69). Probably *The Rose and Crown*, Lawrence Street.

Crown, St Sampson's Square

Mentioned 1817 (YCh 19 6 1817). Licence transferred in 1835 to newly built premises in Parliament Street (YG 24 1 1835). A familiar name for *The Rose and Crown.*

Crown, Walmgate

Previously *The Crown and Cushion.* From 1834 it was called by this more familiar name (Dir). George Hutchinson started brewing there from 1835 when he offered strong and mild ales for sale (YG 5 9 1835). In 1848 he handed over the brewery to a relative, John Foster (YG 7 10 1848) who, by 1867, had changed the name to *The Crown Brewery* (Dir) although the former name made occasional appearances in the street directories until 1895.

Crown and Anchor, King's Staith ¶

Previously *The Anchor*. Mentioned in 1841 under this name (Dir), demolished in 1881 in connection with Clifford Street improvements which included the final completion of the demolition of the Water Lanes area (YEP 10 3 1890).

Crown and Anchor, Low Jubbergate (Market Street)

Mentioned 1822 (YCA F30A) to 1851 (Dir). By 1853 it had become *The Market Street Tavern* and later *The Manchester Tavern* and *The Londesborough Arms.*

Crown and Cushion, North Street

Previously *The Leopard* and *The Tiger*, by 1848 it had gained this name but was usually referred to by the more familiar and unofficial name of *The Crown* (Dir). The Chief Constable, however, referred to it by this, its official name in his 1902 report (CC).

Crown and Cushion, Trinity Lane

Mentioned 1849 (YG 31 1 1849).

Crown and Cushion, Walmgate

Mentioned in 1818 (Dir). From 1834 it was called by the more familiar name of *The Crown* (Dir). Later *The Crown Brewery (Hotel).*

Crown and Harp, Mount Ephraim ¶

Previously *The Hudson's Arms* it had been given this name by 1860 (YG 7 4 1860). In 1902 it had the appearance of two four–roomed cottages made into one building. All the rooms were small. There were four bedrooms on the upper floor but travellers could not be accommodated. The ground floor consisted of a smoke room, a bar and two kitchens. The family and customers had to share the sole WC. No refreshments, other than drink, were served (CC). It was closed on 7 October 1937 (YCA Acc. 189).

Crown Brewery Inn or Hotel, Walmgate

Previously *The Crown and Cushion*. From 1834 it was called by the more familiar name of *The Crown* (Dir). It was first known as *The Crown Brewery* by 1867 although brewing had been carried out there since 1835 (YG 5 9 1835). Nevertheless the previous name was still used until 1895, a year before it had added 'Hotel' to its title (Dir) after brewing had ceased. In 1902 it had two attics which were not in use, four bedrooms and a club room upstairs. Four travellers could be accommodated. On the ground floor were a smoke room, a dram shop and a private kitchen from which food could be supplied if required. There was only one WC in a narrow covered passage opposite the door of the kitchen and anybody wishing to use it had to pass through the kitchen. Adjacent to the door of the WC was a cupboard where food was kept (CC). On 7 February 1947 it was referred for compensation and the premises closed on 8 November 1949 (YCA Acc. 189).

Crowned Lion, Micklegate

During a dispute concerning the rent it was stated that John Broket's ancestors had been tenants 'time out of mind' 1475x1483 (PRO C1/464/28).

Crystal Palace Hotel, Holgate Road ¶

Earliest mention 1872 although Alf Dickinson had had wine and spirit vaults in the premises from 1851 (Dir). Named after the exhibition which had opened in 1851 in Hyde Park, London. In 1902 it had four bedrooms, one set aside for travellers. On the ground floor were two smoke rooms, a club room, and a bar. Two private kitchens were located in the cellars, from which food could be supplied if required (CC). Since then the ground floor has been remodelled at a lower level. The entrance steps have been removed and the upper part of the cellars has been incorporated into the new rooms at pavement level. A Grade II listed building (CAMRA2).

Crystal Palace, Swinegate

Previously *The Lord Nelson*. When the memories of the national hero had faded and the exhibition of 1851 was to the fore, its name was changed. This had happened by 1855 when complaints were made at the Brewster Sessions about the use of the concert room. Removal of the licence was threatened if there were further complaints (YG 1 9 1855). Last mention 1858 (Dir). By 1861 the premises were being used by Tetley's as an ale and porter store (Dir).

County Hospital, Wheldrake

Mentioned 1823 to 1840 when William Young was the licensed victualler (Dir).

Cup, Micklegate

A familiar name for *The Golden Cup*. In use from 1822 to 1828 (YCA F30A; F31) and in 1843 (Dir) by which time it had become *Burland's Coffee House*.

Cup and Compass, Trinity Lane

Previously *The Square and Compass* but had changed to this name by 1830 (Dir). It was, however, referred to by its previous name when offered for sale in 1831 (YG 9 7 1831). Later *The Cricket Ground* and *The Cricketers' Arms*.

Cup and Feather, Castlegate

Mentioned in 1614 when Anthony Bowes was sent to prison for drinking there during sermon time (YCA B34 f. 57).

Cups, Micklegate
Mentioned in 1795 (YCA K69).

Curriers' Arms, Girdlergate (Church Street)
Previously *The Three Jolly Butchers,* Christopher Bean, the licensee, renamed it in 1828 Dir). Between 1830 and 1834 a John William Bean opened a new pub in Jubbergate with this name (Dir). The Church Street pub then became *The Jolly Butchers.* Later *The Ebor Vaults.*

Curriers' Arms, Jubbergate
Mentioned in 1834 and 1835 when Joseph William Bean was the landlord (Dir, YG 14 3 1835), having moved from Girdlergate.

Cutt–a–Feather, St Sampson's Square
By 1711 *The Nag's Head.* Also known as *The White Horse Inn* (WRRD).

Cygnet Inn, Price Street ¶
A beer house, earliest mention 1876 (Dir), on the corner of Price Street and Cygnet Street, from which it takes its name. It was leased to Joshua Tetley and Son of Leeds on 13 July 1891 (DNL). In 1902 it had three small attics, three bedrooms and a sitting room upstairs. On the ground floor were a large bar, a bottle and jug department and two private kitchens. There was also a cellar, and the urinal and WC were inside the house (CC). Tetley's rebuilt it on a new site in the 1930s and it was granted a full 'on' licence on 11 February 1960 (YCA Acc. 189).

De Yarburgh Arms, Main Street, Heslington
Previously *The Ship, The Fox, The Yarburgh Arms,* later *The Deramore Arms.* Mentioned 1895 to 1953 (Dir). The 'De' was added to the name, following an earlier change by the family.

Dean Court Hotel, Duncombe Place
Just after the First World War the central and largest of three buildings, built *c.*1864 by the Dean and Chapter of York, was acquired by the Thwaites family who opened it as Thwaites Hotel. Subsequently the other two buildings were added to the original hotel, as well as other buildings on either side in Duncombe Place and Petergate (YEP 5 3 1988). It had gained this name by 1939 (Dir) and was granted a full 'on' licence on 11 April 1962 (YCA Acc. 189).

Deramore Arms, Main Street, Heslington
Previously *The Ship, The Fox, The Yarburgh Arms,* and *The Deramore Arms.* George Deramore, on succeeding his brother as second Baron Deramore in 1890, changed his name once again in 1892, to De Yarburgh–Bateson (Murray2 p. 69). The owners of the pub did not then think at that time that a further change to the name of their establishment was warranted but finally recognised the ennoblement of the family with the present name in February 1967 (YEP 6 Feb 1967).

Derwent Inn, Elvington
A beer house run by William Jefferson, grocer, mentioned between 1902 and 1921 but by name only in 1909 (Dir).

Derwent Arms, The Village, Osbaldwick
Previously *The Black Bull*, changed to this name in 1937 (Wilde p. 108).

Dick Turpin, Moorcroft Lane
Opened 19 May 1965 on the special removal of the licence from *The Cross Keys*, Penley's Grove Street, which had been in suspense since 19 11 1960. (YCA Acc. 189, YEP 20 5 1965).

Dog, Feasegate
Mentioned in 1795 (YCA K69), a familiar name for *The Black Dog*.

Dog, Low Jubbergate
Mentioned in 1846 (Dir), a familiar name for *The Black Dog.*

Dog, North Street
For sale in 1780 (YCo 18 4 1780). Mentioned in 1783 (YCA K69).

Dog, St Margaret, Walmgate, parish
Mentioned in 1795 (YCA K69).

Dog, St Saviourgate
Previously *The Pointer Dog*, mentioned in 1785, 1787 and 1795 (Cooper2 p. 44, YCA K69). Later *The White Dog* and *The Spotted Dog.*

Dog and Gun, Hungate
Mentioned 1818 to 1851 (Dir). Name changed to *The Sportsman* in 1852.

Dormouse, Shipton Road
Built by Bass Taverns in the grounds of Clifton Hospital, opened January 1997 (YEP 28 11 1997).

Dove Inn, Jackson Street ¶
A beerhouse, mentioned in 1872 (Dir). In 1902 it had two bedrooms and a sitting room above a shop, taproom and kitchen. It had no pantry and food was kept in the beer cellar. The Chief Constable thought that this was not a suitable arrangement and noted it for the attention of the Licensing Justices (CC). Nevertheless some improvements must have been made as it remained open until 25 1 1951 (YCA Acc. 189). Compensation was agreed at £4880 of which the tenant received 10% and the value of the fixtures (YEP 11 11 1950).

Dragon
Mentioned in 1639, the sign of the Dragon, run by 'Ouseman', the post master, where excellent ordinaries [dinners] were to be had (Palliser p. 20). Possibly the same establishment as the next.

Dragon, Lopp Lane
A tapster house, mentioned in 1484 when John Tynley, during a dice game, left a piece of gold on the board and went outside to urinate. On his return the gold had gone so he went to the Council Chamber to make a complaint to the Lord Mayor (Attreed p.311).

Dray, Haymarket
Mentioned in 1818 (Dir).

Drovers' Arms, Lawrence Row
Mentioned in 1867 (Dir), an alternative name for *The Green Tree*.

Duke of Cumberland's Head, Ouse Bridge Foot
Mentioned 1782 (YEP 24 12 1782). Named after the Duke of Cumberland, the victor at the battle of Culloden in 1745. Possibly *The Duke's Head*, Bridge Street, although this was in existence well before this event. Mentioned in 1805 at the death of its owner, William Scruton (YCo 25 2 1805).

Duke of Wellington, Goodramgate
Previously *The Wellington*, and *The Marquis of Wellington*, later *The Wellington* again. Mentioned in 1830 and 1839 (YG 16 1 1830, 9 11 1839). Arthur Wellesley 1769–1852, Commander in Chief of the British forces in the Peninsula, was created Viscount Wellington in September 1809, Earl of Wellington in February 1812, Marquis of Wellington in October 1812 and, finally, Duke of Wellington in May 1814 after defeating the French at Toulouse in April that year. After the escape of Napoleon he was appointed Commander in Chief of the Forces on the Continent leading to the final victory at Waterloo on 18 June 1815. He was Prime Minister on two occasions, 1828–30 and in 1834. The owners of this pub were rather tardy in changing its name to match the Duke's progress through the ranks of the peerage. Also known as *The Lord Wellington* (Dir 1828).

Duke of Wellington, Holtby
Mentioned in 1857 (Dir) but earlier known as *The Lord Wellington.*

Duke of Wellington, Jubbergate
Not mentioned in 1818 (Dir) but described in 1819, when it was offered for sale as being no longer in use (YG 12 6 1819). For origin of name see previous.

Duke of York, 54 Aldwark
Actually *The Duke's Head* (YCA K95) but it is mentioned under this name in 1823 and 1830 (Dir). Later *The Old Duke's Head*. Frederick, second son of George III, was created 11th Duke of York in 1784, a title he held until he died in 1827. Appointed Commander in Chief of the British Army in 1795 he resigned in 1809 because of a personal scandal. However he was reappointed in 1811 and was, by his reforms of the army, instrumental in securing Wellington's victories over the French. He was known as the Soldier's Friend and it would seem that the name of the pub was chosen some time after the triumph at Waterloo.

Duke of York, Walmgate
First mentioned in 1795 (YH 15 8 1795) it would appear to be named in honour of the Grand Old Duke of York (see previous entry). Unlike its namesake in Aldwark it kept this name for all its life closing on 1 January 1898, one of three licences surrendered in consideration of a new licence being granted to the Tadcaster Tower Brewery Co. for a new house, *The Jubilee*, Balfour Street (YCA Acc. 189).

Duke William, St Mary, Castlegate, parish
Mentioned in 1783 (YCA K69). It cannot be named after William, third son of George III, who was not created Duke of Clarence and St Andrews until 1789 and succeeded his brother, George IV, as William IV in 1830. However, in view of its proximity to Clifford's Tower, it is probably named for William, Duke of Normandy, who became William I in 1066.

Duke's Coffee House, Bridge Street (Briggate)
The Sign of *The Duke's Head*, commonly called Duke's Coffee House (YCo 2 7 1751), a name which had already been mentioned the previous year when George Berry advertised the sale of spirituous liquors (YCo 6 2 1750). Later *The Old Duke's Coffee House*. See also *The Duke of Cumberland's Head*.

Duke's Head, 53 Aldwark
First mentioned in 1838 as *The Old Duke's Head* with Robert Merrington as licensee. However he had made his first appearance in 1822 in *The Duke's Head* at 54 Aldwark and had left there by 1834 as John Rounding was then licensee. Robert Merrington then reappeared at *The Old Duke's Head* at 53 Aldwark in 1838. It would seem that he sold out to John Rounding but a few years later decided to return to the street and open a pub next door to his former premises at 54 Aldwark. The two establishments then vied for the right to be considered the senior and both, at various times, added 'Old' to their names. The problem was solved by the disappearance of this pub after 1858 when Thomas Dimmock was the licensee (Dir).

Duke's Head, 54 Aldwark
Mentioned in 1795 (YCA K69). In 1823 and 1830 it was known as *The Duke of York* (Dir). In 1834 John Rounding was the licensee in succession to Robert Merrington who, a few years later, opened another *Duke's Head* at 53 Aldwark. This house was then variously called *The Original Duke's Head*, 1841 and 1849, and *The Old Duke's Head*, 1846 and 1851. After the disappearance of its rival after 1858 it had the field to itself and, for the rest of its life, there was only one Duke's Head in Aldwark (Dir). A three storey house in 1902, it had three attics, four bedrooms on the floor below, with three beds set aside for travellers and, on the ground floor, a smoke room, a bar, a taproom and a very small kitchen. Customers very seldom asked for food. The family had to share the WC with the customers (CC). It was referred for compensation by the Licensing Justices in 1903 (YCA Acc. 189, YG 21 2 1903) and closed soon after.

Duke's Head, Bridge Street
Earliest mention in John Webster's diary 1688 (Malden). Commonly known as *The Duke's Coffee House* in 1751 (YCo 2 7 1751) and then by 1794 *The Old Duke's Coffee House* (YCh 12 6 1794). In the official records , however, between 1783 and 1795 it is recorded under its proper name (YCA K69, Cooper2 p. 42). Probably also known as *The Duke of Cumberland's Head* after 1745 (YCo 24 12 1782).

Duke's Head, Jubbergate
Mentioned in 1795 (YCA K69).

Duke's Head, St Helen, Stonegate, parish
Mentioned in 1783 (YCA K69).

Duke's Head, Shambles End
In existence at some time between 1675 and 1710 (JohnsonB p. 55).

Dukes of York, Low Ousegate
Previously *The Board, Hillyard's Wine Lodge, The Lodge,* using this name between 1986 (Thomson) and 1996 (YEP 6 5 1996). Next *O'Neills.*

Dun Cow, Hope Street
An alternative name for *The Brown Cow*, in use in 1848 and 1855 (Dir).

Dun Horse, Petergate
Mentioned in 1782 when it was for sale on the bankruptcy of its publican, John Thompson (YCo 5 11 1782), 1795 (YCA K69) and 1806 (YCo 11 8 1806).

Durham Ox, North Street Postern, without
Mentioned 1843 to 1872 (Dir).

Dyson's Family and Commercial Hotel, Bootham ¶
By 1896 Henry Dyson, lately proprietor of *Scawin's Railway Hotel*, had taken over as licensee of *The Exhibition Hotel* and tried to rename it. It is described in 1898 and later, as Dyson's late Exhibition Hotel (Dir) and although he painted his name in large letters on its façade this change was resisted in popular and official usage.

Eagle Tavern, Goodramgate
Previously *The Glovers' Arms* and *The Gardeners' Arms*. Gained this name by 1850 (YG 12 1 1850), and offered for sale in 1870 when it apparently closed. At this time the premises included a former brewhouse (YG 3 9 1870). Also called *The Spread Eagle* (Dir 1867).

Eagle, Parliament Street
Mentioned 1841 to 1857 (Dir). Later *The Clock and Eagle* and *The Clock*.

Eagle and Child, Pavement
Mentioned on 15 August 1537 when the body of Robert Aske, leader of the Pilgrimage of Grace, was taken there after decapitation and before being taken to Clifford's Tower in chains (Benson2). The sign is based on the heraldic crest of the Stanley, Earls of Derby family and relates to an incident when the illegitimate son of an ancestor was found under a tree in which an eagle was nesting, and subsequently adopted as his heir. (Dunkling p. 81).

Eagle and Child, 15 (Great) Shambles ¶
Mentioned in 1764 (YCo 23 10 1764). For a time, between 1841 and 1849, it was called *The Reuben's Head* by the licensee who had previously kept another house with that name at 3 Shambles (Dir). The pub premises were behind the buildings fronting the street in the Shambles and were reached by a passage between them. In 1902 the pub had four bedrooms, one reserved for travellers, and a club room upstairs. Below was a smoke room, a small and dark bar, a licensed kitchen, which was used by customers, and a small private kitchen used by the family, which once had been the scullery (CC). It was referred for compensation on 10 March 1925. This was confirmed on 21 March 1925 and it closed soon afterwards.

Earl of Dublin, Gillygate
Previously *The Three Arrows*, gained this name by 1851 (Dir) presumably in honour of Albert Edward, Prince of Wales, for whom this title was revived on 17 January 1850 'to hold to him and his heirs, Kings of the United Kingdom of Great Britain and Ireland for ever'. Mentioned in 1864 (YG 6 2 1864) and by 1867 had become *The Cricketers' Arms* (Dir).

Ebor Tavern, Inn or Vaults, Aldwark ¶
Mentioned in 1841 (Dir), adjacent to the Ebor Brewery, an organisation established in 1836 by Joseph Hunt. In 1902 the licensed premises, used solely for drinking purposes, consisted of a smoke room and a dram shop on the ground floor. Above was a billiard hall not connected with the other rooms (CC). It closed in April 1968 and the premises were demolished some time afterwards (YEP 2 4 1968) opening up a view from Aldwark of the Merchant Taylors' Hall.

Ebor Hotel, Bishopthorpe
Previously *The Brown Cow*, it gained this name by 1881 (Dir). On 7 January 1884 The Tadcaster Tower Brewery Company gained possession of the hotel (Avis p. 79) but sold it later in the year to John Simpson. The premises then consisted of a club room, a small sitting room, bar, main sitting room, snug, cellar, kitchen, scullery, dairy, brewhouse, stable and hayloft. Twenty years later, on 21 April 1904, now in the possession of Mrs Simpson, the brewery bought it back again (Brayley p. 3).

Ebor Vaults, Bishopthorpe Road
A beerhouse, first mention 1872 when George Piercy was described as a grocer and beerseller. By 1896 it had become an 'off' licence only (Dir).

Ebor Vaults, Church Street ¶
Previously *The Three Jolly Butchers, The Curriers' Arms* and *The Jolly Butchers*. It had gained this name by 1861 (Dir). In 1902 it had four bedrooms, two available for travellers, a sitting room and a club room upstairs. There was a smoke room, a bar and a private kitchen on the ground floor. Food could be supplied if required. The family and the customers shared the sole WC (CC). It was referred for compensation in 1950 which was fixed at £4380, with 105 to the tenant (YEP 11 10 1950). The house closed on 25 January 1951 (YCA Acc. 189).

Ebor Brewery, Straker's Passage
Mention 1838 (Dir).

Ebor Inn, Tanner Row
An alternative name for *The Old Ebor*, in use in 1902 (CC).

Ebor Tavern (and Brewery), Tanner's Moat
Located close to North Street Postern, the earliest mention was in 1840 when Edward Calvert transferred his business from *The Lamb Coffee House* (YG 6 6 1840) to what was first known as *The Railway and Ebor Tavern* although by 1843 the 'Railway' element was dropped. Last mention 1855 when Edward Calvert was still the proprietor (Dir). The tavern, together with several cottages and an old iron foundry was purchased by HI Rowntree for £1000 in 1862 and replaced in 1888 by a six storey building (Vernon pp. 73 & 89).

Ebor Commercial House, Tanner Row
A beerhouse, by 1881 called *The Old Ebor*, but first appearing under this name in 1872 (Dir).

Eclipse, High Petergate
Previously *Carr's Coffee House*, *The Chapter Coffee House* and later *The Board, The Chapter Coffee House* again and, finally, *The York Arms*. It used this name between 1818 and 1834 (Dir). Eclipse, a chestnut racehorse by Marske out of Splilletta, was foaled by the Duke of Cumberland in 1764, the year of the great eclipse. It died in 1789. Eclipse was never beaten, its victories including an easy win at a Great Subscription race at York in 1770. It later earned its eventual owner, Captain O'Kelly, over £25,000 in stud fees at 30 guineas a time (Fairfax p. 85, Pick pp. 42 & 430).

Eden Berys, Goodramgate
Mentioned on 14/15 April 1483 (Attreed p. 707).

Edinboro Arms, Fishergate ¶
Previously *The Edinboro Castle* and *The Edinburgh Arms*. Gained this name by 1846, although the previous name made occasional appearances particularly in street directories which were not produced locally (Dir). In 1874 a new building to the designs of WG Penty was built on the opposite corner of Victoria Street (YCL Y942 7418 FIS). In 1902 it had four bedrooms, one set aside for travellers although very rarely used, and a sitting room upstairs. On the ground floor were a smoke room, a vault, a taproom, a private room and a kitchen from which food could be supplied if required – in all a very suitable house for the business (CC). In 1976 the name was changed to The Edinboro (YEP 2 11 1976) and then in 1987 *The Edinburgh* (YEP 19 5 1987).

Edinboro Castle, Fishergate
Opened by 1839 in a building on the corner of Victoria Street (YG 30 3 1839, Wilson p. 122). By 1841 known as *The Edinburgh Arms* (Dir).

Edinburgh Arms, Fishergate
Previously *The Edinboro Castle* but by 1841 had gained this name (Dir). From 1846 also known as the Edinboro Arms which, after 1881, became the universally accepted name, except for Kelly's Directories which persisted with 'Edinburgh' spelling (Dir). However in 1987 it reverted formally to *The Edinburgh* (YEP 19 5 1987).

Edward VII, King's Square
A name adopted by *The Grapes* for a short period after the accession of Albert Edward, Prince of Wales, as Edward VII in 1901. Not recorded in any street directories but the name can be seen on a contemporary photograph.

Edward VII, Nunnery Lane
Originally a beerhouse known as *Wright's House* it had gained this name in commemoration of the accession of Edward VII by 1905 (Dir) and probably simultaneously with the decision made at the Brewster Sessions in 1903 to grant Frank Reynolds, the licensee, a full 'on' licence on his fourth application on consideration of the surrender of that of *Jacob's Well* (Peacock p. 22, YCA Acc. 189).

Edwards, George Hudson Street
Previously *The Adelphi* and *The Railway King* it gained this name in 1997 after it was acquired by the Edwards Group. A Grade II listed building (CAMRA2). Next *Reflex*.

Elephant, Skeldergate
A shortened name for *The Elephant and Castle* recorded in John Cossins' notebook in preparation for the publication of his New and Exact Plan of York in 1727 (Murray3 p. 58).

Elephant and Castle, Peasholme Green
Mentioned in 1639 (Palliser p. 19). The name probably derives from the crest of the Cutlers' Company granted in 1622 – *An elephant Argent armed and harnessed Or bearing on its back a castle Or.* The ingenious pun on *Infanta de Castile* said to date from the Peninsular War is clearly not a candidate for the origin of this name.

Elephant and Castle, Skeldergate ¶
Earliest mention under the full name 1730 (Benson p. 164) but known earlier as *The Elephant.* The terminus for the coach to Wharfedale and the Union coach to Knaresborough and Harrogate. When the premises were offered for sale in 1882 they contained a brewhouse (YG 1 7 1882). In 1902 it had ten bedrooms, including some for the accommodation of travellers, a drawing room and a clubroom upstairs. On the ground floor there were a concert room, a billiard room, a bar, a private room and a good kitchen from which food was supplied if customers requested it. Apart from the main building were a taproom and vaults (CC). The licence was referred for compensation on 10 February 1958 (YCA Acc. 189). The house closed shortly afterwards and was eventually demolished.

Elephant and Falcon, Skeldergate
Previously *The Old Post House*, taken by Joseph Andrich in 1745, who gave it this name.

Ellington's Wine Bar, Stonebow
Previously *Fazer's Fun Bar*, it was given this name in 1991 (YEP 14 5 1991). Next *Fibbers.*

Ellis's Hotel, Low Ousegate
Previously *Harrison's Coffee House, The Coffee House. The Coach and Horses* and *The Commercial Coffee House.* Mentioned in 1834 and 1841 (Dir). Next *The Coach and Horses* again.

Elm Bank Hotel, Driffield Terrace
The town house, designed by JB and W Atkinson for William Benson Richardson, solicitor, in 1872, was reordered by WG and AJ Penty in 1897 for Sidney Leetham, corn miller. At this time the Art Nouveau decoration and furnishing of the interior, designed by George Walton, was introduced. In 1962 it was converted into a hotel and given a full 'on' licence on 11 April that year (YCA Acc. 189). The furniture has long gone elsewhere but much of Walton's decoration still remains.

Engine Drivers' Rest, Mount Ephraim
A beerhouse, opened by 1846, but not necessarily under this name which first appears in 1872 (Dir). In 1902 it was described as a very small house 'nothing more than a four roomed cottage'. There were two bedrooms upstairs, a smoke room, a kitchen and a small back kitchen on the ground floor and a cellar below. The WC was shared by the family and the customers. The Chief Constable specially noted it for the attention of the Licensing Justices (CC). It was not until 1908 that the renewal of the licence was opposed. In

evidence the Chief Constable at the Brewster Sessions said that the pub had been visited on no less than 17 occasions when no customers were found using the place. The landlord explained that since the NER had moved its locomotive works and workmen to Darlington in 1905 there was no chance of making a success of the business (Peacock p. 156). It was referred for compensation on 11 March 1908 and the licence was extinguished on 5 October that year (YCA Acc. 189).

Etridge's Royal Hotel, Museum Street

A coaching house, previously *Gibson's, Bluitt's* and *Ringrose's*. Thomas Etridge, an innkeeper from Cumberland House, Pall Mall, London, succeeded John Ringrose as the hotelier in 1803 (YCo 5 12 1803) and substituted his surname in the title but with the additional of 'Royal'. The reason for this latter alteration is not clear unless it relates to the visit of Christian IV, King of Denmark in 1768. In 1818 it was described as a first rate and excellent inn, admirably conducted and frequented by some of the principal families in the county (Hargrove p. 466). Etridge died on 1 December 1855 at the age of 83 (MI St Stephen's, Acomb). The hotel had been offered for sale, unsuccessfully, in 1854 (YG 4 3 1854), the furniture was sold in 1856 (YG 12 1 1856). In 1859 it was described as empty and to be sold (YG 23 4 1859). It was demolished in 1860 as part of the improvements to the approaches to the new bridge to be built at Lendal (YG 7 4 1860). *Thomas's Hotel* was built on part of its site.

Exchange Hotel, St Sampson's Square ¶

Earliest mention 1846 (Dir). It closed on 7 October 1931 (YCA Acc. 189), the landlord having been declared redundant in May that year (YG 15 5 1931).

Exhibition, Bootham ¶

Previously *The Bird in Hand*, it had first gained this name by 1881 (Dir) and then again in 1892, after a period as *Churchill's Hotel* (YEP 13 12 1980). It was also known in the early years of the 20th century as *Dyson's Commercial and Family Hotel*. In 1902 the Chief Constable considered it to be a very good commercial hotel with six or seven bedrooms set aside for travellers. There was also a coffee room upstairs and, on the ground floor, two small bars, a serving bar, a sitting room and a private kitchen from which food could be supplied if required by customers (CC). In 1967 the brewery intended to transfer the licence to a new public house to be opened in Lindsey Avenue, Acomb, *The Pack of Cards*, as it was proposed to demolish the hotel as part of the Gillygate scheme, part of the inner ring road proposal, a plan that was eventually abandoned because of public opposition (YEP 27 1 1967). A Grade II listed building (CAMRA2).

Falcon, Micklegate ¶

Mentioned in 1715 in a law suit between Sir Peter Vavasour and his wife. Lady Jane Vavasour. It was alleged that she met her lover William Parker, her husband's steward, there (BI CP I 661). It was described by Francis Drake in 1736 as one of two inns of good resort in this street (Drake p. 280). By 1818 it was a very excellent inn the only one of consequence in the street (Hargrove p. 181). It was rebuilt 1842/3 (RCHME III p. 127) but it was not until 1850 that Thomas Waller announced the reopening of the inn 'which has been rebuilt and newly refurbished (YG 16 11 1850). In 1880 the wooden falcon was added to its frontage as an inn sign (YEP 10 11 1975). While not so euphoric as previous reporters the Chief Constable, in 1902, thought it a suitable house for its business. It had five bedrooms, all used by the family, a billiard room and a sitting room upstairs. On the ground floor were a smoke room, a dram shop and a private kitchen from which customers could obtain food (CC). A Grade II listed building (CAMRA2). Also known as *The Old Faulcon*. Later *Rumours*.

Falcon, Spurriergate
Mentioned in 1764 (YCo 2 10 1764).

Fat Ox, Cattle Market, Fawcett Street
One of six pubs opened in what was to become Fawcett Street in the immediate vicinity of the new cattle market opened outside the walls in 1827. Mentioned in 1837 (YG 27 6 1837). The premises included a brewery when offered for sale in 1857 (YG 3 October 1857). On the corner of Victoria Street (OS1851), by 1867 it had been renamed *The Woolpack* (Dir).

Fat Ox, Groves
Mentioned 1845 (YG 5 7 1845), to be let in 1850 (YG 25 5 1850). Possibly an alternative name for *The Castle Howard Ox*.

Faulcon, North Street
Mentioned on 11 May and 23 September 1727 when visited by Darcy Dawes, son of Archbishop Sir William Dawes (Dawes).

Fazer's Fun Bar, Stonebow
New pub opened on 20 August 1985 in premises previously occupied by Fingal's Restaurant. Next *Ellington's Wine Bar, Fibbers*.

Fibbers, Stonebow
Previously *Fazer's Fun Bar, Ellington's Wine Bar*. A live music bar, opened with this name on 14 August 1992 and closed, because of cash flow problems, on 13 August 2002 (YEP 14 8 2002). Purchased by Channelfly and reopened on 26 August 2002 (YEP 20 8 2002).

Fighting Cocks, Walmgate
Mentioned 1746 (YCo 17 3 1746) and 1770 (Benson p. 167).

Firkin, St Helen on the Walls parish
Mentioned in 1783, 85 and 87 (YCA K69, Cooper2 p. 44).

Firkin, St Sampson's parish
Mentioned in 1783 and 7 (YCA K69, Cooper2 p. 44).

Firkin, Walmgate
Mentioned in 1780 (YCo 21 11 1780) and 1783, 87 and 95 (YCA K69, Cooper2 p. 46).

First Hussar, North Street
Previously *The Yorkshire Tavern, The Yorkshire Hussar* and *The Other Tap and Spile*. Purchased by Century Inns and given this name in 1997. The new licensee was 'the first real hussar in York' to run the pub (YEP 17 11 1997).

Fishergate Tavern, Fishergate
A beerhouse opened prior to 1869 (YCA Acc. 189) but first mentioned in 1872 and with this name in 1876 and 1881 (Dir). By 1902 it had become *The Brunswick Tavern*.

George Hotel, Coney Street, 1855

George IV, Redeness Street, 1960

Gimcrack Hotel, Fulford Road, 1980

Globe, Shambles, 1935

Golden Ball, St Mary's Row, Victor Street, 1900

Golden Ball, St Mary's Row, Victor Street, 1935

Golden Barrel, Walmgate, 1940

Golden Lion, Church Street (Girdlergate), 1906   Golden Lion, St Sampson's Square, 1950

Golden Lion, St Sampson's Square, 1881 when the Salvation Army held its first meeting in York

Grapes, King Street, 1906

Grapes, King's Square, 1906

Grapes, Tanner Row, 1906

Great Northern Hotel, George Hudson Street (Hudson Street, Railway Street), 1935

Green Tree, Lawrence Row, Barbican Road, 1906 *Greyhound, Spurriergate, 1957*

Half Moon, Blake Street, 1929

Half Moon, Blake Street, 1930

Ham and Firkin, Walmgate, 1906

Hand and Heart, St Sampson's Square, 1900

Harker's York Hotel, St Helen's Square, 1927

Harry's Café Bar, Micklegate, 1985

Haymarket Tavern, Haymarket, 1928

Hopgrove, Malton Road, 1934. The new Hopgrove is being built behind the old pub

Horseshoe Inn, Osbaldwick, 1909

Imperial, Kingsway North, 1984

Jacob's Well, Trinity Lane, 1900　　　　*John Bull, Layerthorpe, 1935*

John Bull, Layerthorpe, 1992

Jolly Bacchus, Bar Lane, Micklegate, 1852, photographed by William Pumphrey

Jubilee, Balfour Street, 1906

King William, Walmgate, 1921

King's Arms, Bilton Street, 1906

King's Arms Hotel, Fossgate, 1925

King's Head, Feasegate, 1922

Kingston, Tanner Row, 1900

Leeds Arms, Haymarket, 1910

Leeman Hotel, Stamford Street, 1935

Lendal Bridge Hotel, Tanners' Moat, 1909

Fisherman's Arms, Acaster Malbis ¶
Previously *The Fishing Boat* but from 1823 (YCA F30A) to 1857 (Dir) it used this name. It closed as licensed premises shortly after the latter date for want of trade but became the village shop (Appleby pp. 44/5).

Fishing Boat, Acaster Malbis
Recorded by this name in the licensing records of 1822 but thereafter called *The Fisherman's Arms* (YCA F30A).

Five Lions, St Helen, Stonegate, parish
Mentioned in 1783, 85, 87 and 95 (YCA Acc. 189, Cooper2 p. 42).

Five Lions, Walmgate ¶
Previously *The City Arms*, by 1818 it had gained this name (Dir). In 1902 it had nine furnished bedrooms and provided good sleeping accommodation for travellers. On the ground floor were a smoke room, a bar and a large dining room used by ladies on market days as well as a private sitting room and kitchen, in all a good market house (CC). A Grade II listed building (CAMRA2).

Flag and Whistle, Huntington Road
A competition was held to decide the name of this specially built public house just outside the boundary of New Earswick, an otherwise dry village (YEP 17 8 1981). It was won by Mrs Kathleen Leng who was inspired by the railway station which once stood on the site. It opened on 6 May 1982 (YEP 5 5 1982).

Flares, Tanner Row
Previously *The Brewers Arms* which was given a 1970s psychedelic look and renamed in March 2002 (YEP 26 10 2002).

Flying Dutchman, Grape Lane
A beerhouse, previously *The Bloomsbury*, gained this name by 1855 (Dir). Like Bloomsbury, Flying Dutchman was a race horse, by Bay Middleton out of Barbelle and, owned by Lord Eglinton. It was also, in 1849, a Derby winner as well as the St Leger in the same year (Fairfax p. 348). Last mention 1867 (Dir).

Flying Dutchman, Swinegate
Proposals to rebuild part of building in 1860 (YCL 942.7418 SWI).

Flying Dutchman, Tanner Row
Mentioned in 1857 (Dir).

Flying Dutchman, Terry Avenue ¶
A converted Dutch motor ship, 130ft long, built in the 1940s, brought to York to replace *The Barge* which sank in August 1984 (YEP 26 9 1984). A licence was granted in December 1984 and it opened to the public on 1 July 1985 (YEP 13 12 1984). It had only been granted planning permission for twelve months and an extension was turned down (YEP 18 7 1986). Named after a phantom ship which, because of a murder committed on board, was supposed to haunt the sea in a perpetual attempt to make Table Bay. A sighting of it was said to presage impending disaster.

Flying Horse, Coppergate
Mentioned in 1783, 87 and 95 (YCA K69, Cooper2 p. 45). Advertised to let in 1868 (YG 18 7 1868) but there would appear to have been no response as it makes no more appearances in the street directories after this.

Flying Legends, Stirling Road, Clifton Moor
A new pub on the trading estate built on the site of Clifton Airfield, it opened in summer 1992 (YEP 8 4 1992). After some altercation about the originally proposed name, an aircraft which had never been based at Clifton Airfield, this less contentious one was chosen.

Foresters' Arms, Skeldergate
Previously *The Labourer* and *The Three Tuns*, it had gained this name by 1840 (YG 4 7 1840). By 1861 it had become *The Prince of Wales* (Dir).

Fortunate Tar, King's Staith
An alternative name for *The Jolly Sailor*. Mentioned under this name in 1840 (YG 28 3 1840). When it was for sale with three adjoining houses in 1848 it was described as being on the north side of Far Water Lane fronting the Staith, (YG 27 5 1848). Also mentioned in 1849 and 1855 (Dir).

Fortunate Tar, North Street
An alternative name for *The British Tar* (Dir 1879).

Fortune of War, Low Ousegate
Previously, in 1742, *The Old Fortune of War* (YCo 1 6 1742), which implies that there were two houses in the city with this name at that time. It had reverted to this name by 1763 (YCo 8 11 1763). Last appearance on Dr White's map 1782.

Fossway, Huntington Road
Previously *The Bridge*, given this name by 1993 (Thomson).

Foundry Tavern, George Street
A beerhouse, mentioned in 1872 (Dir).

Fountain, Coney Street
'To be lett, publick house' 1748 (YCo 6 12 1748). Called The Fountain Coffee House when the tenant, Joseph Phillips, moved to *The Wildman Inn*, Petergate in 1752 (YCo 5 5 1752). Last mention 1753 (YCo 3 7 1753).

Four Alls, Malton Road, Stockton on the Forest
Originally a beerhouse, mentioned in 1876 when its location was described as Sandburn Mill (Dir). The name relates to the medieval times when it was thought the world was divided into four parts chosen by God

Kings who ruled all
Knights who fought for all
Priests who prayed for all
Peasants who worked for all

A later version of this theme was

The King who governs all
The Parson who prays for all
The Soldier who fights for all
The Farmer who pays for all

William Morris, working on Marxist principles, used the nobleman, the gentleman, the merchant and the poor. See also *The Rose and Crown* which may have been an alternative or temporary name for this establishment in 1884.

Fox, Goodramgate

Earliest mention 1830. Known as *The Beech Tree* from 1848 to 1872 but reverted to its previous name by 1876 (Dir). Also known as *The Lord Byron* (Cooper2 p. 49). The licence was surrendered by Thackwrays so that they could obtain an 'off' spirit licence (YG 7 9 1895). After it lapsed in October the house closed (YCA Acc.189).

Fox, Main Street, Heslington

Previously *The Ship*, mentioned under this name from 1828 to 1849 (Dir). Next *The Yarburgh Arms*, later *The De Yarburgh Arms* and *The Deramore Arms*. Also known as *The Fox and Hounds*.

Fox Inn, Holgate Road ¶

Previously *The Cross Keys*, it changed to this name, shortly prior to 1841 (Dir). The old building was taken down and a new one erected on the same site in 1878 (Cooper p. 49) after the voluntary liquidation of the affairs of Ann Cowton, the innkeeper (YG 20 1 1877). Joshua Tetley & Sons of Leeds purchased it for £16,000 in 1899 (YEP 20 Feb 1986). In 1902 it had five bedrooms, all occupied by the family, and a club room upstairs. Below were two smoke rooms, a dram shop, a small private room and a kitchen from which food could be supplied if required. The Chief Constable thought it a suitable house for carrying on the business of a licensed victualler (CC). Now a Grade II listed building, it was designated a Tetley's heritage inn in 1984 and restored the next year (CAMRA).

Fox, Nether Poppleton ¶

Mentioned in 1822 (YCA F30A). Licence transferred in 1898 to premises on the opposite side of the road with extensive grounds leading down to the Ouse. The original building was renamed Kilburn House. The second premises were demolished in 1965 and rebuilt further back from Church Lane to provide car parking. Closed 31 January 1997 (Davies2 pp. 38-45). Alternatively known as *The Cross Keys*.

Fox, Petergate ¶

Mentioned in 1769 (YCo 20 6 1769). In 1902 it had eight bedrooms, four of which were uninhabitable. The remaining four were all used by the family so no travellers could be accommodated. On the ground floor were a smoke room, a taproom, a serving bar, a private kitchen and scullery. Food could be supplied if required by customers who had to share the sole WC with the family. The licence was surrendered on 8 March 1955 (YCA Acc. 189) and it closed the following day (YEP 8 3 1955). Its owner, Church Schools Ltd obtained permission to demolish it (YEP 8 9 1955) and parts of it were incorporated into the new building erected in its place for the then York College for Girls.

Fox, Stockton on the Forest
First mentioned 1823 (Dir).

Fox, Tadcaster Road, Dringhouses
First mentioned in 1822 when the owner was Benjamin Leaf, a builder (YCA F30A; YEP 10 10 1997). Rebuilt by Anelay's in 1900 to a design by Samuel Needham (Pocock p. 25, 31). It was transferred from the Tadcaster Division of the West Riding County Council on 1 April 1937 on the extension of York boundaries (YCA Acc. 189). After refurbishment it reopened on 28 October 1997 under the new name of *The Fox and Roman* (YEP 10 Oct 1997).

Fox and Hounds, Aldwark
Mentioned by TP Cooper as a house that had closed during the 19th century (Cooper p. 78).

Fox and Hounds, Heslington
An alternative name for *The Fox*, in use in 1834 and 1843 (Dir).

Fox and Hounds, without Micklegate Bar (Blossom Street)
Mentioned in 1822 to 1825 (YCA F30A). A alternative name for *The Punch Bowl*.

Fox and Hounds, Top Lane, Copmanthorpe
Mentioned in 1867 (Dir). Extensively redesigned in 1978 (YEP 15 6 1978).

Fox and Roman, Tadcaster Road, Dringhouses
Previously *The Fox*, it reopened on 28 October 1997, after refurbishment, under this name. (YEP 10 Oct 1997).

Free Gardeners' Arms, Townend Street
Mentioned 1841 to 1855 (Dir). A name derived from the Order of Ancient Free Gardeners, Lancashire Union, founded c.1820, soon spreading into Yorkshire. It was a Friendly Society, an organisation set up to provide help with medical and funeral costs as well as social contact for working men. By 1858 it had become *The Trumpet* (Dir). Also known as *The Gardeners' Arms* (Dir 1846).

Freemasons' Arms, Coffee House, Little Blake Street
Opened as a coffee house in 1806 (YCo 23 6 1806) but by 1818 had substituted 'Arms' for 'Coffee House' in its title (Dir). In 1834 its licensee of over 16 years, John Lawn, was refused a renewal of his licence by the magistrates (YG 13 9 1834). By its next mention in 1838 it had changed its name to *The Golden Eagle* (Dir).

Freemasons' Arms, Townend Street
As it is mentioned only in 1843 (Dir) it is possibly an error by the directory compiler who confused it with *The Free Gardeners' Arms* which doesn't appear in that year but does in the editions before and afterwards.

Friendly Tavern, Dennis Street, Piccadilly ¶
A pre–1869 beerhouse (YCA Acc. 189). In 1902 it had four bedrooms, some of which were very damp and thus not habitable. On the ground floor were a taproom and a kitchen with a cellar below. The Chief Constable thought it a very poor house. The kitchen was very small and licensed so the family had to eat their food among the customers as well as

sharing the sole WC with them. He specially noted it for the attention of the Licensing Justices (CC). It was rebuilt at the end of Rectory Buildings in a Tudor style. Referred for compensation on 4 March 1926 (YCA Acc. 189), it closed shortly afterwards.

Frog Hall Tavern, Layerthorpe ¶
First mentioned in 1828 when John Kilby paid the Corporation an annual rent of £10 for it (YCA E78A). The derivation of its unusual name is clouded in obscurity. One untenable theory is that it is a racehorse name. In 1902 it had three bedrooms and a small closet upstairs, all used by the family. On the ground floor were a smoke room, a taproom, a small serving bar, a private kitchen and a scullery. Food could be supplied if asked for (CC). Rebuilt on a set back building line 1927, business being continued in a temporary public house nearby (S&B 2 10 1926, 3 1 1927). When it closed on 12 January 2002 to make way for a drive–through Macdonald's and Video Store (YEP 14 1 2002) it had three bedrooms, a lounge bar, a public bar and a games room (YEP 31 10 2002).

Fulford Arms, Fulford Road
Previously The Barrack Tavern it was renamed *The Fulford Arms* in 1976 (YEP 9 6 1976) when an heraldic sign was painted depicting the elements of the arms of a west country family named Fulford.

Full Moon, Walmgate ¶
Previously *The Barley Corn* and *The Hope and Anchor*. By 1838 Thomas Moon had become the licensee and he was responsible for the next change of name. Occasionally known by the more familiar name of *The Moon* (Dir 1841, 1876). It was rebuilt shortly before 1902 and it then had five bedrooms, two or three of which were available to let out to travellers. On the ground floor were a smoke room, a dram shop, a serving bar and a private kitchen from which dinners or teas could be supplied to customers. There was also a cellar (CC). JJ Hunt & Co. applied to remove its licence to new premises to be erected opposite the Corporation Housing Estate on Bell Farm and was given a conditional grant on 2 March 1938 (YEP 25 3 1938). It closed on 22 May 1939 when the licence of *The Garrick Head*, Petergate, was voluntarily surrendered at the same time (YCA Acc. 189).

Gallows House, The Mount
Previously *The New Inn*, it had been given this name by 1733 (Benson p. 166), a reference to its proximity to the Tyburn on the Knavesmire. In the 19th century it had become a starch factory and kennels for the York and Ainsty Hunt. In 1855 it was given a new licence under the name of *The White House*.

Garden Gate, Carmelite Street ¶
A pre–1869 beerhouse (YCA Acc. 189), previously *The Ship Inn* (and possibly *The Whale Fishery*), it gained this name between 1885 and 1902 (Dir, CC). This name possibly refers to the fact that Carmelite Street led to Garden Place. In 1902 it had only two bedrooms upstairs while the ground floor consisted of a smoke room, which was also the family's living room, a kitchen and a small back kitchen. The WC, shared by family and customers, was located, together with a urinal, in a yard open to the street in front of the house (CC). Perhaps in view of this report some of these defects were remedied in 1903 (YCA Y942 7418 GAR). Nevertheless the renewal of the licence was opposed, unsuccessfully, in 1908. On trade grounds this attempt does not seem justified as, over the previous six years, its average yearly sales were 539½ barrels of beer, £45 14s 2d worth of bottled beer and stout,

and £25 of minerals and cigars (Peacock pp. 113–5). Further structural improvements were made in 1925 but it was referred for compensation on 26 February 1937. This was paid on 31 January 1938 when the house closed (YCA Acc. 189). Also known by the nickname *The Rat Pit* (Cooper p. 46).

Gardeners' Arms, Goodramgate
Previously *The Glovers' Arms,* it had gained this name by 1841 (Dir) and was still using it in 1849 when it was for sale with its brewhouse (YG 16 6 1849). By 1850 it had been renamed *The Eagle Tavern* (YG 12 1 1850).

Gardeners' Arms, Marygate
Previously *The Minster*, then *The York Minster,* it gained this name by 1851 and was still using it in 1881, then by 1887 it reverted to *The Minster* (Dir).

Gardeners' Arms, Townend Street
A familiar name for *The Free Gardeners' Arms* (Dir 1846).

Garrick Coffee House, Petergate
Kept by Mr Richardson in 1829 and offered for sale by auction 1841 (YG 9 5 1829, 26 6 1841). An alternative name for *The Garrick's Head.*

Garrick's Head, Petergate ¶
An establishment with theatrical connections named after David Garrick 1717–79, the actor. Earliest mention 1783 (YCA K69). It occupied a medieval timber framed and jettied building which caused the Chief Constable to comment in 1902 that the rooms were small, had low ceilings and were badly lighted. It had four bedrooms, one of which was available for travellers, a sitting room and club room upstairs. On the ground floor were a smoke room, a taproom and a small living room where presumably food was prepared if required. There was also a cellar and the WC was shared by the family and the customers (CC). JJ Hunt & Co voluntarily surrendered the licence as well as that of *The Full Moon*, Walmgate, in order to obtain a new one for *The Bridge Inn*, Huntington Road. It closed for the sale of intoxicants on 20 May 1939 (YCA Acc. 189) but remained open as a hotel for some years after.

Gate, Middle Water Lane
Mentioned 1834 to 1841. By 1843 it had become *The Green Tree* (Dir).

George, Apollo Street
Mentioned as a beerhouse in 1872 (Dir). In July 1857 three houses in Apollo Street were offered for sale, two of which had been joined together as a beerhouse. The sale also included brewing plant (YG 25 7 1857). These cottages would appear to have been built on a two–up and two–down arrangement since in 1902 the premises comprised three bedrooms and a sitting room upstairs and a smoke room, a taproom and private kitchens on the ground floor. There was also a cellar, and the WC was shared by the family and the customers (CC). It was referred for compensation on 26 February 1937 and closed soon afterwards (YCA Acc. 189).

George, Bootham Bar, within
Mentioned in 1516 (Benson p. 166).

George, Coney Street (1)
Mentioned as *Hospicium Georgii* in the will of Richard Roderham, Chancellor of Exeter Cathedral, proved on 17 September 1455 (Raine p. 155).

George Hotel, Coney Street (2) ¶
Previously *The George and Dragon*. Built on a messuage which had once been occupied by *The Bear* and afterwards by *The Golden Lion* which had gone by 1596 (Davies pp. 63–4). Kept by Thomas Kaye, Sheriff of York 1603/4, from 1606, on the death of John Bilbowe, until his own death in 1624 (PR).Mentioned in 1622 in a poem by John Taylor, describing a voyage in an open boat from London to York (Palliser p. 14). Mentioned in 1688 in John Webster's diary (Malden). In 1736 described as one of three principal inns in the city (Drake p. 331). A coaching house, with a wide gateway and spacious inner quadrangle, its trade was considerably affected by the coming of the railways to the city in 1839, but it struggled on as a commercial hotel for a few years and then, on 30 May 1855 it was offered for sale by auction (YG 10 May 1855). Later that year the wainscotting, stained glass and antique oak furniture from the State Dining Room were sold (YG 3 10 1855). Thomas Winn moved to manage a new hotel, *The George*, Tanner Row on 6 June 1855 (EH) leaving a Miss Sarah Ann Senior to continue to run it as a family hotel. It was finally offered for sale in 1866 in five lots (YG 7 4 1866) which mainly became shops. One column and a circular bow window above are all that remain of this hotel today.

George, Pavement (All Saints, Pavement, parish)
Mentioned in 1783, 87 and 95 (YCA K69, Cooper2 p 45).

George, Pavement (Fossgate, Hosier Lane End) St Crux parish
Because of changes in the street layouts occasioned by the enlargement of Pavement market the address of this house has changed on a number of occasions. Earliest mention in an advertisement in 1733 (YG 14 8 1733). Its name had been changed to *The Old George* by 1749 to avoid confusion with another establishment with the same name in the locality (see previous), although it was occasionally still known as The George.

George, Petergate
Mentioned in 1516 (Benson p. 166).

George, St Michael, Spurriergate, parish
Probably in First Water Lane, mentioned in 1783 and 87 (YCA K69, Cooper2 p.45).

George, Tanner Row
A new hotel built opposite the railway station by William Hotham, a brewer of George Street and opened 6 June 1855 under the management of Thomas Winn of *The George*, Coney Street, who called it Winn's George Hotel (EH). By 1861 the management had passed to John Holliday, manager of *The Station Hotel* (Dir) and it was renamed *The North Eastern Hotel* after the railway company which had been created in 1854.

George III, Colliergate
Mentioned in 1772 (YCo 21 1 1772). George III ruled from 1760 to 1820.

George IV, Redeness Street ¶
A beerhouse first mentioned in 1834 (Dir). In 1902 it was described as a very suitable house for the business. It had five bedrooms upstairs and, below, a smoke room, a

taproom, a sitting room, a kitchen and a scullery. It also had a cellar (CC). It, along with all the houses around, was demolished in 1962 and on 2 October that year the licence was placed in suspense (YCA Acc. 189). George IV ruled from 1820 to 1830.

George and Dragon, Coney Street
A messuage in this street had once been occupied by *The Bear* and afterwards *The Golden Lion*, which had gone by 1596 (Davies pp. 63–64). On this messuage this inn, later *The George,* was built (Benson2, Cooper2 p. 5).

George and Dragon, Jubbergate
Mentioned in 1783, 85, 87 and 95 (YCA K69, Cooper2 p. 45).

George and Dragon, North Street
Mentioned in 1767 and 1774 (YCo 3 11 1767, 22 3 1774).

George and Dragon (1), Pavement
For a period from at least 1782 (Dr White's Map) to 1798 (Dir) *The Old George* was occasionally known by this name.

George and Dragon (2), Pavement
Earliest mention 1818 (Dir, YCh 19 11 1818), it was demolished in 1835 (YG 19 9 1835) and was rebuilt a few years later on a new site. From at least 1841 (Dir) until his death in 1859 the licensee was William Hutchinson (YG 11 6 1859). His wife continued the business for a few years until 1863 when she put it up for sale (YG 1 3 1863) and the site was purchased by Rowntree's as a grocery store [now Pizza Hut] (Cooper p. 46).

Gibson's Hotel, Museum Street
'A publick house of great resort though without a sign ...... the house is kept by Mr George Gibson, and his stables, sufficient for 200 horses, or more, are in Mint Yard' (Drake p. 337). By 1767 it had become *Bluitt's Hotel* and later *Etridge's Royal Hotel.*

Gibson's Vault, Low Petergate
Previously *The Board,* its proprietor in 1823 was Robert Gibson, a wine and spirit merchant. In 1843 he was succeeded by William Gibson who was followed after 1858 by a number of other people until 1872 (Dir). It was located next door to *The Londesborough Arms.*

Gillygate, Gillygate
Previously *The Waggon and Horses*, its name changed 17 April 2003 after it was acquired by the Exhibition Group and given a makeover (YEP 19 4 2003).

Gimcrack Hotel, Fulford Road ¶
Originally a private house called Ousefield, it opened as a pub on 1 December 1936. It had been granted an 'on' licence on 6 February 1936 when the licence was removed from *The King's Arms Hotel*, Fossgate and that of *The New Walk Tavern* was surrendered. The grant was confirmed on 6 April 1936 (YCA Acc. 189). An application was made, and later withdrawn, after a public outcry, in 2002 to demolish it and replace it with 19 three storey town houses (YEP 15 1 2002). Closed 26 September 2002 as its owners, the brewers, Tom Cobleigh, considered it did not fit into their commercial strategy (YEP 26 & 27 9 2002). Gimcrack was a grey horse by Cripple out of Miss Elliot who started his racing career as a

four year old in 1764 and continued to 1771. During this period he won 27 out of 35 races, but never at York where he ran twice and suffered his only unplaced result (Pick p. 49). The Ancient Fraternitie of Ye Gimcracks (now the Gimcrack Club) was founded in York in his honour in 1770 and he has also given his name to the Gimcrack Stakes founded in 1846 and run on the Knavesmire.

Glass House, Cattle Market, Fawcett Street
One of the names for a pub known, in addition, as *The York Glass Works, The York Glass House, The York Glass Makers' Arms* and finally *The Glass Makers' Arms*. Known by this name in 1846, 51 and 58 (Dir). It owed its name to its proximity to the glass works in Fishergate.

Glass Makers' Arms, Fawcett Street
Previously known, at various times, as *The York Glass Works, The York Glass House, The Glass House, The York Glass Makers' Arms*, it was first called by this name in 1867 (Dir). In 1902 it had four bedrooms, two of which were available for travellers. On the ground floor were a smoke room, a bar and a private kitchen from which food could be supplied if required. The urinal was overlooked from adjacent cottages and the Chief Constable recommended that a screen should be provided (CC). At the Brewster Sessions in 1913 it was referred for compensation and it closed on 6 October 1913 (YCA Acc. 189).

Globe, Bishophill
Mentioned 1817 (YCo 26 6 1817). Possibly *The Golden Ball.*

Globe, Colliergate
Mentioned 1770 (Benson p. 167).

Globe, Coppergate
Mentioned in 1768 (YCo 6 12 1768).

Globe, North Street
Mentioned in 1787 (Cooper2 p. 44).

Globe (1), Shambles (Great Flesh Shambles)
Mentioned on a trade token in 1666 (Benson3 p. 88) and in a lease 1768 (YCA E94 f. 97). Later became a private house in the occupation of John Pallister, Currier, to be let 1770 (YCo 3 4 1770).

Globe (2), Shambles ¶
Earliest mention 1805 (Dir). In 1902 it had four bedrooms, none used by travellers, and a club room upstairs. The ground floor consisted of a smoke room, a taproom, a bar and a private kitchen. It also had a cellar. The sole WC was shared by family and customers (CC). It was closed in 1936 (YG 8 3 1936) having been refused for compensation (YCA Acc. 189). Occasionally called *The Old Globe* (Dir 1843).

Globe (3), Shambles
Mentioned 1818 and 1823 (Dir). Richard Peaker was shown as licensee in the latter year. The official records show him at *The Cross Keys* in 1822 and 1823 (F30A). As the latter name had been in use since 1745, The Globe must have been an alternative or familiar name.

Glovers' Arms, Goodramgate

Possibly previously *The Queen Caroline*. Mentioned 1823 (YCA F30A) to 1841 (YG 11 9 1841) but in 1828 apparently called *The Grove* (Dir). When it was offered for sale in 1837 the premises included a brewhouse (YG 18 2 1837). Next *The Gardeners' Arms,* and *The Eagle.*

Goat, Thursday Market (St Sampson's Square)

Mentioned in John Cossins' notebook 1727 (Murray3 p. 59).

Golden Anchor, High Jubbergate

Mentioned 1756 (YCo 10 8 1756).

Golden Anchor, North Street

Mentioned 1773 (YCo 7 12 1773).

Golden Anchor, Queen's Staith

Mentioned in 1764 and 1767 (YCo 6 3 1764, 16 6 1767). Next *The Anchor.*

Golden Ball, Dale Street, Nunnery Lane

Beerhouse, licence granted to Mrs Mary Joy 1837 (YG 16 9 1837). Mentioned in 1838 (Dir). Next *The Wheatsheaf, The Barley Sheaf, The Crown* and *The Wheatsheaf* again.

Golden Ball, Fetter Lane

Mentioned in 1688 in John Webster's diary in Bishophill Junior parish (Malden) and then in 1783 (YCA K69). Still using the name in 1830 (YG 20 3 1830) but it is also called *The Golden Lion* (mistakenly?) in that year (Dir). By 1834 it had become *The King William IV.*

Golden Ball, Peter Lane Little

Alehouse, to be sold 1763 (YCo 5 4 1763). Mentioned in a lease 27 April 1774 (YCA E94 f. 155).

Golden Ball, St Mary's Row, Victor Street ¶

Mentioned in 1773 when house next door became a school (YCo 8 6 1773) and in 1795 (YCA K69). In 1902 it had three bedrooms, all occupied by the family, and a bathroom upstairs. On the ground floor were a smoke room, vaults and two private kitchens. At the bottom of the yard was a clubroom which was used for playing brasses. There was only one WC shared by the family and the customers (CC). It was extensively refurbished by John Smith & Son in 1929 (CAMRA).

Golden Barrel, Walmgate ¶

Mentioned in 1649 in connection with an execution. The criminals were on their way to the gallows at Green Dykes and, passing this house, were given some mint water to revive them (Knipe p. 27). In 1902 it had three bedrooms, all used by the family, and a sitting room upstairs. Below were a smoke room, a bar, a taproom and a private kitchen. Food was not supplied but if customers required it the landlord sent them to the coffee house opposite (CC). It closed in March 1935 (YG 8 March 1935). The building it occupied latterly was once the Old Rectory House of St Margaret, Walmgate, built in the graveyard of St Peter le Willow church (Cooper p. 34). Also known as *The Barrel[l].*

Golden Cup Coffee House, Micklegate
Previously *The Rose and Crown, The Crown* and *The Grapes* then taken by William Burland and renamed *Burland's Coffee House* (YG 23 10 1824) but known at the same time as *The Cup* (YCA F30A), a name which reappeared in 1843 (Dir). Next *Burland's Hotel* and then *The Crown* once again.

Golden Eagle, Little Blake Street
Previously *The Freemasons' Arms*, it gained this name by 1838. Last mention 1841 (Dir).

Golden Fleece, Pavement
Earliest mention 1666 on a trade token (Benson3 p. 86). Mentioned in 1733 as *The Fleece*, a place where common carriers could be found (Gent). Mistakenly called *The Golden Hart* in 1851 by Ordnance Surveyors (OS). In 1902 it was described as a very old property with plenty of room in it. It had no front door onto the street and was approached by a long passage from Pavement. There were two attics, ten bedrooms, five set aside for travellers, a dining room and a drawing room on the upper floors. On the ground floor were a smoke room, a bar, a licensed kitchen, a small private room and a private kitchen. There was also a cellar. Meals were provided if required by customers (CC). A Grade II listed building (CAMRA2).

Golden Hart, Pavement
A name mistakenly given to *The Golden Fleece* by the Ordnance Surveyors in 1851 (OS).

Golden Lion, Church Street (Girdlergate) ¶
In 1711 Thomas Hessay took out a lease on the property from Abraham Goodgione for £71 1s 6d and subsequently turned it into an alehouse (Johnson p. 23). Mentioned in 1745 (YCo 25 3 1745). In 1902 it had five bedrooms, three available for travellers. On the ground floor were a smoke room, a dram shop, a small and badly lit snug, a bottling department, and a kitchen from which food could be supplied. There was also a cellar. The customers and the family shared the only WC (CC). In 1970 an application from JW Cameron & Co. to demolish the old pub and rebuild a new one, was approved (YEP 29 5 1970). It reopened in 1971 under the name of *The 1900*, to celebrate the 1900th anniversary of the founding of the city (YEP 16 1 1971). It reverted to its former name in 1983 (YEP 23 3 1983).

Golden Lion, Coney Street
A messuage in this street had once been occupied by *The Bear* and afterwards The Golden Lion, which had gone by 1596 (Davies pp. 63–64). On this messuage *The George and Dragon*, later *The George* was built (Benson2, Cooper2 p. 5).

Golden Lion, Fetter Lane
The Golden Ball in Fetter Lane was also (mistakenly?) called by this name in 1830 (Dir).

Golden Lion, St Andrewgate
Mentioned 1783, 85, 87 and 95 (YCA K69, Cooper2 p. 44).

Golden Lion, St Sampson's Square ¶
Mentioned in 1729 when it was bought by Thomas Crosby Innholder. It was already called *The Golden Lyon* at this time (YCA E93 f. 4b). Mentioned in 1733 as a place where common carriers could be found (Gent). Sold in 1819 on the bankruptcy of John Kilby

(YG 26 6 1819). In 1845 the landlord offered home brewed ale (YG 19 4 1845) and when it was put up for sale in 1866 the property included a brewhouse (YG 29 9 1866). In 1902 five bedrooms, two available for travellers, a club room and a sitting room upstairs. Below were two smoke rooms, a bar parlour and a licensed kitchen as well as a private kitchen. Food could be supplied if required (CC). It was acquired by WP Brown's in Aug 1973 and closed a few months later (YEP 4 8 1973). It reopened in 1977 as a tea house (YEP 21 9 1977).

Golden Punch Bowl, Stonegate

An alternative name for *The Punch Bowl*, used in 1761 (Benson p. 164) and 1799 (Bill head).

Golden Slipper, Goodramgate (¶ see Royal Oak)

Previously *The Shoe* and *The Slipper,* using this name by 1823 (Dir) although continuing to be called *The Slipper* in licensing records until at least 1828 (YCA F30A; F31). In 1902 it had five bedrooms, two of which were very damp and uninhabitable, and a sitting room upstairs. The ground floor comprised a smoke room, a small taproom and a dram shop. There was also a cellar. Although no mention of a kitchen, food could be supplied if required (CC). It became a Grade II listed building in 1954 (YG 23 7 1954). In 1983 the brewers made changes to the interior without first getting listed building consent (YEP 21 12 1983). Familiarly known as *The Slipper* 1872 (YG 23 11 1872) and 1902 (CC).

Gotty's, Love Lane

A familiar name for *The New Walk Tavern*, after Albert Gott, landlord in 1907 (Wilson p. 27).

Granby, St Peter the Little parish

Mentioned in 1783, 85, 87 and 95 (YCA K69, Cooper2 p. 45). In 1818 it was called *Granby's Punch House* and by 1819 *The Marquis of Granby*. In 1843 it was referred to as *Granby's Punch Bowl* (Dir). Later *The Griffin.*

Granby's Punch Bowl, Peter Lane

Previously *The Granby, Granby's Punch House* and *The Marquis of Granby,* it was referred to by this name in 1843 (Dir). Later *The Griffin.*

Granby's Punch House, Peter Lane

Previously *The Granby,* it was known by this name in 1818 (Dir). Later *The Marquis of Granby* and *The Griffin.*

Grandstand, Knavesmire

Earliest mention 1811 (YCo 24 6 1811). In 1902 it was owned by the York Race Committee and was described as a suitable house for the business. It had six bedrooms, all used by the family, and five licensed rooms on the ground floor as well as good private kitchens. The licence was allowed to lapse at the Brewster Sessions in February 1911 (YCA Acc. 189).

Grapes, Feasegate

Mentioned between 1822 (YCA F30A) and 1845 (YG 5 7 1845). Also known as *The London Coffee House.*

Grapes, King Street ¶

Previously *The Black Boy* in First Water Lane, but when this street was widened in 1852 and renamed King Street it gained this name (Johnson p. 27). In 1902 it had four bedrooms, one let off to travellers and a sitting room on the upper floor. Below were a smoke room, a dram shop and a private kitchen from which food could be supplied if required. There was also a cellar. Previously the Chief Constable had not thought the house suitable but, since making his report, considerable alterations and improvements had been made (CC).

Grapes, King's Square ¶

A pre–1869 beerhouse (YCA Acc.189), first mentioned in 1867 (Dir). In 1902 it had upstairs three bedrooms, a sitting room and a private kitchen. There were only two rooms on the ground floor, a taproom and a very dark kitchen only lit by a skylight. While there was a urinal inside the house, there was no WC available for the customers. The Chief Constable thought it a very poor house and specially noted it for the attention of the Licensing Justices (CC). Renewal of its licence was opposed, unsuccessfully, in 1906. Although one of the worst six houses in York it was wholly protected by its pre–1869 status and could only be objected to on grounds of necessity (Peacock p. 92). Eventually in 1921 it was referred for compensation and closed on 7 October that year (YG 12 3 1921, YCA Acc. 189). It was also known, for a time, as *The Edward VII*. Familiarly known as *The Sawdust 'Ole*.

Grapes, Micklegate

Previously *The Crown*, then between 1818 and 1838 it was using this name simultaneously with *Burland's Coffee House* (Dir). Next *The Golden Cup* then *Burland's Coffee House, The Cup, Burland's Hotel* and then *The Crown* once again.

Grapes, Petergate

Also known as *Baynes' Hotel, Tomlinson's Hotel, Jackson's Hotel* and *Thomas's Hotel*. Using this name by 1822 when William Baynes was the licensee (YCA F30A), 1855 (The Grapes Hotel), 1867 (Dir) and still in 1874 when it was offered for sale. The property then included a very compact brewhouse (YG 5 12 1874). Next *The Londesborough Arms*. It is probable that this name was in use continuously from 1822 to 1874.

Grapes, Tanner Row ¶

Previously *The Railway Coffee House, The Refreshment Inn, The North Eastern Refreshment Inn,* and *The Railway Inn*, it gained this name by 1881 (Dir) after the centre of railway activity had moved in 1877 to a new station and hotel outside the walls. In 1902 it had eight bedrooms, five of which were set apart for travellers. The ground floor comprised of a smoke room, a bar, and two private kitchens. Food could be supplied if required. The entrance to the house was from a side passage shared with Cutforth Brothers of Micklegate (CC). It closed in 1978 and reopened as Jeeves Restaurant later that year (YEP 13 12 1978).

Great Northern Hotel, George Hudson Street (Hudson Street, Railway Street) ¶

One of several hotels built in the vicinity of the Old Railway Station to provide facilities for travellers, opened in 1852 under the management of Mrs Ann Shaw who moved from *The Crown Hotel*, Micklegate (YG 14 8 1852). In 1902 it had 21 bedrooms, 18 of which were for guests. Additionally it had a commercial room, a dining room, a drawing room, a smoke room, a bar, vaults, private kitchens and a private sitting room. Meals were supplied if required (CC). The top two floors, part of the original hotel, were removed in 1965 (YEP 15 July 1965). After renovation it was reopened as *The Pageant* in 1966 (YEP 3 11 1966). It reverted to its original name in 1984 (YEP 10 5 1984) and was renamed *Merlins* by 1994.

Green Dragon, Davygate
Mentioned 1742 (YCA E94) and 1750/1 (YCo 5 3 1750/1).

Green Tree, Beckfield Lane
Opened 12 December 1958 (YEP 11 12 1958), the licence having been transferred from *The Coach and Horses*, Swinegate, a transfer which was agreed on 10 April 1956. The licence of *The Green Tree*, Lawrence Row, Barbican Road, was surrendered at the same time (YCA Acc. 189).

Green Tree, Lawrence Row, Barbican Road ¶
Previously *The Yew Tree*, gained this name by 1841 (Dir). A house used a good deal by cattle dealers who stayed there for two or three nights during the fortnightly cattle fairs in the nearby cattle market. In 1902 five of the seven bedrooms were let to them. In addition to the bedrooms there was a sitting room upstairs. On the ground floor were a smoke room, a bar, a licensed kitchen and two private kitchens. Meals were provided when required (CC). It closed on 11 December 1958, its licence having been surrendered on 27 October 1958, on the opening of *The Green Tree*, Beckfield Lane, whose licence was transferred from *The Coach and Horses*, Swinegate (YCA Acc. 189). It was also known as *The Drovers' Arms* (Dir 1867).

Green Tree, Middle Water Lane
Previously *The Gate*, gained this name by 1843 (Dir). A notorious brothel and lodging house, at the 1861 census it had 55 residents. It was last mentioned in the same year when James Gibson, the landlord, was charged with having prostitutes living on the premises (Finnegan pp. 39, 112).

Green Tree, Minster Close (Yard)
An alternative name for *The Sycamore Tree* (Cooper p. 21).

Green Tree, St Andrewgate
Closed before 1846 (Cooper p. 57).

Green Tree, Water End, Clifton
Mentioned 1825 (YG 22 10 1825) and 1830 (Dir). Possibly another name for *The Sycamore.*

Grenadier, Jubbergate
Mentioned in 1822 to 1827 (YCA F30A, F31).

Grey Horse, Acomb Green
Previously *The Grey Orville*, by 1823 it was using this name (YCA F30A). Later *The Sun.*

Grey Horse, Clifton
Mentioned 1823 (Dir). Next *The Grey Mare*, *The Old Grey Mare* and *Ye Olde Grey Mare.*

Grey Horse, Elvington

Previously *The Bay Horse* but by 1840 had gained this name (Dir). Had the directory compiler been confused by the rhyme of Bay and Grey, or had the sign become so dirty that the original colour of the horse could no longer be discerned?

Grey Horse, Little Blake Street (Lop Lane)

Mentioned 1754 (YCo 5 March 1754).

Grey Horse, North Street

Previously *The Sawyers' Arms*, gained this name by 1846 (Dir). Also called *The Grey Mare*, by 1861 it had become *The Neptune* (Dir). Later *The Newcastle Arms.*

Grey Marcia, Front Street, Acomb

Mentioned in 1857, 1867 and 1889 (Dir), an alternative name for *The Marcia*, a grey mare (Orton p. 258).

Grey Mare, Bishopthorpe

First mentioned in the licensing records of 1822 as The Grey Mare (Martia). This alternative name, a positive indication of which grey mare was intended, was dropped the next year (YCA F30A). With the exception of 1838, when the name is given as The Marque, the pub continues to use this name until at least 1857 (Dir). By 1866 it had abandoned it in favour of *The Marcia* (Brayley p. 4).

Grey Mare, Clifton

Previously *The Grey Horse* and *The Old Grey Mare*, it had gained this name by 1855 but had reverted to The Old Grey Mare by 1879 (Dir). Later *Ye Olde Grey Mare.*

Grey Mare, Front Street, Acomb

Previously *The Square and Compasses* and *The Marcia*, this name was used between 1823 and 1838 (YCA F30A, F31; Dir), a reference to Marcia, a grey mare (Orton p. 258). By 1843 it had reverted to *The Marcia* or occasionally, in 1857 and 1889 *The Grey Marcia* (Dir). Later *The Poacher*.

Grey Mare, North Street

A name being used in 1851 and 1855 by *The Grey Horse* (Dir).

Grey Orville, Acomb

Mentioned in October 1822 (YCA F30A). Lord Fitzwilliam's bay colt Orville by Beningborough out of Evelina won the St Leger at Doncaster in 1802 (Orton p. 263). By 1823 it had become *The Grey Horse* and later *The Sun.*

Greyhound, Acomb

Previously known as *The Hare and Hounds* and *The Greyhound and Hare.* Mentioned 1838 (Dir).

Greyhound, Dunnington

First mentioned in 1823 (Dir).

Greyhound, Newgate

A beerhouse, mentioned between 1838 and 1872 (Dir). Previously *The Pig and Whistle* (Cooper p. 49).

Greyhound, North Street
Sold in 1819 on the bankruptcy of John Kilby (YG 28 8 1819).

Greyhound, Spurriergate ¶
Mentioned in 1772 (YCo 28 7 1772) and marked on Dr White's Map of 1782. In 1841 it moved to a new building, designed by JB and W Atkinson for Robert Brogden, brewer, of Tockwith (RCHME V p. 220b). The bedrooms in 1843 were described as being 'large and airy and fitted up with every convenience that could be desired' (Dir 1843 Advt). In 1902 it was described as a long narrow house. It had seven bedrooms, four of which were available for travellers, and two sitting rooms upstairs. On the ground floor, above a large cellar, were a smoke room, a dram shop and a living kitchen from which food could be supplied if required. The urinal was situated between the smoke room and the kitchen and there was no WC for customers (CC). It was offered for sale in a block with three other properties in Spurriergate in 1957 (YEP 6 9 1957). It closed on 31 March 1958, compensation being agreed the next day (YCA Acc. 189).

Greyhound, St Sampson's Square (Thursday Market)
Mentioned in 1818 (Dir). Sold in 1819 on the bankruptcy of John Kilby (YG 26 6 1819). Last mention 1838 (Dir) before its name was changed to *The Reindeer* (or *The Stag*). Later *The Hand and Heart, The Bradford Arms* and *The Hand and Heart* again.

Greyhound, Trinity Lane
Originally a familiar name for *The Hare and Greyhound*, first mentioned in 1777 (YCo 10 10 1777) and interchangeable with *The Greyhound and Hare* and *The Hare and Hound*. By 1823 this had become the accepted name of the house (YCA F30A). Last mention 1838 (Dir). Also known as *The Upholsterers' Arms* (Dir 1823) or *The Upholders' Arms* (YCA F30A).

Greyhound and Hare, Acomb
An alternative name for *The Hare and Hounds,* mentioned in 1823 (Dir). Later *The Greyhound.*

Greyhound and Hare, Trinity Lane
The original name of *The Greyhound*, interchangeable with *The Hare and Greyhound*. Earliest mention 1747 (YCo 28 4 1747). Mentioned in 1784 (YCo 18 5 1784).

Grid Iron, Lendal
Mentioned in 1824 (YCA F30A). The gridiron is the attribute of St Leonard after whom the nearby medieval hospital was named. Also known as *The Coffee House.*

Griffin, Peter Lane
A beerhouse, previously *The Granby, Granby's Punch House* and *The Marquis of Granby*, it gained this name by 1851 (Dir). When it was offered for sale in 1855 the property included a brewhouse (YG 16 6 1855). Last mention 1863 when it was to let (YG 10 10 1863).

Grob and Ducat, Rougier Street
In 1927 *The Old Ebor* was closed but the redundant publican continued to run it as a café. It was revived as a public house on 2 June 1976 under this new name (YEP 2 6 1976). Its name was changed to *The Richard III* in December 1980 (YEP 13 12 1980). Later *Macmillans.*

Light Horseman, Fishergate, 1910

Lion and Lamb, Blossom Street, 1974

Little John, Castlegate, 1940

Locomotive, Watson Street, 1935

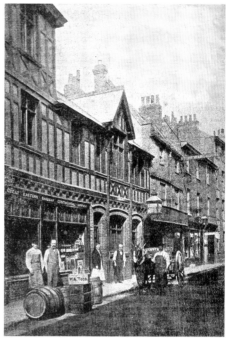

Londesborough Arms, Petergate, 1980

London Hotel, Davygate, 1900

Lord Collingwood, Upper Poppleton, 1906

Lord Nelson, Walmgate, 1906

Lowther Hotel,
King's Staith, 1935

Magpie, Penley's Grove Street, 1960

Mail Coach, St Sampson's Square, 1929

Marcia, Bishopthorpe, 1911

Marcia, Front Street, Acomb, 1935

Market Tavern, Coppergate, 1910   *Market Tavern, Coppergate, 1927*

Masons' Arms, Fishergate, 1906

Melbourne Hotel, Cemetery Road, 1927

Minster Inn, Marygate, 1930

Mount Hotel, The Mount, 1935

Nag's Head, Askham Bryan, 1908

Nag's Head, Micklegate, 1906

New Walk Tavern, Love Lane, 1935

Old Ebor Tavern, Tanner Row, 1907

Old George Hotel, Fossgate or Pavement or Whipmawhopmagate, 1947

Old Grey Mare, Clifton, 1935

Old Malt Shovel, 12 Walmgate, 1947

Old Malt Shovel, 12 Walmgate, 1890

*Old Turk's Head, King's Court,
King's Square (Haymarket), 1890*

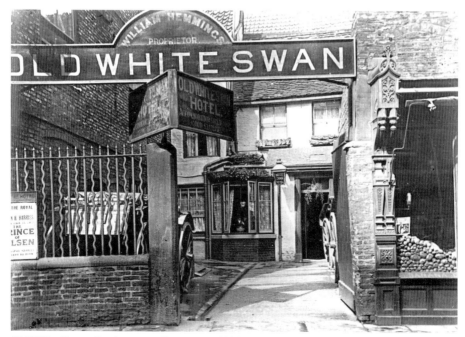

Old White Swan, Goodramgate (Petergate), 1906

Other Tap and Spile, North Street, 1990

Ouse Bridge Tavern, King's Staith, 1885

Pack Horse, Micklegate, 1950

Pack Horse, Skeldergate, 1935

Pavement Vaults, Pavement, 1960

Phoenix, George Street, 1935

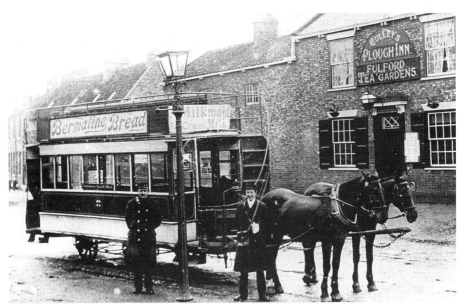

Plough, Main Street, Fulford, 1906

Plough, Main Street, Fulford, 1930

Plumber's Arms, Skeldergate, 1950

Punch Bowl, Blossom Street, 1906

Punch Bowl, Lowther Street, 1950

Punch Bowl, Stonegate, 1906

Punch Bowl, Stonegate, 1984

Grove, Goodramgate
Mentioned in 1828 (Dir) but almost certainly an error by the street directory compiler as the building it occupied was *The Glovers' Arms* both before and after this date.

Grove House, Cole Street, Groves
Mentioned 1837 (YG 10 6 1837) to 1855 (Dir). There was, at this time, a large villa in the area called Grove House, on whose grounds the later extensions to the Groves were built.

Gun, Museum Street
A familiar name for *The Cannon* but given authority by its inclusion on the 1852 Ordnance Survey Map. The surveyor must have asked a passer–by the name of the establishment and been told its colloquial name.

Haha Bar & Canteen, New Street
Opened in 2000 (Thomson).

Haigh's Vaults, High Petergate
A pre–1869 beerhouse operating with a six day licence in 1900 (YCA Acc. 189) owned by George Wolstenholme, wine and spirit merchant in 1872 (Dir). In 1893 TB Haigh claimed that his business, formerly Wolstenholme's which he had taken over by 1887, had been established in 1800 (Dir).

Half Moon, Barker Hill, Jewbury
An alehouse, first mentioned in 1841 (Dir). Its licence was not renewed on 7 September 1894 and the house was pulled down soon afterwards (YCA Acc. 189).

Half Moon, Blake Street ¶
Mentioned in 1783, 85, 87 and 95 (YCA K69, Cooper2 p.42). In 1902 it had three attics which were not in use and five bedrooms, all occupied by members of the family. On the ground floor were two smoke rooms, a dram shop, a private room and kitchens from which food could be supplied if required (CC). It underwent extensive structural alterations, including a new façade in 1930 (date on rainwater head). It was taken over by Fortes in 1968 (YEP 10 10 1968) and reopened the next year as a Henekey Inn (YEP 15 4 1969). After its closure in 1978 (YEP 7 7 1978) it became part of Macdonald's hamburger franchise chain.

Half Moon, Goodramgate
Mentioned 1780 (YCo 3 10 1780) and 1783 (YCA K69).

Half Moon, Marygate
Adjoining Manor Shore (now Museum Gardens Gate), mentioned in a baptism at St Olave's Church in 1771 (PR).

Half Moon, Strensall
John Linfoot, a bricklayer, was publican here by 1815 (Mitchell p. 15). First mentioned in a street directory 1823 (Dir).

Half Moon, Trinity Lane
A beerhouse, previously *The Square and Compasses, The Cup and Compass, The Cricket Ground, The Cricketers' Arms* then *The Seven Stars,* it gained this name by 1872 (Dir). In 1902 all the rooms were described as small. On the upper floors were six bedrooms, above

a smoke room, a kitchen and a scullery where all the cooking was done for family and customers who also shared a single WC. There was also a cellar (CC). It was referred to the Compensation Authority in March 1910 and renewal of the licence was refused on 26 May that year (YCA Acc. 189).

Ham and Firkin, Walmgate ¶
Mentioned 1761 (YCo 27 10 1761). In 1902 it had five bedrooms, two of which were set apart for travellers, and a sitting room upstairs. Below were a smoke room, a taproom, a market room, a private kitchen, from which dinners could be supplied, and a small private room. There was also a cellar (CC). It was referred for compensation on 12 March and closed on 1 October 1923 (YCA Acc. 189).

Hammer and Pincers, Huntington
Previously and later *The Blacksmiths' Arms*, it was using this name in 1872 and 1876 (Dir), probably a familiar name based on the blacksmith's tools displayed on the sign.

Hand and Grapes, Briggate (Bridge Street)
Mentioned in 1787 (Cooper2 p. 42) and 1795 (YCA K69).

Hand and Heart, St Sampson's Square ¶
Previously *The Greyhound* and *The Reindeer* (or *The Stag*), it had gained this name by 1843 (Dir). By 1875 it had become *The Bradford Arms* (Davison p. 43), but after 1876 it had become *The Hand and Heart* again (Dir). It was a timber framed jettied building which in 1902 was described as a very old property with small and badly lit rooms. It had six bedrooms, some of which were used to accommodate up to ten travellers and a large club room upstairs. Downstairs was a smoke room, a bar, a taproom and a private kitchen from which food could be supplied. The urinal combined with a WC was in a public passage which ran at the side of the house. The family also had to use these facilities (CC). The Tadcaster Tower Brewery Co. surrendered the licence at the 1903 Brewster Sessions (YCA Acc. 189) and its premises were absorbed by *The Black Bull* next door.

Hand and Whip, Castlegate
Mentioned in 1770 (Benson p. 167).

Hansom Cab, Market Street
Previously *The Burns' Hotel*, reopened with this name in 1975 after the frontage had been renovated (YEP 12 3 1975). Named after Joseph Aloysius Hansom 1803–1882, a York born architect, whose name is associated with the invention of the Hansom Cab. A Grade II listed building (CAMRA2).

Harcourt Arms, Church Street
Previously *The Blacksmiths' Arms*, it gained this name by 1851 (Dir) and was renamed *The Talbot* by the landlord, George Osborne, shortly before he moved to The Plough, Fulford, in 1865.

Hare and Greyhound, Trinity Lane
A name interchangeable with *The Hare and Greyhound*.

Hare and Hounds, Acomb
Mentioned from 1822 and 1828 (YCA F30A, F31), also known as *The Greyhound and Hare*. Later *The Greyhound*.

Hare and Hounds, Huntington
Mentioned from 1823 to 1872 (Dir).

Hare and Hounds, Monk Bar
Previously and later *The Minster*. Mentioned in 1750 (YCo 13 3 1750). The next year the licensee, Christopher Barthorpe, the City Huntsman, moved to *The Old George*, Pavement and took this name with him (YCo 18 2 1751).

Hare and Hounds, Pavement
When Christopher Barthorpe, the City Huntsman, moved to here from *The Hare and Hounds*, Monk Bar, he brought this name with him (YCo 18 2 1750). It was offered for let in 1756 (YCo 17 2 1756) when, no doubt, it reverted to its previous name.

Hare and Hounds, Walmgate
Mentioned in 1742 (YCo 19 1 1742).

Harker's Café Bar, St Helen's Square
Opened in May 1995 in premises originally built for the Yorkshire Insurance Company and taking a name once used by a hotel on the opposite side of the Square.

Harker's York Hotel, St Helen's Square ¶
Previously *The York Tavern* (Dir) and *The Royal Sussex Hotel* (Benson2). It was given this name by Christopher Harker, at one time butler to Colonel Harry Croft of Stillington, shortly after he moved here in 1850 from *The White Horse*, Coppergate (YG 5 1 1850). This name was retained, after his death on 22 June 1870, by subsequent tenants. In 1902 it had 30 bedrooms for travellers, as well as others for staff, and three sitting rooms upstairs. On the ground floor were three public rooms, a private room and kitchens. In addition there were also vaults detached from the hotel in Davygate (CC). It was demolished in 1929 to create an enlarged square and the last tenants transferred the name to a large villa on Tadcaster Road, Dringhouses, called the Hollies when they turned it into a new hotel (YG 2 1 1929). The licence was transferred to *The Tang Hall Hotel* on 6 January 1930 (YCA Acc. 189).

Harker's Hotel, Tadcaster Road, Dringhouses
Shortly before the demolition of *Harker's York Hotel*, St Helen's Square, the last tenants, Mrs Rasdal and Mrs Witham, moved to The Hollies and brought this name with them (YG 2 1 1929). The Hollies was built for John Close by the North Eastern Railway Co. as a replacement for North Lodge which had to be demolished to make way for the new railway station opened outside the walls in 1877. In 1946 it was renamed The Chase Hotel. Transferred from Tadcaster District of the West Riding County Council on 1 April 1937 on the inclusion of Dringhouses into the city (YCA Acc. 189).

Harp, Fossgate
A familiar name for *The Hibernian*, no doubt, from its sign which will have depicted an Irish harp. Mentioned in 1846 and 47 (YG 19 12 1846, 27 2 1847).

Harp, Middle Water Lane
A beerhouse, mentioned from 1861 to 1872 (Dir).

Harrison's Coffee House, Low Ousegate
Mentioned 1748 (YCo 26 1 1747/8) and 1785 when Bernard Watson was 'pleased to advertise his gravy and pease soup' (YCo 27 12 1785). Next *The Coffee House, The Coach and Horses, The Commercial Coffee House, Ellis's Hotel* and *The Coach and Horses* again.

Harry's Café Bar, Micklegate ¶
Opened 18 July 1984 (advertising brochure), encompassing the site of *The Barefoot*. During 2002 it was given a £400,000 overhaul and reopened as *The Bedroom* on 20 December 2002 (YEP 20 12 2002).

Harty Chalk, Micklegate
A phonetic spelling of *The Artichoke* recorded in 1795 (YCA K69).

Hawk's Crest, Goodramgate
In Lady Row 1796 to 1819 (RCHME V p 144a).

Haymarket Tavern, Haymarket ¶
Previously *The Shoulder of Mutton* and *The Tower of London*, it had gained this name by 1861 (Dir). When it was offered for sale in 1895 the property included a brewhouse (YG 1 6 1895). In 1902 it had six bedrooms, only three of which were furnished. Below were a smoke room, in which all the cooking was done, a dram shop, a kitchen and a small private sitting room. There was also a cellar (CC). It closed on 9 June 1932 when its licence was transferred to *The Knavesmire Hotel* (YCA Acc. 189).

Heart and Crown, Stonegate
Mentioned 1754 (YCo 16 4 1754).

Helmet, Coney Street
Mentioned in 1653 in connection with a burial at St Martin le Grand (PR) and in 1673 (Benson p. 166).

Hibernian, Fossgate
Near Foss Bridge, mentioned in 1843 (YG 14 10 1843) and 1848 (Dir). Familiarly known as *The Harp*. Next *The Lincoln Arms*.

Highland Deer, Penley's Grove Street
An alternative name for *The Highland Red Deer* (Dir 1846).

Highland Red Deer, Penley's Grove Street
A beerhouse, mentioned from 1843 to 1867 and called *The Highland Deer* in 1846. By 1872 it was called *The Reindeer* (Dir).

Highlander, Jubbergate
A beerhouse, mentioned 1834 to 1841 (Dir).

Hillyard's Wine Lodge, Low Ousegate
Previously *The Board*, gained this name by 1963 (Dir). Next by 1974 *The Lodge* and then *Yates' Wine Lodge, Dukes of York, O'Neills*.

Hole in the Wall, High Petergate
Previously *Wolstenholme's Dram Shop*, *Haigh's Vaults*, *Petergate Wine and Spirit Stores and Bar* and *The Board*, gained this name when it re–opened on 9 December 1981 after structural repairs to its façade as *The Hole in the Wall* (YEP 8 12 1981).

Hole in the Wall, Minster Close (Yard)
A building close to the Minster on the north side of the nave, mentioned in connection with a baptism in 1748 (PR). It was demolished in 1816 together with St Peter's Prison (Hargrove, p. 126).

Hop Pole Inn, Malton Road
A name mistakenly (?) given to *The Hopgrove* in 1889 and 1893 (Dir).

Hope and Anchor, Walmgate
Mentioned in 1830, by 1838 its name had been changed to *The Full Moon* (Dir).

Hopgrove, Malton Road ¶
Mentioned in 1857. In 1889 and 1893 it is mistakenly (?) called *The Hop Pole Inn* (Dir). A large road house, built on land behind the original building, replaced it in the 1930s. In 1997 it became *The Stockton on the Forest.*

Horse, Main Street, Fulford
An alternative name for *The Bay Horse* (Dir 1828).

Horse, Main Street, Heslington
Previously *The Robin Hood*, gained this name by 1828 (Dir). Later *The Chestnut Horse, The Bay Horse* and *The Charles XII.*

Horse, Middlethorpe
Previously *The Board*, it was using this name between 1826 and 1828 (YCA F31). Later *The Horseshoe.*

Horse and Groom, Aldwark
Mentioned in 1795 (YCA K29), probably an alternative name for *The Horse and Jockey.*

Horse and Groom, Little Stonegate
Mentioned in 1822 (YCA F30A) and 1838 (Dir), an alternative name for *The Horse and Jockey.*

Horse and Groom, Minster Yard
In existence at the beginning of the 19th century, later known as *The Buck* (Cooper p. 21).

Horse and Groom, Mint Yard
When it was offered for let in 1810 it had been open for five years previously (YCo 12 3 1810). Mentioned in 1823 (Dir) but shown in the licensing records in 1882 as *The Bay Horse* (YCA F30A).

Horse and Groom, Monkgate
Mentioned in 1783, 85, 87 and 95 (YCA K69, Cooper2 p. 44).

Horse and Groom, near The Mount
Mentioned in 1765 when it was to let (YCo 2 7 1765) and 1783 (YCA K69).

Horse and Groom, St John, Ousebridge, parish
Mentioned in 1783 (YCA K69).

Horse and Jockey, Aldwark
Mentioned in 1823 (Dir). Sometimes known as *The Horse and Groom.*

Horse and Jockey, Jubbergate (Market Street)
Mentioned in 1838, it had become *The Turf Coffee House* by 1841 (Dir). Next *The Turf Tavern* and *The Alexandra.*

Horse and Jockey, Little Stonegate
Mentioned between 1826 when it was for sale (YG 4 11 1826) and 1858 (Dir). Sometimes known as *The Horse and Groom.* By 1861 it had become a beerhouse, *The Shakespeare Tavern.*

Horse and Jockey, Micklegate
Mentioned in 1841 (Dir).

Horse and Jockey, Murton
Previously *The Jerry*, gained this name by 1843. Next, by 1857, *The Bay Horse* (Dir).

Horse Barefoot, Micklegate
An alternative name for *The Barefoot* (Dir 1841).

Horse Bloomsbury, Grape Lane
An alternative name for *The Bloomsbury* (Dir 1841).

Horse Cotherstone, Hungate
An alternative name for *The Cotherstone* (Dir 1849 & 1855).

Horseshoe, Coppergate
A house of this name was mentioned without a street location in the Accounts of the Innholders' Company on 28 December 1697 (BI MTA.17/1 p.123b). The first positively identifiable mention is in 1742 (YCo 4 5 1742). Last mention in 1838 (Dir).

Horseshoe, Dunnington
Previously *The Smith* then *The Blacksmiths's Arms* which between 1872 and 1876 was using this name (Dir).

Horseshoe, Middlethorpe
Previously *The Board* and *The Horse*, it had gained this name by 1838 (Dir) after which it is no longer mentioned.

Horseshoe, Naburn
Mentioned in 1823 and 1840, by 1857 it had become *The Blacksmiths' Arms* (Dir).

Horseshoe Inn, Osbaldwick ¶
The later name for *The Blacksmiths' Arms* based, no doubt, on the emblem on the pub sign. It was in use as an alternative name at various times from 1843 and exclusively from 1893 until its closure in the early 1930s (Dir).

Hound, St Michael le Belfrey parish
Mentioned 1787 (Cooper2 p. 43).

Hudson's Arms, Mount Ephraim
Mentioned 1848 to 1855 (Dir). By 1860 it had changed its name to *The Crown and Harp* (YG 7 4 1860). Mount Ephraim was an area inhabited largely by railwaymen of George Hudson's company, the York and North Midland Railway. After his fall from grace in 1849 his name was expunged from institutions in the city but not, it seems, immediately by his workers who waited until his company had been replaced by the North Eastern Railway.

Hudson's Arms, North Street
Mentioned in 1848 (Dir).

Huntsman, Fossgate
Mentioned in a lease 14 March 1764 under the name or sign of the Huntsman near the bridge in the parish of Fossgate (YCA E94 f. 57).

Imperial, Kingsway North ¶
Opened 4 June 1937, its licence transferred from *The Bell*, Micklegate, on 24 May that year. The licence of *The Alexandra*, Market Street, was voluntarily surrendered at the same time (YCA Acc. 189). It was closed in July 1994 and demolished five months later (YEP 28 12 1994).

Independent, Lowther Street
Previously *The Punch Bowl*, it gained its new name on 11 December 2001 (YEP 11 12 2001).

Jackson's Hotel, Petergate
Although called *The Grapes* from 1822 to 1874 it was also known as *Baynes' Coffee House, Baynes' Hotel* then *Tomlinson's Hotel* before it changed its name when W Jackson became proprietor in 1844 (YG 27 1 1844). In 1853 it became *Thomas's Hotel*. Next, having reverted to *The Grapes* for a time, *The Londesborough Arms*.

Jacob's Well, Trinity Lane ¶
First mentioned 1822 (YCA F30A). A building belonging to the Feoffees of Holy Trinity, Micklegate, its name derives from its biblical counterpart in Samaria about which Jesus said 'Whosoever drinketh of this water shall thirst again' (John 4,13). In 1902 it had four bedrooms, none available for travellers, a sitting room and a kitchen upstairs. On the ground floor were a smoke room, a taproom used as a kitchen and dining room, and a bar. There was also a cellar and the sole WC was shared by family and customers (CC). The licence was surrendered at the Brewster Sessions in 1903 in exchange for a full 'on' licence being granted to *The Edward VII* in Nunnery Lane (YCA Acc. 189).

Jerry, Murton
Mentioned in 1840 (Dir). Next *The Horse and Jockey.*

Jerry Inn, without Walmgate Bar
For sale in 1838 (YG 27 10 1838).

John Bull, Layerthorpe ¶
First mentioned in 1824 (YCA F30A). In 1902 it had three bedrooms, none available for travellers, a sitting room and a spirit store upstairs. Below were a smoke room, a bar, a

snug and a private kitchen from which food could be supplied if required. All the rooms were very small and there was a brewhouse attached in which the landlord brewed his own ale (CC). At the Brewster Sessions in 1903 the renewal of its licence was, unsuccessfully, opposed. In its defence it was stated that there had never been a conviction recorded against any landlord since it had been opened over 70 years previously. It was a free house which brewed 108 gallons of beer a week (Peacock p. 64). It was rebuilt in 1937 on an adjacent site, designed in the office of Sir Bertram Wilson, for 54 years architect to John Smith & Co. (YEP 22 9 1993). It closed in 1978 and was purchased from the brewery by Peter Turnbull. He agreed to its reopening on a short–term lease in December 1982 and, after a hard fought battle by its regulars and staff, he repossessed the pub which closed on 28 May 1994, to be demolished and replaced by a car show room (YEP 28 5 1994).

Joiners' Arms, Goodramgate
A beerhouse, previously *The Bay Horse* and *The Square and Compasses*, mentioned from 1851 to 1858. The name is probably a colloquial, based on the portrayal of woodworking tools on the sign of *The Square and Compasses*.

Joiners' Arms, Holy Trinity, Goodramgate parish
Mentioned in 1787 (Cooper2 p. 44).

Joiners' Arms, Newgate
Mentioned 1740 when it was to let (YCo 30 9 1740).

Joiners' Arms, Spencer Street
A pre–1869 beer house (YCA Acc. 189), first mentioned in 1867 (Dir). In 1902 it had three bedrooms upstairs above a smoke room and a taproom, which was used as a kitchen. There was also a cellar. The family, customers and the occupants of the private house next door shared a privy in the yard (CC). It was referred for compensation in June 1921 (YG 25 6 1921) and closed on 7 October that year (YCA Acc. 189).

Joiners' Arms, Walmgate
Mentioned in 1783, 87 and 95 (YCA K69, Cooper2 p. 46).

Joiners' Arms, Wesley Place
Previously *The Square and Compass,* it was using this name, probably as a familiar name, at various times between 1851 and 1872. It had reverted to its previous name by 1876 (Dir).

Jolly Bacchus, Bar Lane, Micklegate ¶
Mentioned on a trade token in 1666 (Benson3 p. 86), in 1688 in John Webster's diary (Malden) and then in 1783, 87 and 95 (YCA K69, Cooper2 p. 43). In 1812 Joseph Thackray paid the Corporation £10 10s 0d for one year's rent. The rent had risen to £30 by 1828. (YCA E78A). It was purchased for street improvements in January 1873 (YG 18 1 1873) and the licence was transferred to *The Melbourne*, a beer house in Melbourne Terrace, in August that year (YG 9 8 1873). Also known as *The Bacchus* and *The Boy and Barrel.*

Jolly Butchers, Church Street (Girdlergate)
Previously *The Three Jolly Butchers*, it had become *The Currier's Arms* by 1828 but by 1834 reverted to a slight variation of its previous name after dropping the 'Three' (Dir). At

the Brewster Sessions in 1855 the licensee was commended for making improvements but was informed that more were required (YG 1 9 1855). By 1861 it had become *The Ebor Vaults* (Dir).

Jolly Porter, Grape Lane
Mentioned in 1783, 85, 87 and 95 (YCA K69, Cooper2 p. 42).

Jolly Sailor, Far Water Lane (Friargate)
Previously *The Mariner*, it had gained this name by 1795 (YCA K69). Last mention 1851 although it appeared under its alternative name of *The Fortunate Tar* at various times between 1840 and 1855 (Dir).

Jolly Sailor, Lendal
Mentioned in 1770 (YCo 28 8 1770) and 1783, 85 and 87 (YCA K69, Cooper2 p. 42).

Jolly Sailor, Skeldergate
Mentioned 1818 to 1879 (Dir). Demolished to make room for the approaches to Skeldergate Bridge (Cooper p. 67).

Jonah Landed, Coppergate
Earliest mention 1733 as a place where common carriers could be found (Gent). For sale in 1747 (YCo 13 1 1747).

Jubilee, Balfour Street ¶
Opened in 1897 and named in celebration of Queen Victoria's diamond jubilee. The directors of the Tadcaster Tower Brewery had started their discussions on providing a new public house in this area in 1884 and were willing to transfer the licence of *The Sun Inn*, Tanner Row, their worst house (Avis pp. 89/90, 96). To gain a licence for the new house they in fact surrendered, at the Brewster Sessions in 1897, three others, those of *The Duke of York*, Walmgate, *The Nag's Head*, Fossgate, and *The Shoulder of Mutton*, Shambles (YCA Acc. 189). In 1902 the new house, which had opened on 1 January 1898 and was considered to be suitable for the business, had seven bedrooms, two set aside for travellers and a club or singing room upstairs. On the ground floor were a smoke room, a bar, a snug, a taproom, a bottle and jug department and a private kitchen from which food could be supplied if required (CC).

Judges' Lodgings, Lendal
Bar in basement of the hotel opened to non–residents October 1979 (YEP 11 10 1979).

Julius Caesar, Petergate
Mentioned 1754 (YCo 23 4 1754).

Junction, Leeman Road
Opened in 14 Dec 1994 in premises which were formerly the Phoenix Working Men's Club (YEP 16 12 1994).

Keel, King's Staith
A beerhouse, previously *The Old Ouse Bridge*, *The New Bridge* and *The Labour in Vain*. A beerhouse mentioned in 1836 (YG 27 2 1836) and in 1846 when at the Brewster Sessions an application by John Graves for the renewal of his licence was refused (YG 29 8 1846). He was subsequently fined for allowing drinking 'at an untimely hour' (YG 12 9 1846).

Keel, Marygate
Mentioned 1818 (Dir).

Kennedy's Café Bar, Little Stonegate
Mentioned in 2000 (Thomson). Newly opened 2001 (YEP 6 1 2001).

Keregan's, Stonegate
An alternative name for *The Billiard Table.*

Keystones, Monkgate
Previously *The Bay Horse* and sometimes known as *The Bay Malton*. Given this name in 1996 (YEP 12 Dec 1995).

King William, Walmgate ¶
Named after King William IV 1830–37, earliest mention 1835 when a beerhouse licence was refused to John Perry (YG 16 9 1835). As he was the licensee in 1838 (Dir) he must have overcome the objections. By 1902 it had been granted a full licence. At this time it had two attics, five bedrooms, two of which could, if necessary, be used for travellers, a sitting room and a spirit room upstairs. Below were a smoke room, a bar and a private kitchen from which food could be supplied if required. There was a brass room in the yard (CC). It closed in 1958 and the licence was transferred to *The King William*, Barkston Avenue which opened on 28 October that year. The licence of *The Blue Bell*, Walmgate was surrendered at the same time. (YCA Acc. 189). The façade and interior were acquired by the Castle Museum who rebuilt them in Half Moon Court which was opened by Barbara Kelly on 17 June 1963.

King William, Barkston Avenue
Opened on 28 October 1958 after the transfer to it of the licence of *The King William*, Walmgate (YCA Acc. 189).

King William IV, Fetter Lane
Previously *The Golden Ball* and *The Golden Lion*, it had gained this name by 1834 (Dir). In 1902 it had three poor bedrooms, all used by the family, and a club room upstairs. On the ground floor were a smoke room, a very small bar and snug, and a private kitchen from which food could be supplied if required (CC). It was referred for compensation on 9 March 1927. This was agreed on 13 June and it closed on 30 September that year (YCA Acc. 189, YG 16 7 1927).

King William IV, Layerthorpe
A beerhouse, to be sold or let in 1831 (YG 19 11 1831). A brewhouse was erected on the premises in 1866 (YG 31 3 1866). In 1902 it had four bedrooms, a smoke room, a bar, a kitchen and a private sitting room. There was also a cellar. The family and customers shared the sole WC (CC). The licence was surrendered at the same time as that of *St Peter's Vaults* was transferred to *The Acomb* Hotel. It closed on 20 June 1940 (YCA Acc. 189).

King of Prussia, North Street
Mentioned in 1770 (Benson p. 167).

King's Arms, Askham Bryan
Mentioned in 1838 (Dir).

King's Arms, Bilton Street ¶
Mentioned in 1838 (Dir). It was described in 1902 as only a four roomed cottage much too small for licensed premises. It had only two bedrooms, a smoke room and a kitchen but no pantry. It did, however, have a cellar. There was no urinal only a WC shared by the family and customers. The Chief Constable specially noted it for the attention of the Licensing Justices (CC). It was referred to the compensation authorities in 1921 and closed on 7 October that year (YCA Acc. 189).

King's Arms Hotel, Fossgate ¶
Mentioned in 1764 (YCo 6 3 1764). In 1774 it was called *The Old King's Arms* (YCo 17 5 1774). In 1876, when the hotel was offered for sale, the premises included four cottages and a brewhouse (YG 2 9 1876). In 1902 it was a large spacious house but only four of the bedrooms were furnished, including one which was available for travellers. There were three smoke rooms, a dram shop and private kitchens (CC). It closed on 30 November 1936 and the licence was transferred to *The Gimcrack*, Fulford Road (YCA Acc. 189).

King's Arms, King's Staith
An early 17th century building, it had become a public house by 1783 (YCA K69). In 1867 the licensee, George Duckitt, changed its name to *The Ouse Bridge Tavern* (Johnson p. 31, Dir), a name which it retained until 1974 when, on 28 March, it reopened after refurbishment under its original name (YEP 26 3 1974). A Grade II listed building (CAMRA2).

King's Head, Colliergate
Mentioned in 1770 (Benson p. 167).

King's Head, Feasegate ¶
First mentioned in 1838, apparently having moved from Thursday Market when William Dawson became licensee (Dir) after the death of the previous tenant, John Pew, coal merchant who died in September 1837 (YG 30 9 1837). In 1841 it is shown in St Sampson's Square (Dir), probably an error by the compiler of the street directory. In 1902 it had six bedrooms, two set aside for travellers, a sitting room and a club room upstairs. On the ground floor were a smoke room, a bar and a private kitchen from which food could be supplied if required (CC). The premises closed on 8 March 1958 and the licence was surrendered two days later (YCA Acc. 189).

King's Head, Stonegate
Described as the house formerly known as the King's Head in a lease on 13 May 1762 (E94 f. 41b) but still extant in 1783, 85 and 87 (YCA K69, Cooper2 p. 42). A 15th century building, altered and cased in brick in the mid 18th century, still in existence at 15 Stonegate (RCHME V p. 228a).

King's Head, Thursday Market (St Sampson's Square)
Mentioned in a lease 4 May 1748 (YCA E93 p. 203). Last mentioned in 1834 after which it appears to have moved to Feasegate (Dir).

Kingston, Tanner Row ¶
A pre–1869 beerhouse (YCA Acc. 189) first mentioned in the street directories in 1872 (Dir). The Kingston was a railway engine which ran on the Hull and Selby Railway at its

opening ceremony on 1 July 1840. In 1902 it had three attics, five bedrooms and a club room on the upper floors. Below were a smoke room, a bar and a private kitchen. There was a yard some distance from the house reached by a public passage where the urinal and WC were. The customers, however, frequently chose to urinate in the passage (CC). A full 'on' licence was granted on 14 February 1961 (YCA Acc. 189). The pub was closed in 1984 and demolished to make way for extensions to the insurance company office (ER).

Kites, Grape Lane
Originally a restaurant, awarded a licence as a café–bar as well in 1999 (YEP 11 2 1999).

Knavesmire, Albemarle Road
After many years of trying, permission was finally given in April 1931 for the building of a public house to serve the South Bank area (YG 11 4 1931). The licence was granted on 2 June 1932, transferred from *The Haymarket Tavern*, Haymarket, and it opened on 9 June. The licence of *The Rose and Crown*, Aldwark, was surrendered at the same time (YCA Acc. 189).

Knife and Steel, Swinegate
Mentioned in 1795 (YCA K69).

Labour in Vain, George Street
In 1830 the John Jolly was the licensee of a pub with the same name on King's Staith. His widow, Ann Jolly, then appeared in 1839 here in George Street (YG 30 3 1839), having taken the name with her and leaving her former pub to change its name to *The Keel* (Dir). The, now non–politically correct, sign board of this house (Cooper p. 61) depicted a woman scrubbing a black boy with the legend underneath:

> You may wash him and scrub him from morning to night
> Your labour's in vain, black will never come white.

Its name was changed to *The Phoenix* by 1867 (Dir).

Labour in Vain, King's Staith
Previously *The Old Ouse Bridge* and *The New Bridge*. Mentioned in 1830, when John Jolly was licensee. By 1836 it had become *The Keel* (Dir).

Labourer, Skeldergate
Mentioned in 1822 and 1830 (YCA F30A, F31). Also known as *The Labouring Man.* Later *The Three Tuns, The Foresters' Arms,* and *The Prince of Wales.*

Labouring Man, Skeldergate
An alternative name for *The Labourer* (Dir 1828).

Lamb, St Dennis parish
Mentioned in 1783 and 87 (YCA K69, Cooper2 p. 46).

Lamb, St Margaret parish
Mentioned in 1783 (YCA K69).

Lamb, Tanner Row
Mentioned in 1787 and 95 (Cooper2 p. 42, YCA K69). When it was offered for sale in 1870 the property included a brewhouse (YG 8 1 1870). In 1902 it had six bedrooms, four

of which were available for travellers. Below were a smoke room, a singing room, a bar and a kitchen from which food could be supplied if required. There was also a cellar (CC). It was referred to the compensation authorities in March and renewal of the licence was refused on 26 May 1910 (YCA Acc. 189). Also known as *The Lamb Coffee House* (YG 2 12 1843).

Lamb Coffee House, Tanner Row
Mentioned in 1843 (YG 2 12 1843). See above.

Lamb, Walmgate
Mentioned in 1787 and 95 (YCA K69, Cooper2 p. 46).

Last Drop, Colliergate
York Brewery Co. were granted planning permission in January 2000 for its first tied house which opened on 2 August that year (YEP 7 1 2000, 2 8 2000). The name, no doubt intended to refer to the products of the brewery sold there, inspired the hanging theme of naming for all subsequent pubs opened by the brewery.

Lawson's Beerhouse, Alma Terrace
A beerhouse, opened by William Lawson, builder by 1867 (Dir). By 1881 it had become *The Wellington*. Later *The Sir Colin Campbell* and *The Wellington* again.

Leeds Arms, Haymarket ¶
Previously *The Clifford's Tower*, mentioned 1827 (YCA F31). When George Hill, the licensee of some forty years, died in 1874 and the property was put up for sale it included a brewhouse (YG 14 3 1874). In 1902 it was described as an old property and had two attics, three bedrooms, all occupied by the family, and a club room on the upper floors. On the ground floor, above the cellar were a smoke room, a dram shop, a taproom and a private kitchen from which food could be supplied if required. There was no urinal and the buildings were in bad repair (CC). This must have led to the renewal of the licence being opposed, at first successfully, at the 1903 Brewster Sessions (Peacock p.66) but later, on appeal, it was renewed (YG 11 4 1903). It closed in March 1935 (YG 8 3 1935, YCA Acc. 189) but other uses were found for the building which was not demolished until 1966 (YEP 24 4 1966).

Leeman Hotel, Stamford Street ¶
After the death of George Leeman, three times Lord Mayor of York, MP for the city, chairman of the NER and thorn in the flesh of George Hudson, on 21 August 1880 a statue of him was erected by public subscription on Station Road and, at the same time, Thief Lane was renamed Leeman Road. Thus, when a new public house was built in the housing development at the end of Leeman Road, it was appropriate that it should be named after him. It was opened between 1885 and 1887. In 1902 it had a box room, three bedrooms, a billiard room and a sitting room upstairs. On the ground floor were a smoke room, a singing room, a taproom and a private kitchen from which food could be supplied. There was also a cellar (CC).

Lendal Bridge Hotel, Tanners' Moat ¶
Previously *The Railway Tavern*, it gained this name by 1885 although Lendal Bridge opened in 1863 and the main railway activity moved to the new station outside the walls in 1877. In 1902 it had three bedrooms, all occupied by the family, a sitting room and a

settling room upstairs. Below were a smoke room, a serving bar, a kitchen licensed as a taproom, as well as a small back kitchen. Food could be supplied if required. There was also a cellar and a sole WC shared by the family and customers (CC). Later *The Maltings.*

Lendal Cellars, Lendal
A new public house opened on 24 Jan 1984 (YEP 20 1 1984) in the cellars that were below the former house of the Oldfield family, wine merchants and post masters (Johnson p. 7).

Leopard Inn, Aldwark
While TP Cooper suggested that this, and *The Spotted Dog* were earlier names for *The Bay Horse* (Cooper p. 77), both houses are listed in 1843, the earliest mention of The Leopard. It was offered for sale in 1858 (YG 5 6 1858), 12 years after *The Bay Horse* had closed (Dir). This is also the last time it is mentioned (Dir).

Leopard, Coney Street
Earliest mention 1778 (YCo 17 1 1778). It was built in a passage leading off Coney Street and thus had no frontage to the street. In 1902 the Chief Constable thought it a very poor house with badly lit rooms but did not note it for the special attention of the Licensing Justices. Upstairs there were four bedrooms, of which one or two could be made available to travellers, as well as a sitting room and a kitchen. On the ground floor, however, there were just two rooms, a smoke room and a bar. Food could be supplied if required. By 1906 the Chief Constable had decided it was one of the worst six houses in York and opposed the renewal of the licence on the grounds of non–necessity. A soldiers' pub, it took £603 a year, paying £344 to the brewery and £10 to the compensation fund. The representatives of the pub claimed compensation of £1345 5s 0d based on the rent paid by the tenant at 18 years purchase, trade profits at 10 years purchase and the estimated rental value of the building without licence at 14 years purchase. In the end the Commissioners of Inland Revenue fixed the compensation at £960, £200 for the tenant and the balance for the lessees. (Peacock pp. 92 & 115). As well as refusing to renew the licence, permission to transfer it to 122 Haxby Road for a new establishment to be known as The White Cross Hotel was also refused (YG 17 2 1906). The licence was to expire on 5 April 1907 (YCA Acc. 189) and the building was demolished in 1924 (YG 22 11 1924).

Leopard, Coppergate
Earliest mention 1750 when an exhibition of strange creatures found in Liverpool was held there (YCo 15 5 1750). Thomas Eagle, the tenant in 1838 advertised his 'pure unadulterated home–brewed ale of great strength' (YG 24 2 1838). The inn together with its brewhouse were offered for sale in 1877 (YG 3 11 1877). Last mentioned in 1887 (Dir). Name changed by 1889 to *The Market Tavern* (Dir).

Leopard Inn, High Ousegate
Mentioned in 1749 (YCo 11 4 1748) and 1830 when it is called *The Little Leopard* (Dir) to distinguish it from others with the same name.

Leopard, North Street
A beerhouse, licence granted to John Masser in 1837 (YG 16 9 1837). This name was interchangeable with *The Tiger* (Dir), a commentary on the ability of the sign painter to depict a wild animal he had never seen or, alternately, of the pub's more bibulous

customers to recognise the beast intended. The confusion was sorted out by 1848 when it changed its name to *The Crown and Cushion*.

Leopard Inn, Pavement
To be let 1783 (YCo 23 9 1783). Sold in 1819 on the bankruptcy of John Kilby. It was then held on a 40 year lease from the Dean and Chapter of York, which had started on 1 June 1816, at a rent of £1 15s 0d a year (YG 28 8 1819). At its last mention in 1834 the licensee is William English who next appears in 1838 at The *Leopard*, Shambles (Dir). He appears to have transferred the name to new premises. Also known as *The Panther* (Dir 1823), another case of the beast on the sign not being recognisable – see *The Leopard*, North Street.

Leopard Inn, Shambles
Previously located in Pavement (see above) but had moved here by 1838 (Dir). When it was offered for sale in 1849 the property included a brewhouse (YG 24 3 1849). Last mention 1858 (Dir).

Light Horseman, Fishergate ¶
Mentioned 1819 (YG 19 6 1819), built on a site behind the present house (OS 1852) where *The Well House* once stood (Kaner p. 15), probably shortly after the Cavalry Barracks was built in 1796. Rebuilt on a site nearer the road in the 1870s as a purpose built public house (CAMRA). In 1902 it had five bedrooms, all occupied by the family, and a club room upstairs. On the ground floor were a smoke room, a bar parlour, a large bar, two private rooms and a kitchen. There was also a cellar (CC).

Light Horseman, Grape Lane
Mentioned in 1838 (Dir), according to TP Cooper it was previously *The Rifleman* (Cooper p. 79), a pub which is not mentioned after 1824.

Lincoln Arms, Fossgate
Previously *The Hibernian*, using this name by 1851 (YCA Poor Law Application Book).

Lion, Haxby
A familiar name for *The Red Lion*, in use in various years between 1899 and 1902 (Dir).

Lion and Cat, High Ousegate
Mentioned 1743 and 1755 (YCo 4 10 1743, 21 10 1755).

Lion and Lamb, Blossom Street ¶
Mentioned in 1783, 85, 87 and 95 (YCA K69, Cooper2 p. 43). In 1902 it had ten bedrooms, three available for travellers, and a club room upstairs. Below were two smoke rooms, a dram shop, a small private room and private kitchens from which food could be supplied if required (CC). In 1987 it was renamed *The Nickel and Dime* (YEP 17 1 1987) and closed after planning permission sought to convert it into offices (YEP 2 11 1988).

Little Black Bull, Davygate
Mentioned in 1783, 85, 87 and 95 (YCA K69, Cooper2 p. 43), a later name for *The Black Bull*, probably to avoid confusion with another pub of the same name in St Sampson's Square.

Little Coach, Micklegate
A nickname given to *The Coach and Horses*, Micklegate, to distinguish it from The *Coach and Horses,* Nessgate.

Little John, Castlegate ¶
Previously *The Robin Hood*, its name had been changed to this by 1893 (Dir). A couplet was devised to make its customers aware of what had happened:

> Robin Hood is dead and gone
> Now come and drink with Little John.

In 1902 it had eight bedrooms, two were occupied by the family and only three of the remainder were furnished for travellers. On the ground floor were a smoke room, a bar, a very small and dark snug and a private kitchen from which food could be supplied. There was no WC for the customers and the urinal was inside the house and required better ventilation (CC). A Grade II listed building (CAMRA2).

Little Leopard, High Ousegate
Previously *The Leopard*, gained this name by 1830, the only time it is mentioned (Dir).

Locomotive, Watson Street ¶
Mentioned in 1851 (Dir). In 1902 it had four bedrooms and a drawing room upstairs. Below were a smoke room, a taproom, a bar and a private sitting room but no separate kitchen. Nevertheless food could be supplied if required (CC).

Lodge, 16 Low Ousegate
Previously *The Board*, then *Hillyard's Wine Lodge*, it was given this name by 1974 (Dir), later *Yates' Wine Lodge, Dukes of York* and *O'Neills.*.

Londesborough Arms, Market Street
Previously *The Crown and Anchor, The Market Street Tavern* and *The Manchester Tavern*, gained this name by 1867, the only time it is mentioned (Dir).

Londesborough Arms, Petergate ¶
Previously *Baynes' Coffee House, Baynes' Hotel, Tomlinson's Hotel, Jackson's Hotel* and *Thomas's Hotel,* it had gained this name by 1876 (Dir). There is a possible connection in this with George Hudson, who had attended a meeting there in 1833. He had purchased Londesborough Park, near Market Weighton, from the Duke of Devonshire in 1845, hoping to establish a family seat there. On his downfall in 1849 it was bought by Albert Denison who was created Baron Londesborough in 1850 and whose arms latterly appeared on the pub sign. In 1902 there were four bedrooms, none available for travellers, two other small rooms and a club room upstairs. Below were two smoke rooms, a dram shop, a private sitting room and kitchens from which food could be supplied (CC). It closed in October 1984 (YEP 10 9 1984).

London Hotel, Davygate ¶
Previously *The Turf Coffee House* and *The Cricketers' Resort* it was renamed after being rebuilt in Tudoresque style to the designs of WG Penty in 1890. In 1902 the premises were used solely for drinking. It had three bedrooms, a sitting room, a billiard room and a kitchen upstairs. On the ground floor were a smoke room and a vault above the cellar. The urinal was inside and the customers and family shared the sole WC (CC). It was pulled

Queen Inn, Lawrence Street, 1906

Queen's Hotel, Micklegate, 1963

Queen's Head, Bootham Square, 1934

Queen's Head, Fossgate, 1960

Railway Hotel Tap, Station Road, 1898

Red Lion, Goodramgate, 1921. Although long closed the position of its sign board can be clearly seen

Red Lion, Haxby, 1906

Red Lion, Micklegate, 1930

Red Lion, Walmgate (Merchantgate), 1916

Reindeer, Penley's Grove Street, 1929

Richard III, Rougier Street, 1985

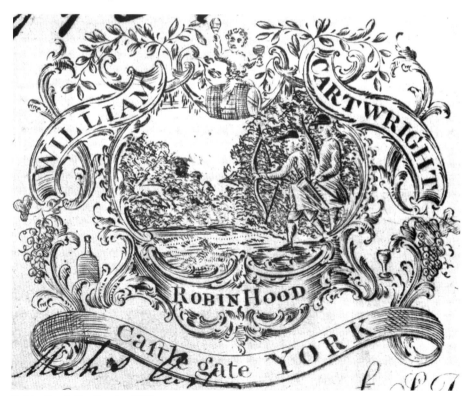

Robin Hood, Castlegate, 1788

Rose and Crown, Aldwark, 1910

Royal Oak, Copmanthorpe, 1906

Royal Oak, Goodramgate, 1906

Saddle, Main Street, Fulford, 1924

Sailor with Wooden Leg, Low Ousegate, 1810   *St Peter's Vaults, Walmgate, 1905*

Sea Horse, Fawcett Street (Cattle Market), 1995

Ship, First Water Lane (later King Street), King's Staith, 1905

Ship, Strensall, 1906

Shoulder of Mutton, Heworth (Green) Moor, 1906

Slip Inn, Clementhorpe, 1906

Slip, (Heworth Moor) Malton Road, 1930

Sportsman, Caroline Street, 1935

Spotted Cow, Barbican Road, 1906

Spread Eagle, Walmgate, 1906

Square and Compass, Long Close Lane, 1906

158

Star and Garter, Nessgate, 1896

Sun Inn, Acomb Green, 1935

Sycamore, Water End, Clifton, 1929, when it was no longer a pub

Talbot Inn, Church Street, 1955

Tam O'Shanter, Lawrence Street, 1935

Tang Hall Hotel, Fourth Avenue, 1950

Thomas's Hotel, Museum Street, 1900

Three Cranes, St Sampson's Square, 1906

Three Tuns, Coppergate, 1935

down in 1939 as part of a scheme to widen Davygate. It was proposed to transfer the licence to The Embassy Hotel on The Mount (YEP 5 9 1938) but, in the event it was granted on 8 February 1939 to Betty's Café having closed on 4 April 1938 (YCA Acc. 189).

London Coffee House, Feasegate
Mentioned 1825 (YG 30 4 1825) to 1846 (Dir). Also known as *The Grapes.*

Lord Byron, Goodramgate
A name given, according to TP Cooper, to a house known variously as *The Beech Tree* and *The Fox* (Cooper2 p 49).

Lord Collingwood, Upper Poppleton ¶
First mentioned in 1823 (Dir), named after vice-admiral Cuthbert Collingwood, 1750-1810. He commenced his naval career in 1761, and, serving as second in command to Lord Nelson at the Battle of Trafalgar in 1805, took command of the fleet after the latter's death. After the battle he was raised to the peerage as a baron. He died at sea during the blockade of Toulon and was brought home to be buried in St Paul's Cathedral (DNB).

Lord John Cavendish, Fossgate
Mentioned 1795 (YCA K69). Lord John Cavendish, 1732–96, was the fourth son of the third duke of Devonshire. He was MP for York from 1768 to 1790 and Chancellor of the Exchequer in 1782 and 83 (DNB).

Lord Hawke, Walmgate
An alternative name for *The Admiral Hawke* (YG 8 1 1831).

Lord Nelson, Goodramgate
Mentioned 1818 (Dir) to 1828 (YCA F30A). Horatio Nelson entered the Navy in 1770 and rose to the rank of Vice Admiral by 1801. For his action against the French in Aboukir Bay in 1798 he was created Baron Nelson. He commanded the attack on Copenhagen in 1801 and afterwards was created Viscount Nelson. He died on 21 October 1805 in the battle off Cape Trafalgar on the deck on his flag ship, Victory, having been struck down by a sniper's bullet. He was accorded a public funeral and was buried in St Paul's Cathedral on 9 January 1806. His brother, William, was created Earl Nelson on 20 November 1805 in consideration of the eminent services of Horatio (DNB).

Lord Nelson, High Jubbergate
Mentioned 1822 (YCA F30A) to 1828 (Dir).

Lord Nelson, Little Shambles
Mentioned 1818 (Dir) to 1824 (YCA F30A).

Lord Nelson, Navigation Road
A beerhouse, mentioned 1834 (Dir). In 1902 it was described as a clean and suitable house for the business with three bedrooms, a smoke room, a bar, a cellar and a private cellar kitchen (CC). It closed on 7 October 1931 (YCA Acc. 189).

Lord Nelson, Nether Poppleton
Earliest mention by name 1822 when John Taylor was landlord (YCA F30A) although he is recorded as a licensee in the village in 1821 (Davies2 p. 31).

Lord Nelson, Patrick Pool
Mentioned 1834 (Dir) to 1836 when it was for sale (YG 12 3 1836).

Lord Nelson, Swinegate
Mentioned 1827 (YCA F30A) to 1851 when renewal of its licence was postponed (YG 30 8 1851). By 1855 it had become *The Crystal Palace.*

Lord Nelson, Walmgate ¶
Earliest mentioned 1812 (YCo 31 8 1812). In 1902 the premises were described as new and suitable for the business. It had six bedrooms, only three of which were furnished, and a club room upstairs. On the ground floor, above a cellar, were a smoke room, a dram shop and a kitchen (CC). It was closed in 1981 and became the area sales office for Bass North as it was no longer economically viable. Preference was given to upgrading *The Five Lions* nearby (YEP 23 9 1982). Familiarly known as *The Nelson.*

Lord Wellington, Goodramgate
An alternative name used in 1828 for a public house (Dir) known variously as *The Wellington*, *The Marquis of Wellington*, and *The Duke of Wellington.*

Lord Wellington, Holtby
Mentioned in 1823 and 1840 (Dir). Later called *The Duke of Wellington* which was probably its official name.

Lottery, St Nicholas Place, Osbaldwick Lane, Hull Road
Mentioned 1840 (YG 8 8 1840) and 1843 (Dir).

Lowther Hotel, King's Staith ¶
Built in 1884 on a site previously occupied by *The Crown and Anchor*. It was designed by W Brown, architect of Clifford Street, whose plans were approved by the Corporation in October 1884. It was named after James Lowther, MP for York, 1865 to 1880. In 1902 it had five bedrooms, a sitting room, a large club room and a billiard room upstairs. On the ground floor were a smoke room, a large bar, and two private kitchens from which food could be supplied if required. There was also a cellar (CC).

Macmillans, Rougier Street
A café bar, previously *The Grob and Ducat* and then *The Richard III,* it reopened with this name in April 1990 (YEP 4 4 1990). See also *The Old Ebor.*

Magnet, Osbaldwick Lane
Built in 1934 by John Smith & Co, designed in the office of Sir Bertram Wilson, for 54 years the company architect (CAMRA).

Magpie, Penley's Grove Street ¶
At first, a familiar name for *The Magpie and Stump*, but eventually adopted as its official name. This name was first mentioned in 1876 and used exclusively after 1905 (Dir). The licence was placed in suspension on 8 August 1961 after the original building was demolished as part of a Groves improvement scheme (YCA Acc. 189). Planning permission was granted for the building of a new licensed hotel (YEP 25 5 1962). The licence transferred and brought into operation in the new premises 31 October 1962 (YCA Acc. 189).

Magpie and Stump, Penley's Grove Street

First mentioned in 1838 and from 1876 familiarly known as *The Magpie* (Dir). Its premises contained a brewhouse (YG 19 10 1861, 14 1 1871). In 1902 it had three bedrooms, all occupied by the family, a smoke room, a bar, two kitchens, a sitting room and a cellar. Food could be supplied if required. Although not a large house the Chief Constable thought it suitable for the business done (CC). After 1905 it was exclusively known as *The Magpie* (Dir).

Mail Coach, St Sampson's Square ¶

Previously *The Barrel Churn, The Cooper, The Barrel* and *The Coach and Horses*, it had gained this name by 1834 (Dir). The premises also contained a brewhouse (YG 15 5 1858, YG 1 10 1888). In 1902 it was described as an old property with small rooms. It had three bedrooms, all occupied by the family, and a sitting room upstairs. On the ground floor were a bar, a snug, and a kitchen from which food could be supplied if required. There was also a private kitchen, detached from the main building, and a cellar (CC). It was completely rebuilt in a Tudoresque style in 1930 (Johnson p. 40). It closed in 1970 to undergo a £10,000 refurbishment (YEP 18 9 1970). The modernised building was renamed *The Roman Bath*, commemorating the presence of the remains of a Roman bath–house in its cellars and reopened in September 1971 (YEP 3 9 1971).

Malt Shovel, Bedern

Mentioned in 1834 (Davison p.37) and 1836 (YG 12 3 1836).

Malt Shovel, Fossgate

To be sold at *The Black Dog*, Jubbergate 4 August 1763 (YCo 19 7 1763). In 1902 it was described as a very poor house, being very old with small rooms, low ceilings and badly lit. It had two uninhabitable attics and two bedrooms, both used by the family, upstairs. While below were a smoke room, a snug, a bar, a kitchen and a cellar. The WC was in the yard but badly situated (CC). Renewal of its licence was consequently refused at the Brewster Sessions in 1903 (Peacock p. 66) with the result that it was surrendered (YCA Acc. 189).

Malt Shovel, Heworth Road

Public house, for sale by auction 1835 (YG 6 6 1835).

Malt Shovel, Little Shambles

Previously *The Parrot*, gained this name by 1787 (Cooper2 p.44). Last mention 1872 (Dir).

Malt Shovel, St Martin cum Gregory parish

Mentioned in 1783 (YCA K69).

Malt Shovel, 12 Walmgate

For sale in 1775 (YCh 10 3 1775). In 1828 and afterwards it was sometimes known as *The Old Malt Shovel* to distinguish it from the other house in the street with the same name. Although there were occasional lapses to the former name, by 1851 the revised name was firmly established (Dir).

Malt Shovel, 66 Walmgate

Mentioned in 1783 (YCA K69). The rivalry with the other *Malt Shovel* in Walmgate led to this one also, for a period between 1841 and 1848, claiming the earlier date of foundation with the name *The Old Malt Shovel*. The matter was resolved by 1851 when its name was changed to *The Bricklayers' Arms* (Dir). Later renamed *The Spread Eagle.*

Maltings, Tanner Row
Previously *The Railway Tavern* and *The Lendal Bridge* it gained this name in October 1992 (YEP 29 6 2002).

Man and Horse, St Peter the Little parish
Mentioned in 1783 (YCA K69).

Man and Horses, All Saints, North Street, parish
Mentioned 1787 (Cooper2 p. 42).

Manchester Tavern, Low Jubbergate (Market Street)
Previously *The Crown and Anchor* and *The Market Tavern,* it gained this name after 1853 and by 1858 (Dir). It was offered for sale in 1863 (YG 17 1 1863) and by 1867 it had become *The Londesborough Arms.*

Marcia (Marque, Martia), Bishopthorpe ¶
Although mentioned in the licensing records of 1822 as having two names, this one and *The Grey Mare*, it was the latter by which it was almost universally known until some time after 1857 (Dir). By 1866 the other name had been abandoned. It was remodelled and given a new front in 1930 by WJ Simpson (Brayley p. 4). Mr Garforth's Marcia, a grey mare, by Coriander out of Faith was a successful racehorse in York meetings in 1902 (Orton pp. 258 & 263).

Marcia, Front Street, Acomb ¶
Previously *The Square and Compasses*, by 25 April 1817 (AMCR) its name had been changed to *The Marcia* to celebrate a successful racehorse who was a grey mare (see above). Between 1823 and 1838 it was referred to as *The Grey Mare* (YCA F30A, F31; Dir). By 1843 it had reverted to *The Marcia*. It was occasionally, in 1857 and 1889, called *The Grey Marcia* (Dir). It was rebuilt on a larger scale, probably in the early years of the twentieth century. Transferred from the Tadcaster Licensing District 1 April 1937 on the extension of city boundaries (YCA Acc. 189). In 1998 it became *The Poacher.*

Mariner, Far Water Lane (Friargate)
Mentioned in 1783 and 87. By 1795 it had become *The Jolly Sailor* (YCA K69, Cooper2 p. 45).

Market Tavern, Coppergate ¶
Previously *The Leopard*, last mentioned in 1887 (Dir). By the next year it had gained this name after the arrival of ex Sergeant Major Culham of the 9th Lancers who was given the tenancy on 13 February 1888 on the recommendation of Albert Victor, Duke of Clarence. Its owners, the Tadcaster Tower Brewery, were soon concerned about his slack ways. After he was sacked in 1889 it was discovered that he had pawned his licence! (Avis pp. 114, 147 & 163). In 1902 it had two non–habitable attics used as lumber rooms, three bedrooms, all used by the family, and one sitting room in the upper floors. On the ground floor there were two smoke rooms, a bar and a kitchen from which food could be supplied if required. There was a private kitchen some distance away down a passage which ran along the side of the house. The family and customers shared the sole WC. There was also a cellar (CC). A timber framed and jettied building of the 16th century (RCHME V p. 128a), its rooms were all dark (CC). It was purchased by Wimpey International in Jan 1984 and opened as Russell's Restaurant in October 1985 (YEP 28 10 1985).

Market Tavern, St Sampson's Square
Previously *The Punch Bowl*, it gained this name by September 1855. By that time 54 complaints had been received in the previous year and the licensee was cautioned at the Brewster Sessions that if he continued to allow singing and dancing parties on the premises he would lose his licence (YG 1 9 1855). Last mention 1857 (Dir).

Market Street Tavern, Market Street
Previously *The Crown and Anchor*, by 1853 it had gained this name (YG 2 7 1853). After 1855 its name was changed to *The Manchester Tavern* (Dir). Later *The Londesborough Arms*.

Marquee, Clifton Scope (Water End)
See next.

Marquee Gardens, Clifton Scope (Water End)
Mentioned 1823 to 1855 (Dir).

Marquis of Granby, Peter Lane
Previously *The Granby* or *Granby's Punch House*, first mentioned with this name when it was sold in 1819 on the bankruptcy of John Kilby (YG 26 6 1819). John Manners, Marquis of Granby, who died on 19 October 1770, was Commander in Chief of the British army in 1766. He set up some of his soldiers as landlords of public houses when they left the army. In their gratitude many named their houses after him (Dunkling p. 167). In 1843 it was referred to as *Granby's Punch Bowl* (Dir). By 1851 it had become *The Griffin*, a beerhouse (Dir).

Marquis of Wellington, Goodramgate
Previously *The Wellington*, it had been given this name by 1823, although in 1828 it was known as *The Lord Wellington* (Dir). By 1830 it had been renamed *The Duke of Wellington* to reflect the Iron Duke's elevation in the ranks of the peerage (YG 16 1 1830).

Masons' Arms, Fishergate ¶
Previously *The Quiet Woman*, a beerhouse, its name was changed in 1838 by the landlord, George Tilney, who had been a stonemason. When it was offered for sale in 1878 it had an 'excellent, well–arranged and most complete brewhouse' (YG 10 8 1878). In 1902 it had three bedrooms, one of which was available for travellers, and a sitting room upstairs. Below were a smoke room, a bar, a taproom and a private kitchen from which food could be supplied. There was also a cellar (CC). In 1935 it was completely rebuilt on a new building line set back from the road using, internally, panelling and fireplaces from the recently demolished prison (RCHME II p. 86a). Now a Grade II listed building, after World War 2 the sitting room and lounge bar were joined together to form one big room (CAMRA).

Masons' Arms, Goodramgate
A familiar name for *The Square and Compass*, based on the tradesman's tools displayed on the sign, mentioned in 1823 (Dir).

Maxfield's Hotel, Low Ousegate
Mentioned in 1830 (Dir).

Maypole, Clifton
Mentioned in 1647 when Elizabeth and Helen Drysdale of Tadcaster were executed at St Leonard's Gallows, Green Dykes, for wilfully and deliberately poisoning with oxalic acid two young men who 'were paying their addresses' to them at the house on 16 February (Knipe p. 25). Its name is an indication that it must have been located adjacent to Clifton Green, possibly a predecessor of *The Old Grey Mare.*

McGregor's House (Tavern), Low Ousegate
A beerhouse with a six day licence, also known as *The Board.* Earliest mention 1849 (YG 4 8 1849) when its draft and bottled ale was advertised for sale. Named after its original owner, Charles McGregor. In 1902 it had four bedrooms, all used by the family, a sitting room and a kitchen upstairs. On the ground floor were a taproom and a smoke room. There was a warehouse in the very small back yard used as a storeroom (CC). It was referred for compensation on 12 March and closed on 1 October 1923 (YG 17 3 1923, YCA Acc. 189).

Melbourne Hotel, Cemetery Road ¶
A beerhouse, first mentioned in 1867 (Dir). When *The Jolly Bacchus*, Bar Lane, Micklegate was purchased for street improvements in January 1873 (YG 18 1 1873) its full licence was transferred here in August that year (YG 9 8 1873), where it subsequently spread into two adjacent houses. Named after Viscount Melbourne, Prime Minister 1835–41. In 1902 it had four bedrooms, all occupied by the family, a sitting room and a dining room upstairs. Below were a smoke room, a bar parlour, a bar and a private kitchen from which food could be supplied. There was also a cellar (CC) and a brewhouse (YG 10 10 1885).

Merlin's, George Hudson Street
Previously *The Great Northern, The Pageant*, and *The Great Northern* again, it gained this name by August 1994 (YEP 11 8 1994).

Mermaid, St Dennis' parish
Mentioned in 1783 (YCA K69).

Mermaid, St Michael le Belfrey parish
Mentioned in 1783, 85 and 87 (YCA K69, Cooper2 p. 42).

Micklegate, Micklegate
Previously *The Bar Hotel* and *Scruffy Murphy's.* After seven years with an Irish theme it was given a new look and a new name in late 2002 (YEP 22 2 2003).

Mill, Hull Road, Dunnington
A familiar name for *The Windmill.*

Mill, York Road, Wigginton
A familiar name for *The Windmill.*

Millfield, White Rose Close, York Business Park
A Brewers' Fayre and Travel Inn opened in 1997.

Minster Inn, Marygate ¶
First mentioned in 1823, by 1838 it was occasionally called by the alternative name of *The York Minster*. Then by 1851 it had become *The Gardeners' Arms* before reverting by 1887 to its original name (Dir). Built on the narrow strip of land against the walls of St Mary's Abbey and using that wall as part of its structure, it had in 1902 only two small rooms on the ground floor, a smoke room from which an internal urinal had been partitioned off, and a taproom also used as a kitchen from which food was provided if required. Upstairs were three bedrooms, one of which was used as a living room, and there was also a cellar. The Chief Constable thought it a very poor house and specially noted it for the attention of the Licensing Justices (CC). The results of his report were dramatic. Its owners, Tadcaster Tower Brewery Co., engaged the local architect Samuel Needham, to design a new public house (CAMRA). A transfer of the licence was granted on 23 November 1903 for the new house and premises about to be constructed on the opposite side of Marygate which was to be known as The Minster Inn. The licensee, Harriet Ann Palmer, later Keech, transferred from the old pub and presided over her new premises until her death in 1944 (YCA ACC. 189). Its original 1903 layout is still intact with many original features present, nevertheless it has been denied statutory listing (CAMRA).

Minster, Micklegate
A familiar and, eventually, the official name for *The York Minster* which had appeared on John Cossins' New and Exact Plan of the City of York, published in 1727 (Murray3 p. 18). Described by Francis Drake in 1736 under the shortened name as one of two inns of good resort in the street (Drake p. 280). Last mention 1830 when it was taken by Henry Henning (YG 27 3 1830). Also known as *The Minster Coffee House*.

Minster, Monk Bar
To be let in 1739 (YCo 7 8 1739). In 1842 it was described as a good inn with new stable, coachhouse, brewhouse, granaries and good vaults (YCo 10 8 1742). By 1750 Christopher Barthorpe, City Huntsman, had become the licensee and he changed the name to *The Hare and Hounds* (YCo 13 3 1750). After he moved to *The Old George*, Pavement, in 1752 (YCo 18 2 1751) and certainly by 1752, when it was again offered for let, it had reverted to its original name (YCo 7 4 1752).

Minster Coffee House, Micklegate
Previously *The York Minster* and *The Minster,* it was using this as an alternative name from when it was for sale in 1743 (YCo 30 8 1743) until 1823 (YCA F30A).

Mitford Tavern
Mentioned in 1489 (Attreed p. 643).

Mitre, North Street
Mentioned in connection with a robbery 1748 (YCo 7 6 1748).

Mitre, Shipton Road
A new public house, built for Hammond's United Breweries, opened on 20 Dec 1961 (YEP 19 12 1961).

Mitre, Stonegate
Mentioned in 1653 in connection with a burial at St Martin, Coney Street (PR) and in 1673 (Benson p. 166).

Moon, Walmgate
A Familiar name for *The Full Moon.*

Mount Hotel, The Mount ¶
Previously *The Saddle.* Bought by J Smith & Co in 1892 (YEP 5 11 1973) when its name was changed. In 1902 it had three bedrooms, all used by the family, a sitting room and a box room upstairs. On the ground floor were two smoke rooms, a large bar, a small room and a private kitchen. There were also two cellars (CC).

Nag's Head, Askham Bryan ¶
Previously *The Barstow Arms,* changed to this name after 1909 (Dir).

Nag's Head, Fossgate
Mentioned 1783 (YCo 1 4 1783). It closed on 1 January 1898, one of three licences surrendered in consideration of a new licence being granted to the Tadcaster Tower Brewery Co. for a new house, *The Jubilee,* Balfour Street (YCA Acc. 189).

Nag's Head, Heworth Road
First mentioned 1838 (Dir). In 1902 it had three bedrooms, one of which was available for travellers. Downstairs there were a smoke room and two kitchen, one private. Food could be supplied if required. There was also a cellar. All the rooms were small and the family and customers shared the only WC (CC).

Nag's Head, Micklegate ¶
Mentioned in 1772 (Benson p. 164), and 1783, 85, 87 and 95 (YCA K69, Cooper2 p. 43). Sold in 1819 on the bankruptcy of John Kilby (YG 25 9 1819). In 1902 it had four bedrooms, one set aside for travellers, and a clubroom upstairs. Below were a smoke room, a taproom, a bar and a kitchen from which food could be supplied if required. There was also a cellar (CC). A Grade II listed building (CAMRA2).

Nag's Head, Middle Water Lane
Mentioned in 1770 (Benson p. 167), and 1783, 87 and 95 (YCA K69, Cooper2 p. 45).

Nag's Head, St Sampson's Square (Thursday Market)
Mentioned in a lease 1711, previously known as *The Cutt–a–Feather* and *The White Swan* (WRRD D.328.559), closed by 1789 (RCHME V p. 206).

Navigation Tavern, Bishopgate Street (near Skeldergate Postern)
To be let in 1845 (YG 5 7 1845). Closed by 1881 (Dir).

Nelson, Walmgate
Mentioned in 1831 (YG 14 5 1831). A familiar name for *The Lord Nelson.*

Neptune, North Street
Previously *The Sawyers' Arms, The Grey Horse* or *The Grey Mare,* it gained this name by 1861. By 1867 it had become *The Newcastle Arms* (Dir).

Neptune, The Shambles
Previously *The Butchers' Arms,* mentioned in 1824 (YG 3 7 1824) although it did not fully relinquish its alternative name until 1828 (YCA F30A). In 1902 it was approached by a passage way from the street as the room at the front was used by the landlord and his

brother as a cobbler's shop. The rooms were all small and very dark. It had five bedrooms, one or two of which were used by lodgers or travellers, and a clubroom upstairs. On the ground floor were a smoke room and a kitchen, where the members of the family cooked their food but it was also used as a drinking room. The Chief Constable considered it a very poor house and specially noted it for the attention of the Licensing Justices (CC). The result was that the renewal of its licence was refused at the Brewster Sessions in 1903 (YG 21 2 1903, YCA Acc. 189).

New Inn, Grimston
Mentioned from 1843 to 1849 (Dir).

New Inn, The Mount
In existence in 1731 when it appeared on an engraving by John Haynes (RCHME V p. 106b). Next *The Gallows House* and later *The White House.*

New Inn, Rufforth
Mentioned in 1823 (Dir) but the pub has been licensed as *The Tankard* since 1822 (YCA F30A).

New Inn, Tadcaster Road, Askham Richard
When it first appeared in the licensing records in 1822 this pub had no name but in 1824, when George Buckle had succeeded Ann Buckle as the licensee, it had been given this name (YCA F30A). Another Ann Buckle was the licensee in 1857 prolonging the family occupation to at least 35 years. Because of this association the new road house built on the site in 1938 was called *Buckles* (YEP 3 12 1938).

New Bridge Inn, Middle Water Lane, King's Staith
Previously *The Old Ouse Bridge,* it gained this name by 1823 (Dir) after the opening of the new Ouse Bridge in 1820. Next *The Labour in Vain* and *The Keel.* Also known as *The Bridge.*

New Bridge, Tanner Moat
At the bankruptcy sale of the estate of John Kilby in 1819 the building was described as a dwelling house, lately used as a public house, adjacent to the malt kiln, in the occupation of John Fryer Kilby (YG 26 9 1819).

New Bridge Street Hotel, Bridge Street
Previously *Rooke's Dram Shop* it was known by this name between 1834 and 1841. (Dir) It was also using the alternative name of *The Board* from 1830. By 1897 it was generally called *Ye Olde No 5.*

New Market Hotel, Cattle Market
Mentioned in 1838 (Dir), an alternative name for The City Arms.

New Sandhill, Goodramgate
Mentioned in 1821 (YG 7 7 1821) but the next year called *The Sandhill.*

New Slip Inn, Malton Road
Mentioned in 1843 as *The Slip* (Dir) although sometimes known by this name (Dir 1848, 1855). By 1887 it had dropped 'New' for good.

New Turf Tavern, Railway View, Dringhouses
Mentioned 1909 (Dir). The original name for *The Turf Tavern* when it moved to this site.

New Walk Tavern, Love Lane ¶
A pre–1869 beerhouse (YCA Acc. 189). Also known as *Gotty's*, after Albert Gott, landlord in 1907, until its closure (Wilson p. 27). In 1902 it had three bedrooms, a front parlour, a kitchen and a small back kitchen. There was only one privy shared by the customers and the family. While the Chief Constable thought the domestic accommodation very bad and the premises generally very poor he did not make any special recommendations to the licensing magistrates (CC). The licence was voluntarily surrendered in 1936 when the licence of *The King's Arms*, Fossgate, was transferred to *The Gimcrack*. It closed on 30 November 1936 (YCA Acc. 189).

Newcastle Arms, George Street
Previously *The Craven Ox Head*, then *The Craven Ox*, it gained this name by 1867 (Dir). In 1902 it had an unused attic and four bedrooms, all used by the family. On the ground floor were a smoke room, a dram shop, a taproom and a private kitchen. There was also a cellar. The family and the customers shared the WC (CC). The licence was formally surrendered on 9 February 1966 when *The Puss 'n Boots*, Hamilton Drive East, opened (YCA Acc. 189).

Newcastle Arms, North Street
Previously *The Sawyers' Arms, The Grey Horse* or *The Grey Mare* and *The Neptune,* it gained this name by 1867 (Dir). In 1902 it had four bedrooms and, while one was set aside for travellers, sleeping accommodation had never been asked for. On the ground floor were a bar parlour, a bar, and a kitchen from which food was supplied. There was also a cellar. The rooms were very small and the kitchen was used as a drinking room (CC). The renewal of its licence was opposed at the Brewster Sessions in 1907. The licensee, William Martin, was also a muffinman and sold tea, coffee and cocoa as well as intoxicating liquors. The sand barge men who used his house took their previously prepared dinners to be cooked there. Nevertheless his trade amounted to only £12 a week. Compensation of £1100 was paid including £100 to Martin (Peacock p. 114) and the licence was surrendered on 10 October 1907 (YCA Acc. 189).

Newcastle Arms, New York Street (Nunnery Lane)
To be let and entered into immediately 1854 (YG 4 3 1854). Last mention 1861 (Dir).

Nickel and Dime, Blossom Street
Previously *The Lion and Lamb*, closed for refurbishment in 1987 and reopened under this name (YEP 17 1 1987). Closed permanently by 1992 (Thomson).

Nineteen Hundredth, Church Street
Previously and later *The Golden Lion*. In 1970 an application from JW Cameron & Co. to demolish the old pub and rebuild a new one was approved (YEP 29 5 1970). It reopened in 1971 under this name to celebrate the 1900th anniversary of the founding of the city (YEP 16 1 1971). It reverted to its former name in 1983 (YEP 23 3 1983).

Noah's Ark, Goodramgate
In Lady Row (RCHME V p. 144b). To be sold by auction 1878 (YG 18 5 1878).

Noah's Ark, Silver Street
Mentioned in 1783, 85 and 95 (YCA K69). Sold in 1819 on the bankruptcy of John Kilby (YG 26 6 1819). Demolished in 1837 in connection with the enlargement of the market (YG 18 7 1837).

Noah's Ark, St Dennis parish
Mentioned in 1783 and 87 (YCA Acc. 189).

North Eastern Hotel, Tanner Row
Previously *The George*. By 1861 the management had passed to John Holliday, manager of *The Station Hotel* (Dir) and renamed The North Eastern Hotel after the railway company which had been created in 1854. Its licence lapsed in 1899 (YCA Acc. 189) after it had been purchased by the North Eastern Railway Company to house the staff displaced from the former *Scawin's Hotel* when it was demolished to clear the site for the building of the new railway offices.

North Eastern Refreshment Inn, Tanner Row
Previously *The Railway Coffee House, The Refreshment Inn,* it gained this name by 1858. Next, by 1879, *The Railway Inn* and later *The Grapes*. (Dir).

Northern Wall, Fossgate
Previously *The Stonebow* and *The Boulevard,* given this name on 10 December 1993 after a £100,000 refurbishment. The landlord had discovered that his pub was located close to the site of the north wall of a 13th century Carmelite Friary. (YEP 10 12 1993).

Oak, Copmanthorpe
A familiar name for *The Royal Oak.*

Oddfellows' Arms, Hungate
Mentioned 1822 and 23 (YCA F30A).

Oddfellows' Arms, Townend Street
Mentioned 1838 (YG 24 11 1838) and 1841 (Dir).

Oddfellows' Arms, Tanner Row
Previously and later *The Unicorn*, using this name in 1838 and 1841 (Dir). More recently *The Corner Pin.*

Old Black Dog, 59 Jubbergate
Mentioned in a lease 29 August 1757 (YCA 94 f. 14b). The 'Old' had been added to the name to distinguish it from at least one and maybe two other Black Dogs in Jubbergate at the time. By 1823, strangely, with one of the similarly named pubs still in existence, it became *The Black Dog* but revived its earlier name briefly in 1828 (Dir).

Old Duke's Coffee House, Bridge Street
Previously *The Duke's Head* and *The Duke's Coffee House*. Mentioned in 1794 (YCh 12 6 1794).

Old Duke's Head, 53 Aldwark
First mentioned in 1838 with Robert Merrington as licensee. However he made his first appearance in 1823 in *The Duke of York* at 54 Aldwark which by 1834 had become *The*

Duke's Head with John Rounding as licensee. Robert Merrington then reappeared here in 1838. It would appear that he sold out to John Rounding but a few years later decided to return to the street and open a pub at 54 Aldwark next door to his former premises. The two establishments then vied for the right to be considered the senior and both, at various times, add 'Old' to their names. The problem was solved by the disappearance of this pub shortly after 1858 (Dir).

Old Duke's Head, 54 Aldwark
Previously *The Duke's Head* and *The Duke of York* and then by 1834 *The Duke's Head* again. This house then variously called itself *The Original Duke's Head*, 1841 and 1849, and *The Old Duke's Head*, 1846 and 1851, in an attempt to establish its seniority over the other *Duke's Head* at 53 Aldwark. After the disappearance of its rival soon after 1858 it had the field to itself and, for the rest of its life, it reverted to the name of *The Duke's Head*.

Old Ebor, Drake Street, Nunnery Lane
A pre–1869 beerhouse (YCA Acc. 189) using the 'Old' epithet to distinguish it from the various other houses in the city with 'Ebor' in their names. In 1902 it had four bedrooms and two sitting rooms upstairs. Below were a smoke room, a snug, a bar and a private kitchen. There was also a cellar. The family had to share its WC with the customers (CC). The full 'on' licence of *The Pack Horse*, Micklegate was transferred here on the closure of that house on 12 March 1957. (YCA Acc. 189, YEP 3 4 1957).

Old Ebor, Straker's Passage, Fossgate
Mentioned 1843 (Dir) and 1845 (YG 8 2 1845).

Old Ebor Tavern, Tanner Row ¶
A beerhouse, earliest mention 1867, but first appearance under a specific name was as *The Ebor Commercial House* in 1872 (Dir). By 1881 it had become *The Old Ebor*. In 1902 the Chief Constable thought the premises suitable for a beer house. It had an attic and four bedrooms above a smoke room, a bar, a snug, a weigh room and private kitchens. There was also a cellar (CC). It was referred for compensation on 9 March 1927. This was agreed four days later and the licence expired on 30 September 1927 (YG 16 7 1927, YCA Acc. 189). The last licensee, Mrs Clara Inman, continued to use the premises as The Old Ebor Café. In 1976 it was revived as a public house, *The Grob and Ducat*.

Old Faulcon, Micklegate
Mentioned in 1743 (YCo 18 10 1743), an alternative name for *The Falcon* used to avoid confusion with another house with the same name in North Street.

Old Fortune of War, Low Ousegate
Mentioned 1742 (YCo 1 6 1742). The use of 'Old' implies that there were two houses in the city with this name at that time. By 1763 this one had become The *Fortune of War*.

Old George Hotel, Fossgate or Pavement or Whipmawhopmagate ¶
Previously *The George*, it had gained this name, to avoid confusion with another house nearby with the same name, by 1749 when it was to be let (YCo 12 9 1749). Two years later it was renamed *The Hare and Hounds* when it was taken by Christopher Barthorpe, the City Huntsman (YCo 18 2 1751). For a period from at least 1782 (Dr White's Map) to 1798 (Dir) it was known as *The George and Dragon* and sometimes, 1783 to 1795, as *The*

George as well (YCA K69, Cooper p. 46). It would appear that the sign during this period showed the patron saint rather than one of the monarchs. By 1823 it was firmly re–established as *The Old George* (Dir) except in the licensing records where it was still listed as The George between 1822 and 28 (YCA F30A, F31). When it was advertised to be sold or let in 1867 the property was described as part freehold and part leasehold, from the Sub–chanter and Vicars Choral of York on a 40 year lease of which 29 years were still to run (YG 25 10 1867). In 1902 it had upstairs a club or commercial room and 20 bedrooms, of which 16 or 17 were available for travellers. On the ground floor were a bar, two rooms used by commercials, sitting rooms and private kitchens. Described as a good commercial hotel, it supplied the full range of meals to its patrons (CC). It was closed on 30 October 1949 and its business transferred to the *White Swan*, Piccadilly (YEP 13 10 1949). It was demolished in 1950 during the creation of Stonebow (YEP 30 6 1950). The licence was suspended in 1949 and surrendered on 10 April 1956 when *The Clock*, Walmgate, was closed and its licence transferred to *The White Rose*, Cornlands Road (YCA Acc. 189).

Old Globe, Shambles
Mentioned in 1843 (Dir), a name used to avoid confusion with *The Globe (3)* which was, in fact, already closed by this time.

Old Grey Mare, Clifton ¶
Previously *The Grey Horse*, using this name by 1830 and then, by 1855 it became *The Grey Mare* for a period until at least 1876, after which it reverted to The Old Grey Mare (Dir). In 1902 it had an attic, four bedrooms, all used by the family, and a billiard room on the upper floors. Below were two smoke rooms, a taproom, a bar parlour, a dram shop and private kitchens from which food could be supplied. There was also a cellar. The Chief Constable thought the sleeping accommodation was not good but otherwise it was a good suitable house (CC). By 1953 it had become *Ye Olde Grey Mare.*

Old Hawke, St Mary, Castlegate, parish
Mentioned in 1783 (YCA K69).

Old King's Arms, Fossgate
Mentioned in 1774 (YG 17 5 1774). An alternative name for *The King's Arms.*

Old Malt Shovel, 12 Walmgate ¶
Previously *The Malt Shovel.* By 1828 it had been renamed *The Old Malt Shovel* (Dir) to distinguish itself from the other house in the street with the same name. Although there were occasional lapses to the former name, by 1851 the revised name was firmly established (Dir). During the time it belonged to Brett Brothers Brewery, who sold it to JJ Hunt & Co in 1896, a tessellated pavement was installed in the entrance which described it as *Ye Olde Malte Shovel*. In 1902 it had five bedrooms, two of which were available for travellers, a sitting room and a store room upstairs. On the ground floor were a smoke room, a bar, a very small snug, a small room and a private kitchen. The Chief Constable considered that a proper urinal was required (CC). It was referred for compensation in May 1956 (YEP 29 5 1956). This was paid on 24 and it closed on 31 October the same year (YCA Acc. 189).

Old Malt Shovel, 66 Walmgate

Previously *The Malt Shovel*. The rivalry with the other *Malt Shovel* in Walmgate led to this one also, for a period between 1841 and 1848, claiming the earlier date of foundation with the name *The Old Malt Shovel*. The matter was resolved by 1851 when its name was changed to *The Bricklayers' Arms* (Dir). Later renamed *The Spread Eagle*.

Old Orleans, Ousegate

Grand Metropolitan announced in 1988 that they were converting the former Décor 8 premises into a restaurant (YEP 11 3 1988).

Old Ouse Bridge, King's Staith

A beerhouse, later *The New Bridge, The Labour in Vain.* and *The Keel* (Cooper p. 86).

Old Pack Horse, Micklegate

When John Burton moved to the opposite side of Micklegate, next door to St Martin's churchyard, in 1778 he took the name, *The Pack Horse*, with him. His original house then became The Old Pack Horse and was taken by John Simpson (YCo 9 6 1778). Mentioned in 1783 (YCA K69). The new Pack Horse does not seem to have survived very long as it does not appear in any list of licences after 1783. After its demise The Old Pack Horse became *The Pack Horse* again (YCA K69).

Old Post House, Skeldergate

Taken by Joseph Andrich in 1745, who changed the name to *The Elephant and Falcon* (YCo 4 2 1745).

Old Rackitt, Petergate/Swinegate

Mentioned in a deed in 1694 (RCHME V p. 196b) and in 1749 (YCo 27 6 1749), situated in an area between the two streets known as the Rackitt. Also called *The Rackitt*, the name by which it was universally known by 1783 (YCA K69).

Old Sandhill, Colliergate

Previously *The Sandhill* but probably given this name in 1742 when the landlord, William Barwick, moved to *The White Swan* between Petergate and Goodramgate and renamed that house *The White Swan and Sandhill* (YCo 29 6 1742). It was certainly using this name in 1763 (YCo 11 1 1763). It was reached by a narrow passage between the shops in Colliergate (OS). In 1869 it was purchased by the York Rifle Corps and some fittings were sold (YG 22 5 1869). Two years later a new drill hall was built on its site, fronting St Andrewgate (Cooper p. 45). Although it was no longer open to the public, drinks were still supplied to the volunteers (CC) until April 1910 when the licence was allowed to lapse (YCA Acc. 189).

Old Sandhill Tap, St Andrewgate

An adjacent establishment to *The Old Sandhill* in existence in 1852 (OS). By 1858 it was referred to as *The Sandhill Tap* when they had separate licensees (Dir).

Old Sycamore Tree, Minster Close (Yard)

An alternative name for *The Sycamore Tree*, mentioned in 1818 (Dir).

Old Three Cups, 192 Walmgate

An alternative name for one of the two *The Three Cups* which were within 40 yards of each other, mentioned in 1795 (YCA K69).

Old Turk's Head, King's Court, King's Square (Haymarket) ¶

Previously *The Turk's Head Coffee House* which was shortened to *The Turk's Head.* 'Old' had been added to its name by 1783 (YCA K69) presumably to avoid confusion with another pub of the same name, perhaps *The Turk's Head* in Low Ousegate, but this was not in exclusive use until 1846 (Dir). In 1902 it had five bedrooms, four set apart for travellers, and a clubroom upstairs. Below were two smoke rooms, a bar and a kitchen from which food could be supplied if required. The kitchen was so very dark that the gas had to be kept alight all day. The family and customers shared the only WC (CC). At the Brewster Sessions in 1907 the renewal of its licence was successfully opposed. It lapsed on 10 October that year after compensation of £800 had been paid (Peacock pp. 113, 155, YCA Acc.189).

Old White Swan, Goodramgate (Petergate) ¶

Previously *The White Swan, The White Swan and Sandhill* and *The White Swan* again. 'Old' was added to its name by 1885 (Dir) and this became the accepted name although it is occasionally referred to as *The White Swan* in later street directories. From its original building it had grown until it became a complex of nine separate structures, with, at one time, an entrance onto Petergate. In 1902 while it had nine bedrooms, only one was available for travellers and six were only used on special occasions. It also had a large dining room, a bar, a market room, a billiard room, and private kitchens from which food could be supplied. There was no WC available for the customers (CC). In 1984, after a £750,000 restoration the previous year by Bass North, it received an RIBA award (YEP 16 8 1984). A Grade II listed building (CAMRA2).

O'Neills, Low Ousegate

Previously *The Board*, then *Hillyard's Wine Lodge*, *The Lodge*, *Yates' Wine Lodge* and *Dukes of York* it was given this name in 1996 when it reopened as an Irish theme bar (YEP 6 5 1996).

Original Black Dog, Jubbergate

Previously *The Black Dog*, but using this name in 1830 to distinguish itself from another pub with the same name in the street. Later *The Black Dog* again and then finally *The Dog.* (Dir).

Original Duke's Head, 54 Aldwark

Previously *The Duke's Head* and *The Duke of York,* it was using this name at various times between 1841 and 1855 to avoid confusion with another pub of the same name next door. Sometimes called *The Old Duke's Head* in the same period, it reverted to its original name after the disappearance of its rival after 1858 (Dir).

Oscar's, Little Stonegate

A wine bar, opened in February 1982 (YEP 13 2 1982).

Other Tap and Spile, North Street ¶

Previously *The Yorkshire Hussar*, it was bought by Brent, Walker Breweries and opened in 1990 with this name, part of their chain which included *The Tap and Spile*, Monkgate (YEP 6 3 1990). After being purchased by Century Inns it was renamed *The First Hussar* (YEP 17 11 1997).

Ouse Bridge Tavern, King's Staith ¶

Previously *The King's Arms*, in 1867 the licensee, George Duckitt, changed its name to this (Johnson p. 31, Dir). In 1902 it had three bedrooms, all used by the family, a club room, a WC and a kitchen, from which food could be supplied, upstairs. On the ground floor were a taproom, a dram shop and a smoke room. There was no WC for the customers (CC). On 28 March 1974 it reopened after refurbishment under its original name (YEP 26 3 1974).

Ox, Stockton on the Forest

At first sight this would appear to be an error made by the street directory compiler intended to be *The Fox*. However both pubs are listed in 1896 (Dir).

Pack Horse, Fossgate

Earliest mention 1733 as a place where common carriers could be found (Gent). Mentioned in 1783, 87 and 95 (YCA K69).

Pack Horse, Micklegate (1) ¶

Earliest mention 1733 as a place where common carriers could be found (Gent). In 1778 the licensee, John Burton, moved to the opposite side of the street next to the churchyard of St Martin cum Gregory taking the name with him. The original house then became *The Old Packhorse*. By 1787 after the demise of the new *Pack Horse* it reverted to its earlier name (YCA K69). In 1824 the premises were enlarged by the acquisition of the building on its east side (YCA E97 F. 185v) so that in 1902 it had 14 bedrooms, ten set aside for travellers. There were also a large dining room, a smoke room, a bottle and jug department, a snug, a ladies' market room, a taproom and a kitchen which could supply the full range of meals. There was also a cellar (CC). The inn closed on 4 April 1957 (YEP 3 4 1957) when its full 'on' licence was transferred to The Old Ebor, Drake Street, Nunnery Lane (YCA Acc. 189). The building was demolished in 1960 to enable Micklegate to be widened (YEP 23 9 1960).

Pack Horse, Micklegate (2)

In 1778 the licensee of the other *Pack Horse,* John Burton, moved to the opposite side of the street next to the churchyard of St Martin cum Gregory taking the name with him. The original house then became *The Old Packhorse*. The new pub does not seem to have flourished as it does not appear in the list of licences after 1783 (YCA K69).

Pack Horse, Pavement

Mentioned in 1834 (Dir), a mis–identification of *The Black Horse.*

Pack Horse, Skeldergate ¶

Mentioned in 1783, 85, 87 and 95 (YCA K69). In 1902 there were four bedrooms, two set apart for travellers, and a clubroom upstairs. On the ground floor were a smoke room, a serving bar and a taproom. The private kitchen, from which food was supplied, was detached from the house in what had once been a cottage on the opposite side of the yard. There was also a cellar and a brewhouse where the landlord brewed his own ale (CC). It was referred for compensation on 26 February 1937. This was paid on 31 January the next year when the house closed (YCA Acc. 189).

Pack Horse, Tadcaster Road, Askham Bryan

Mentioned in 1881 and 1895 (Dir).

Tiger, (Jubbergate) Market Street, 1906

Trinity House Hotel, Trinity Lane, 1906

Turk's Head, St Andrewgate, 1906

Unicorn Inn, Lord Mayor's Walk, 1935

Unicorn, Tanner Row, 1906

Victoria Inn/Hotel, Cemetery Road, 1906

Victoria Vaults, Nunnery Lane/Dove Street, 1935

Waggon and Horses, Gillygate, 1906

Waggon and Horses, Lawrence Street, 1935

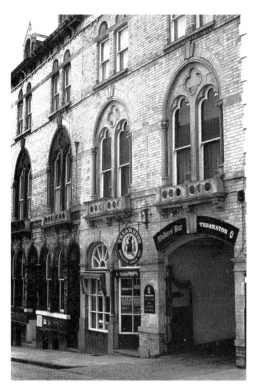

Walker's Bar, Micklegate, 1984

Wenlock Arms, Wheldrake, 1906

Wheatsheaf, Davygate, 1890

Wheatsheaf, Hungate, 1930

White Horse, Bootham, 1880

White Horse, Bootham, 1906

White Horse, Coppergate, 1963

White Horse, Skeldergate, 1906

White House, The Mount, 1960

White Swan, Pavement, 1906

White Swan, Piccadilly, 1923

*Wild Man, Water Lane, 1841,
drawn by Francis Bedford*

Windmill, Askham Bryan, 1900

Windmill, Blossom Street, 1906

Windmill, St George's Field, 1852, photograph by William Pumphrey

Windmill, York Road, Wigginton, 1906

Woodman, Bishopthorpe, 1906

Woodman, Heworth Green, Malton Road, 1921

Woolpack, Fawcett Street (Cattle Market), 1932

Woolpack, St Saviour's Place, 1935

Woolpack, St Saviour's Place, 1970

Ye Olde No 5, Bridge Street, 1906

Ye Olde Starre Inne, Stonegate, 1974

York Arms, High Petergate, 1933

Yorkshireman Inn, Coppergate, 1952

Pack of Cards, Lindsey Avenue
A proposal was made in 1967 to transfer the licence from The Exhibition, Bootham, which was to be closed and demolished for the construction of an Inner Ring Road, to this new pub (YEP 27 1 1967). In the event a new licence was granted on 18 December 1969 (YCA Acc. 189).

Packet House, Skeldergate
Mentioned in 1841 (Dir).

Pageant, George Hudson Street
Previously *The Great Northern Hotel*. After renovation it was reopened as *The Pageant* in 1966 (YEP 3 11 1966). It reverted to its original name in 1984 (YEP 10 5 1984) and was renamed *Merlins* by 1994.

Painted Wagon, Piccadilly
A new public house to be built under the converted ABC Cinema (YEP 17 8 1972).

Painters' Arms, Goodramgate
Mentioned in 1769 (Johnson p. 8) and in 1783 and 85 (YCA K69).

Panther, Pavement
Mentioned 1823 (Dir), an alternative name for *The Leopard.*

Paragon Inn, Cattle Market, Fawcett Street/Paragon Street
Offered for sale with a brewhouse in 1851 (YG 15 3 1851), it became *The Cattle Market Inn* by 1872 (Dir).

Parrot, Little Shambles
Mentioned 1783 and 85 (YCA K69), by 1787 it had changed its name to *The Malt Shovel* (Cooper2 p. 44).

Parrot, St Dennis, Walmgate, parish
Mentioned 1783 (YCA K69).

Pavement Café Bar, New Street
Mentioned 2000 (Thomson), next *The Blue Fly* (YEP 4 11 2002).

Pavement Vaults, Pavement ¶
Previously *The Board*, by 1949 it was also known as *The Pavement Vaults.* It ceased trading on 27 January and the licence was surrendered on 13 February 1963 (YCA Acc.189).

Paviers, St Dennis parish
Mentioned in 1568, a capital messuage, tenement or inn called The Sign of the Paviers (YCA E23 f. 38).

Pavilion, Gentlemen's (White Rose) Cricket Ground, Bootham Stray
In 1902 it had two bedrooms, a private sitting room, a private kitchen, two dressing rooms and a pavilion in which members of the public could buy intoxicating drinks while cricket matches were being played (CC). In February 1916 the licensees, GE Barton, Caterers, did not take up the ale licence for the coming year and the facility lapsed (YCA Acc. 189).

Pavilion, Railway Street (George Hudson Street)
Mentioned 1881 (Dir).

Petergate Spirit Stores and Bar, Petergate
Previously *Wolstenholme's Dram Shop*, and *Haigh's Vaults*, it gained this name by 1902. Later *The Board* and *The Hole in The Wall*.

Pewterers' Arms, Low Ousegate
Mentioned in 1783, 85, 87 and 95 (YCA K69, Cooper2 p. 45). For sale by auction in 1838 (YG 5 5 1838).

Phalanx and Firkin, Micklegate
Previously *The Coach and Horses* but familiarly known as *The Little Coach*, and *The Coach*, before being given this name on 17 October 1996 when it became *The Phalanx and Firkin* (YEP 15 10 1996) following the Firkin Brewery chain's policy of adding an alliterative prefix to their brand title. After being acquired by a new owner and given a makeover it reopened as *The Priory* in March 2003 (YEP 29 3 2003).

Pheasant, New Walk Terrace
Mentioned 1843 (YG 21 10 1843) and demolished c.1845 (Cooper p. 54).

Phoenix, George Street ¶
Previously *The Labour in Vain*, it gained this name by 1867 (Dir). It was practically a new house in 1902 when it had four bedrooms, a sitting room and a kitchen upstairs. On the ground floor were two smoke rooms, a serving bar and a sitting room (CC). A Grade II listed building (CAMRA2).

Pig and Whistle, Newgate
A beerhouse, mentioned between 1838 and 1872 (Dir). Eventually called The Greyhound (Cooper p. 49).

Pigeon, Monk Bar without
Mentioned in 1752. For sale the next year after the death of the licensee, Robert Heppinstall, a good accustomed inn with five coach houses, good stabling, a large yard and other conveniences (YCo 14 4 1752).

Pitcher and Piano, Coney Street
A café bar, opened since 1998 (YEP 22 6 2002).

Plasterers' Arms, St Sampson's parish
Mentioned 1783, 85 and 87 (YCA K69, Cooper2 p. 43).

Plonkers Wine Bar, Cumberland Street
Opened August 1984 (YEP 3 8 1984). Refused a full public house licence in 1987 (YEP 17 3 1987).

Plough, Clifton
First mentioned 1828, by 1846 had become *The Burton Stone Inn* (Dir).

Plough, Main Street, Fulford ¶
Earliest mention 1813 when the licensee, George Tomlinson, advertised accommodation for parties (YCo 9 8 1813). The diarist, William Wodson, played quoits or brasses there in 1825 (Briddon p. 40). Given a face lift, including a shell doorway *c.*1930.

Ploughboy's Rest, Swinegate
Mentioned 1849 (YG 1 12 1849) but is included in the street directories between 1846 to 1855 without a name (Dir).

Plumber's Arms, Skeldergate ¶
A beerhouse with a licence granted before 1869 (YCA Acc. 189), it does not make an appearance in the street directories until 1876 (Dir). Although scheduled for compensation in 1910 the licence was renewed (YG 12 2, 12 3 1910). It closed on 1 January 1964 and, after demolition, was rebuilt. The new upgraded house was granted a full 'on' licence and opened as *The Cock and Bottle* on 19 May 1965 (YCA Acc. 189). Later *The Villiers* and *The Cock and Bottle* again.

Poacher, Front Street, Acomb
Previously *The Square and Compasses, The Marcia, The Grey Mare,* and *The Marcia* again, occasionally *The Grey Marcia.* It gained this name in 1998 (Thomson).

Pointer Dog, St Saviourgate
Mentioned in 1783 but by 1785 had become *The Dog* (YCA K69, Cooper2 p 44). Later *The White Dog* and *The Spotted Dog.*

Postern Gate, Piccadilly
A new pub opened by Wetherspoons in The Travel Lodge at Fishergate Postern on 20 May 2002 (YEP 20 5 2002).

Prince of Wales, Skeldergate
Previously *The Labourer, The Foresters' Arms* and *The Three Tuns,* it had gained this name by 1861 (Dir) – see next. In 1902 it had three bedrooms, one set aside for travellers, a sitting room and a clubroom upstairs. On the ground floor were two smoke rooms, a dram shop and two private kitchens from which food could be supplied (CC). It was referred for compensation in February (YG 15 2 1913) and closed on 6 October 1913 (YCA Acc. 189).

Prince of Wales, Walmgate
Mentioned in 1843 (Dir), named after Albert Edward, Prince of Wales, eldest son of Queen Victoria, who was born on 9 November 1841, succeeded as monarch in 1902 and died in 1910.

Princess Victoria, Bootham Square
Mentioned in 1843 (Dir) but was previously called *The Victoria* and later *The Victoria* again or *The Queen.* By 1858 it had become *The Queen's Head.* Princess Victoria, the heir to the throne, made her first appearance in York in 1835 when she attended the musical festival with her mother, the Duchess of Kent, and became Queen in 1837.

Princess Victoria, Lawrence Street
Previously *The Wheatsheaf* and next, according to TP Cooper (Cooper p. 87) given this name. Later *The Victoria* or *The Queen Victoria, The Queen's Head, The Queen* and *The Rook and Gaskill.*

Printing Press, Swinegate
Mentioned 1822 to 1826 (YCA F30A; F31), alternatively known as *The Stanhope Press.*

Priory, Micklegate
Previously *The Coach and Horse* and *The Phalanx and Firkin,* it was given this name in March 2003 after a makeover by its new owners (YEP 30 3 2003).

Punch Bowl, Blossom Street ¶
Mentioned in 1783, 85, 87 and 95 (YCA K69, Cooper2 p. 43). On 5 April 1811 John Kilby paid the Corporation £42 12s 0d for a lease of seven years (YCA E78A). In 1902 it had seven bedrooms, three set apart for travellers, and a dining room upstairs. Below were a bar, a smoke room, a snug and a private kitchen from which food was supplied. There was also a cellar. The Chief Constable thought that the urinal was too close to the kitchen door (CC). In 1974 the butcher's shop on the corner of Nunnery Lane was incorporated into the premises increasing the bedrooms to 13 in number (YEP 11 5 1974). A Grade II listed building (CAMRA2). Between 1822 and 1825 it was known by the alternative name of *The Fox and Hounds* (YCA F30A).

Punch Bowl, Jubbergate
Mentioned in 1783, 85, 87 and 95 (YCA K69, Cooper2 p. 43). Last mention 1828 (Dir).

Punch Bowl, Lowther Street ¶
First mentioned in 1858 (Dir). In 1902 it had six bedrooms, two set aside for travellers. On the ground floor were a smoke room, a bar parlour, a large bar and a private kitchen from which food could be supplied. There was also a cellar (CC). In 2001 its name was changed to *The Independent.*

Punch Bowl, Micklegate
Mentioned in 1783, 85, 87 and 95 (YCA K69, Cooper2 p. 43). On 25 March 1811 John Kilby commenced renting it from the Corporation at a rental of £36 a year (YCA E78A).

Punch Bowl, Peter Lane
See *Granby's Punch Bowl.*

Punch Bowl, St John, Ousebridge, parish
Mentioned in 1783 (YCA K69).

Punch Bowl, St Sampson's Square
Mentioned in 1783, 85, 87 and 95 (YCA K69, Cooper p. 28). Sold in 1819 on the bankruptcy of John Kilby (YG 26 6 1819). By 1855 it had become *The Market Tavern.*

Punch Bowl, Stonegate ¶
Mentioned in 1761 as *The Golden Punch Bowl* (Benson p. 164). On 12 January the same year the Punch Bowl Lodge of Freemasons received its warrant. It expired in 1764 (Riley p. 25). It was also patronised by the Minster Bell Ringers and in 1765 the tongue from a tenor bell, purchased for £3 7s 6d (Johnson p 38.), was installed as a window support in the

back bar where it still remains (Benson2). A notorious house in the 19th century, on one occasion in 1880 when 24 immoral characters were found on the premises the publican was charged with keeping a disorderly house (YG 27 11 1880). In 1902 it had three unused attics and five bedrooms, three of which, although spare, were not let out to travellers. On the ground floor were a smoke room, a bar, a dram shop and a kitchen from which food was supplied. The rooms were all very dark and badly lit and the family shared its WC with the customers (CC). It was refurbished by the Tadcaster Tower Brewery Co. after a fire in 1930 (CAMRA). The old brick front was replaced by a medieval type jettied timber framed front set back on a new building line. A Grade II listed building (CAMRA2).

Punch Bowl, Walmgate
Mentioned in 1783, 87 and 95 (YCA K69, Cooper3 p. 46).

Puss 'n Boots, Hamilton Drive East
A provisional full 'on' licence was granted for this new pub on 14 February 1961 conditional on the surrender of the licence of *The Newcastle Arms*, George Street. That house did not close until 9 February 1966 and the final licence was granted on the same day (YCA Acc. 189).

Putrid Arms, Skeldergate
It is hard to believe that this name, mentioned in 1818 (Dir), is anything other than a nickname but it is impossible to identify it amongst the other pubs in the street at that time. The reputation of the landlord at the time, Silvester Reed, was apparently not sullied by this association as he went on to hold licences at *The Bay Horse*, Monkgate, and *The Old Sandhill*, Colliergate.

Quakerwood, Woodthorpe
Opened in July 1991, its name was suggested by Ken Tinker, a builder of Acomb, who had, in his youth, known the area in which the pub is located, as Quaker Wood (YEP 24 7 1991).

Queen, Bootham Square
A beerhouse, mentioned in 1834, had become *The Victoria* by 1838. By 1843 it was called *The Princess Victoria* but then the name alternated between *The Victoria*, 1846 and 1851, and *The Queen*, 1849 and 1855 (Dir). Later *The Queen's Head*.

Queen Inn, Lawrence Street ¶
Previously *The Wheatsheaf, The Princess Victoria, The Victoria* or *The Queen Victoria* and *The Queen's Head*, it was using this name by 1858 (Dir). In 1902 it had seven bedrooms, four of which were available for travellers. On the ground floor were a smoke room, a taproom, a dining room, a spirit store and private kitchens from which food was supplied. There was also a cellar. All the rooms had low ceilings (CC). In 2002, taken over by the York Brewery Company, it was renamed *The Rook and Gaskill*.

Queen Caroline, Goodramgate
Mentioned in 1822 (YCA F30A) and 1823 (Dir). Princess Caroline of Brunswick was the first cousin and queen consort of George IV. She died on 7 Aug 1821. Possibly *The Glovers' Arms* next.

Queen Victoria, Lawrence Street
Previously *The Wheatsheaf, The Princess Victoria* or *The Victoria,* it was using this name in 1843 (Dir, YG 16 12 1843) but its shorter name continued to be used until it became *The Queen's Head.* Later *The Queen* and *The Rook and Gaskill.*

Queen's Hotel, Micklegate ¶
Opened by George Adams, late of the Elephant and Castle, Skeldergate, in 1845 (YG 26 4 1845) in the western house of a pair built by two Thompson cousins in the third decade of the 18th century. In 1902 seven of its 12 bedrooms were available for travellers. There was also a bar, a billiard room, a commercial room, a vault, a private room and a kitchen from which the full range of meals were supplied (CC). It was closed in 1971 and planning permission sought to change it into shops (YEP 9 9 1971). Eventually the whole building, including the eastern house was demolished as it had become a danger to the public because of its frailty and, after much controversy, a replica of the original building was erected on the site (Murray3 p. 28).

Queen's Arms, St Saviourgate
Mentioned in 1838 (Dir).

Queen's Head, Bootham Square ¶
A beerhouse, previously *The Victoria, The Princess Victoria*, and *The Queen*, it was using this name 1858 (Dir). In 1902, by which time it had been granted a full licence, it had five bedrooms, two available for travellers. On the ground floor were two smoke rooms and a very small living kitchen. There was also a cellar in which food was kept as there was no pantry. The family shared its WC with the customers (CC). It closed on 1 October 1923 (YCA Acc. 189) and was demolished after being compulsorily purchased in 1934.

Queen's Head, Castlegate
Mentioned in 1761 (YCo 17 2 1761). In 1764 the annual rental of £3 was used for the repair of St Mary's, Castlegate (VCH p. 393). Last mentioned in 1772 (YCo 14 4 1772).

Queen's Head, Coney Street
Mentioned in 1748 (YCo 28 6 1748).

Queen's Head, Fossgate ¶
Previously *The Wellington Coffee House*, mentioned with this name in 1838 (Dir, YG 8 12 1838). In 1902 it had five bedrooms, two set apart for travellers, and a clubroom upstairs. Below were a smoke room, a taproom, a dark and small snug and a private kitchen from which food could be supplied to customers (CC). The next year it was selling 'a vast number of glasses of beer a week' but, nevertheless, an attempt, unsuccessful as it turned out, was made at the Brewster Sessions to oppose the renewal of its licence (Peacock p. 65). It finally succumbed in 1956, closing its doors for the last time on 31 October (YCA Acc. 189) despite the landlord having increased the takings by 500% in the previous months. Even this was not enough to overcome the structural problems which included considerable dampness (YEP 5 3 1956) so compensation was paid to him and the owners on 24 October. The building was demolished in 1964 (YEP 12 2 1964).

Queen's Head, Lawrence Street
Previously *The Wheatsheaf, The Princess Victoria* or *The Queen Victoria* or *The Victoria,* it was using this name in 1857 (Dir). Later *The Queen* and *The Rook and Gaskill.*

Queen's Head, Walmgate
Mentioned in 1838 (Dir)

Queen's Staith Inn, Queen's Staith
Mentioned between 1858 and 1879 (Dir). Later *The Anchor.*

Quiet Woman, Fishergate
A beerhouse, mentioned in 1835 when George Tilney, a stonemason, was refused a licence
(YG 16 9 1835). He seems to have redeemed himself for, in 1838, he was in residence and
changed its name to *The Masons' Arms*.

Rackitt, Petergate
Previously *The Old Rackitt*, universally known by this name by 1783 (YCA K69). For sale
in 1804 (YCo 23 1 1804).

Railway Tavern, Queen Street (Thief Lane)
First mentioned in 1841 (Dir), the railway having arrived at York in 1839 at a temporary
station nearby, outside the walls. The establishment was purchased by the North Eastern
Railway and, by 1855, part of it became the York Railway Library and Reading Room
(YG 2 6 1855). It was finally closed in 1885 to enable the site to be cleared for the building
of the new Railway Institute which opened in 1889 (YG 18 5 1889).

Railway Tavern, Tanners' Moat
First mentioned in 1855 (Dir) and still using this name in 1884 (YEP 24 8 1884). By 1885
it had become *The Lendal Bridge* (Dir). Later *The Maltings.*

Railway Inn, Tanner Row
Previously *The Railway Coffee House, The Refreshment Inn, The North Eastern
Refreshment Inn* it was using this name in 1879. By 1881 it had become *The Grapes* (Dir).

Railway Hotel, Tanner Row
Built opposite the (old) Railway Station in Tanner Row and opened under the
proprietorship of George Britton in 1841 (YG 9 10 1841). A year later Britton was
succeeded by Mrs Sarah Scawin who renamed the hotel *Scawin's Railway Hotel*.

Railway and Ebor Tavern, Tanners' Moat
Located close to North Street Postern, the earliest mention was in 1840 when Edward
Calvert transferred his business from *The Lamb Coffee House* (YG 6 6 1840). By 1843
'Railway' had been dropped from its title and it became *The Ebor* Tavern (Dir).

Railway Coffee House, Tanner Row
Mentioned in 1846 (Dir). Later *The Refreshment Inn, The North Eastern Refreshment Inn,
The Railway Inn* and *The Grapes.*

Railway Hotel Tap, Station Road ¶
Previously the *Railway Tap* (Tanner's Moat), which by 1891 had been taken over by
Scawin's Railway Hotel (Dir). Demolished to make way for the new North Eastern
Railway Offices in 1898.

Railway King, George Hudson Street
Previously *The Adelphi*, it was renamed on 14 December 1971 to commemorate the 100th anniversary of the death of George Hudson, the Railway King (YEP 15 12 1971). At the same time the street, originally Hudson Street, but Railway Street after his downfall in 1849, was renamed George Hudson Street. Later *Edwards* and then *Reflex*.

Railway Tap, Tanner's Moat
In existence in 1852 (OS). John Norrison, a coal merchant had started brewing in 1822 on a site between Tanner Row and Tanners' Moat, near where the (old) railway was to be built in 1841 (YG 9 3 1822). This public house provided an outlet where the brewery's products could be sold to the public, including railway passengers. By 1891 it was part of *Scawin's Railway Hotel* complex and was now called *The Railway Hotel Tap*, Station Road (Dir).

Rat Pit, Carmelite Street
A nickname for *The Garden Gate* (Cooper p. 46).

Recruiting Serjeant, Trinity Lane
Mentioned in 1783, 85, 87 and 95 (YCA K69, Cooper2 p. 43).

Red Calf, High Petergate
Opposite St Michael le Belfry church 1724–40 (RCHME V p. 186), mentioned in 1725/6 (Dawes).

Red Cow, Hope Street
Mentioned in 1835 (YG 26 9 1835), the original name of *The Brown Cow*.

Red Cross
Mentioned in John Webster's diary 1688 (Malden).

Red Hart, Coney Street
Mentioned in 1570 (Benson p. 166).

Red Lion, Askham Bryan
Mentioned 1822 (YCA F30A) to 1867 (Dir).

Red Lion, Church Street (Girdlergate)
Mentioned in 1785 when it was taken by William Fryer (YCo 14 6 1785) but this is a mistake for *The Golden Lion* where Widow Fryer was the licensee in 1785 (Cooper2 p. 44).

Red Lion, Coppergate
Mentioned in 1739 (YCo 30 10 1739).

Red Lion, Goodramgate ¶
A coaching house shown on John Cossins' New and Exact Plan of the City of York, published in 1727 (Murray3 p. 18). When it was offered to let in 1830 the premises included a club and sale room, a good taproom and a private brewery (YG 6 3 1830). After the demise of stage coach travel, its fortunes declined and it was offered for sale in 1866 (YG 22 12 1866) after which it closed as a public house.

Red Lion, Haxby ¶
Earliest mention 1823. More familiarly known as *The Lion* in various years between 1889 and 1901 (Dir).

Red Lion, High Ousegate
To be sold 1763 (YCo 9 8 1763).

Red Lion, Knapton
Earliest mention 1823 (Dir).

Red Lion, Micklegate ¶
Mentioned in John Webster's diary 1688 (Malden). Property of the Vicars' Choral, partly rebuilt and refronted with brick between 1745 and 1748 (RCHME III p. 92). In 1902 it had four bedrooms, one set aside for travellers, and a sitting room upstairs. Below were two smoke rooms, a bar and a private kitchen from which food could be supplied. There was also a cellar (CC). It closed in 1939 when its licence was transferred to a new public house which John Smith & Sons had built in Bishopthorpe Road, *The Winning Post,* which opened on 22 May that year (YCA Acc. 189).

Red Lion, Mint Yard
Mentioned in 1783 (YCA K69).

Red Lion, Peasholme Green (Woolmarket)
Mentioned in 1783, 85, 87 and 95 (YCA K69, Cooper2 p. 69) although an earlier date can be deduced from the death notice of Samuel Smith who had been licensee for more than 50 years. i.e. from at least 1761 (YCo 5 8 1811). Rebuilt after Emanuel Siddall, brewer, had agreed on 9 February 1827 a lease for 50 years with the feoffees of St Saviour's parish (BI MD 98). Last mention 1861 (Dir).

Red Lion, Poppleton
Earliest mention 1822 (YCA F30A). An 18 bedroom motel was added in 1980 and, with the addition of a new bar and lounge in 1982, its transformation from a simple country pub was complete (YEP 11 1 1983). There is a theory that its origins can be traced back to at least 1743. This is based on an entry in John Wesley's diary on 18 February that year while he was journeying north to Newcastle. 'We enquired at Poppleton, a little town three miles beyond York, and hearing there was no other town near, thought it best to call there' at an unspecified house. He then goes on to record that he 'began soon after to speak to our landlord' (Lyth p. 26). This latter term could equally apply to a person who lets a room or the licensee of a public house. On such sparse detail Wesley's resting place in Poppleton and the earlier history of The Red Lion must remain a mystery.

Red Lion, St Margaret, Walmgate, parish
Mentioned in 1783 (YCA K69).

Red Lion, Walmgate (Merchantgate) ¶
Previously *The Three Cups*, its name was changed in 1805 to avoid confusion with another pub of the same name in its immediate vicinity (YCo 13 6 1805). When it was offered for sale in 1849 a brewhouse was included in the premises (YG 11 8 1849). In 1902 it had five bedrooms, two of which were available for travellers. On the ground floor were a smoke room, a taproom, a bar and a private kitchen, from which food could be supplied (CC). Although described as a suitable house for the business an unsuccessful attempt was made the next year to oppose the renewal of its licence (Peacock p. 65). A Grade II listed building (CAMRA2).

Red Lion, Wheldrake
Mentioned 1823 and 1840 (Dir).

Reflex, George Hudson Street
Previously *The Adelphi, The Railway King* and *Edwards,* given this name in July 2003 after a revamp in a 1980s style (YEP 12 7 2003).

Refreshment Inn, Tanner Row
Previously *The Railway Coffee House,* it gained this name by 1846. Next, by 1858, *The North Eastern Refreshment Inn.* Later *The Railway Inn* and eventually *The Grapes.* (Dir).

Reindeer, Penley's Grove Street ¶
A beerhouse, previously *The Highland Red Deer,* also *The Highland Deer.* By 1872 it was using this name (Dir). In 1902 it had four bedrooms, a smoke room, a taproom and a private kitchen. There was no pantry so food was kept on the bedroom landing. The family and the customers shared a privy in a small back yard. The Chief Constable thought that it was not a very good house (CC). It was demolished after a Compulsory Purchase Order in 1958 (YEP 25 9 1958). A new house was built on the site and opened with a full licence, granted on 31 October, on 1 November 1962 (YCA Acc. 189, YEP 31 10 1962).

Reindeer, St Sampson's Square
Previously *The Greyhound,* it was using this name by 1838 (Dir). Also known as *The Stag* (YCo 8 2 1838). Last mention 1842 (YG 21 5 1842). Next *The Hand and Heart* and *The Bradford Arms* and *The Hand and Heart* again.

Reuben's Head, 3 Shambles
Mentioned in 1828 and 1830 when Ralph Smelt was the licensee and in 1838 when it was occupied by W.F. Edgar. By 1834 Ralph Smelt had moved to *The Eagle and Child* at 15 Shambles which, by 1841, he had renamed *The Reuben's Head* (Dir).

Reuben's Head, 15 Shambles
A name given by 1841 to *The Eagle and Child* by Ralph Smelt, who had previously been licensee of a house with the same name at 3 Shambles. By 1851, when R. Hicks was the licensee, it had reverted to its previous name (Dir).

Richard III, Rougier Street ¶
Previously *The Grob and Ducat,* it gained this name on 21 December 1980 (YEP 22 12 1980). Next *Macmillans.*

Rifleman, Coffee Yard, Grape Lane
Mentioned between 1818 (Dir) and 1828 (YCA F31). According to TP Cooper it later became *The Light Horseman* (Cooper p. 79) which is not mentioned until 1838 (Dir). Sometimes known as *The Sharpshooter* (Dir 1828).

Ringrose's Hotel, Museum Street
A coaching house, previously *Gibson's* and *Bluitt's,* it became Ringrose's in 1785 when Bluitt was succeeded by John Ringrose who had been a waiter with him for 12 years (YCo 29 3 1785). Ringrose became free of the Innholders Company on 4 January 1787 (YCA E55). Mentioned in 1799 on the death of John Clark, former head ostler (YH 27 7 1799). Became *Etridge's Royal Hotel* in 1803.

Rising Sun, Skeldergate
Mentioned in 1773 (YCo 8 6 1773).

Ritz Bar, Market Street
Previously Nicholson's Eating House or City Dining Room, on 8 February 1939 it was decided that, as these premises were no longer a bona–fide restaurant, full compensation under the 1910 Act could in future be payable. An application for a full licence was refused on 5 February 1952 (YCA Acc. 189) which must have led to the premises being sold to George Woodcock, confectioner, to be made into a shop (YEP 8 1954). The licence lapsed on 7 Aug 1954.

Riverside Inn, Church Lane, Low Ousegate
Previously *The Tavern in the Town*, mentioned in 1981 and 1989 (YEP 16 7 1981, 12 12 1989). Next *Yates' Wine Lodge.*

Riverside Farm, Shipton Road, Skelton
The former Rawcliffe Farm was converted to a pub and restaurant complex in 1996 (YEP 14 5 1996).

Robin Hood, Castlegate ¶
Mentioned in 1727 when creditors of Christopher Blanchard, the licensee, were sought (YCo 24 2 1727). Mentioned in 1733 as a place where common carriers could be found (Gent). By 1893 it had become *The Little John* (Dir). Although this change seems to be fairly drastic, substituting the name of a member of the band of merry men for its leader, in 1795 both were given joint status. At this time the house was called *The Robin Hood and Little John* (YCA K69).

Robin Hood, Coppergate
Mentioned in 1838 (Dir).

Robin Hood, Heslington
Mentioned in 1823 (Dir). Next *The Horse* and *The Chestnut Horse, The Bay Horse*, and *The Charles XII.*

Robin Hood and Little John, Castlegate
Mentioned in 1795 (YCA K69). Previously and later *The Robin Hood*, eventually *The Little John.*

Roman Bath, St Sampson's Square
Previously *The Barrel Churn, The Cooper, The Barrel, The Coach and Horses* and *The Mail Coach*, it opened with this name in 1971 (YEP 3 9 1971), a reference to the excavated remains of a Roman bathhouse which can be seen in its basement.

Rook and Gaskill, Lawrence Street
Previously *The Wheatsheaf, The Princess Victoria, The Queen Victoria* or *The Victoria, The Queen's Head* and *The Queen*, it was purchased by the York Brewery as its third tied house and reopened on 7 August 2002 (YEP 3 8 2002). Its name follows the hanging theme of its two predecessors, *The Last Drop* and *The Three Legged Mare*, and commemorates Peter Rook and Leonard Gaskill, the last two persons hanged at Greendykes. They were executed on 12 May 1676 for stealing 13 sheep, from John Brown of Driffield (Knipe p. 38). The new name was suggested by Margaret Chicken of Market Weighton (YEP 27 7 2002).

Rooke's Dram Shop, (New) Bridge Street (Briggate)
Mentioned in 1823 in the occupation of Mark Rooke (Dir), but it appears in 1822 without a name (YCA F30A). It was also known as *New Bridge Street Hotel*. A beerhouse with a six day licence (YCA Acc. 189), it had gained the alternative name of *The Board* by 1830. By 1902 it was more generally called *Ye Olde No 5*.

Rose, Coney Street
Previously *The Bull,* it was unoccupied in September 1505 (YCA B9 f. 27) and by 1506 its name had been changed to *The Rose otherwise The Bull*. In 1511 the house was described as being in great decay and ruin (YCA B9 f. 61r).

Rose and Crown, Aldwark ¶
A beerhouse, first mentioned without a name in 1846 (Dir) but by 1859, when it was to be sold, it had been given a title (YG 1 1 1859). In 1902 it was described as a very old property, only a moderate house. It had two bedrooms and a box room upstairs. Below were a smoke room, a snug and a cellar kitchen too small for living in. The smoke room had to be used instead as a living kitchen (CC). The licence was surrendered in 1932 in consideration of the transfer of the licence of *The Haymarket,* Peasholm Green to the *Knavesmire Hotel*, Albemarle Road (YCA Acc. 189). The building was purchased by the Merchant Taylors in 1940 and demolished nine years later to expose their Hall to the street (Mennim pp. 180 & 189). The sign is based on a badge used by Elizabeth I with the motto *Rosa sine spina*.

Rose and Crown, Askham Richard
Earliest mention 1822 (YCA F30A).

Rose and Crown, Blossom Street
Mentioned in a lease on 10 December 1763 as unoccupied (YCA E94 f. 53).

Rose and Crown, Lawrence Street
Built as two houses in the early 18th century (RCHME IV p. 81) and mentioned as a public house in 1786 (YCo 2 5 1786). When it was offered for sale in 1869 the premises included a brewhouse (YG 22 5 1869). In 1902 it had five bedrooms, two set apart for travellers, two attics, a nursery, and a sitting room upstairs. On the ground floor were two smoke rooms, a taproom, a club room and a kitchen from which food could be supplied. There was also a cellar (CC).

Rose and Crown, Marygate
At the bottom of the street, for sale in 1789 (YCo 24 2 1789).

Rose and Crown, Micklegate
See *The Crown.*

Rose and Crown, Middle Water Lane
Mentioned 1795 (YCA K69).

Rose and Crown, (Thursday Market) St Sampson's Square
For sale, including a brewhouse, in 1822 (YG 27 7 1822). The full name of *The Crown*.

Rose and Crown, Stockton on the Forest
On 16 January 1884 a director of the Tadcaster Brewery Co. visited this pub, and after finding Mrs Metcalf, the tenant, the worse for drink, persuaded her to give up her tenancy.

On his return to York he received a message that she had been found dead at the bottom of a staircase (Avis p. 81). This is the only reference to a pub of this name at Stockton on the Forest. A Mrs Medcalf was licensee of *The Four Alls*, Sandburn Mill, and a Thomas Metcalf had been at *The White Swan* in 1872 and 1876 (Dir) so it is possible that either of these pubs was using this name for a short period at this time.

Rose and Thistle, Bedern
Mentioned in 1830 (Dir). The sign is a reference to the union of England and Scotland when James IV of Scotland became James I of England in 1603.

Rose and Thistle, Scarborough Parade, Malton Road
Mentioned in 1834 (Dir).

Royal Hotel, Museum Street
see Etridge's Royal Hotel.

Royal Mail Hotel, St Helen's Square
Mentioned in 1841 (Dir, YG 10 9 1841) and 1843 (Dir).

Royal Oak, Copmanthorpe ¶
Earliest mention 1822 (YCA F30A). Occasionally known as *The Oak*. This is the second most popular pub name after The Red Lion (Dunkling p226) and derives from the incident in 1651 when Charles II hid in the Boscobel Oak, near Shifnal, to escape from Roundhead soldiers after his defeat at the Battle of Worcester. After his restoration to the throne in 1660 his birthday, 29 May, was celebrated as Royal Oak day.

Royal Oak, Goodramgate ¶
Previously *The Blue Boar*, also known as *The Blue Pig*, it was sold in 1819 on bankruptcy of John Kilby (YG 28 8 1819) and bought by Thomas Belt (Johnson p. 41). On his leaving in 1825 it was given this name (YCA F30A). In 1902 it had three bedrooms, a store room, a dining room, a sitting room and a living kitchen upstairs. This kitchen was on the second floor. On the ground floor were two smoke rooms, a service bar and another kitchen from which food was supplied (CC). A Grade II listed building (CAMRA2).

Royal Oak, Micklegate
The Adelphi, then a temperance hotel, was built in 1851 on the site of an earlier public house, *The Royal Oak*, by 1647 called *The Ship* (Johnson p. 7).

Royal Oak, Thursday Market (St Sampson's Square)
Mentioned, to let, in 1778 (YG 17 2 1778). Last mention 1795 (YH 2 5 1795).

Royal Sussex Hotel, St Helen's Square
In 1841 HRH the Duke of Sussex stayed at *The York Tavern*, after which it was given this name (Benson2). Also known as *The Sussex*, although not mentioned in any street directory under either name.

Rumours, Micklegate
Previously *The Falcon*, reopened 2 September 2002, after refurbishment as an 1980s theme pub, with this name (YEP 31 8 2002).

Ruben's Head, 3 & 15 Shambles
See *The Reuben's Head.*

Running Horse, Petergate
Mentioned in 1783, 85, 87 and 95 (YCA K69, Cooper2 p. 42).

Saddle, Askham Richard
Mentioned 1867 (Dir).

Saddle, Main Street, Fulford ¶
The White House, 14 Main Street, was previously a public house, first called *The Blacksmiths' Arms* and, by 1815, The Saddle. When it became a private house a new pub with the same name was built on the opposite side of the road (Briddon pp. 48/9). It was rebuilt in 1857 (YEP 16 10 1979). When it was sold by auction in 1890 the premises included a brewhouse (YG 26 7 1890).

Saddle, The Mount
Earliest mention 1838 (Dir). Rebuilt in 1891 to the designs of W Brown, it was bought by J Smith & Co in 1892 (YEP 5 11 1973) when its name was changed to *The Mount.*

Sailor with Wooden Leg, Low Ousegate ¶
The subject of an early 19th century drawing. Possibly a familiar name based on the depiction of a man with a wooden leg on the inn sign. If so the likely candidate is a public house on King's Staith, known at various times as *The Mariner, The Jolly Sailor* and *The Fortunate Tar,* but it was too far from Low Ousegate to have had an entrance on that street. Certainly it would be a fortunate tar who had lost a leg and would not be required to serve again under the harsh conditions of Nelson's royal navy.

St Crispin's Arms, Church Lane, North Street
See *The Crispin's Arms.*

St George's Tavern, Union Street (Edwin Street after 1890), Margaret Street
A beerhouse in St George's parish mentioned in 1858 (Dir) but not until 1862 with a name (YG 7 6 1862). In 1902 it had two bedrooms, a sitting room and a box room upstairs. Below were a vault, a taproom and a private kitchen. Despite the presence of this kitchen, food was cooked in the taproom. The family and customers shared a WC (CC). It was referred for compensation and closed on 7 October 1927 (YCA Acc.189).

St Helen's Hotel, Davygate
Previously *Addison's Hotel,* given this name in July 1848. Later *The Clarence Hotel.*

St Leonard's Hotel, St Leonard's Place
An alternative name for *The Bird in Hand,* used during the tenancy of Ann Morley (Dir).

St Leonard's Coffee House and Refectory, Little Blake Street (Lop Lane)
Mentioned 1835 (YG 28 8 1835).

St Nicholas, Lawrence Street
Mentioned in 1832 (YG 15 12 1832) and 1852 (OS), so named because of an earlier church of that name in the vicinity, which was destroyed in the siege of York in 1644 (VCH p. 397). By 1854 it had become *The Tam O'Shanter* and alternatively *The Burns' Hotel.*

St Peter's Vaults, Walmgate ¶

Previously *The Spotted Dog,* it had acquired this name by 1867 (Dir). When it was for sale in 1883 the premises included a brewhouse (YG 28 7 1883). In 1902 although it had four bedrooms, travellers were not accommodated. There were also two attics. On the ground floor were two smoke rooms, a bar, and two private kitchens from which food could be supplied. There was also a cellar. The family and customers shared the sole WC (CC). On 5 April 1939 the transfer of its licence to a new house, *The Acomb Hotel,* was confirmed (YG 7 4 1939). The order was made final on 20 June 1940 when the new establishment opened and the licence of *The King William IV,* Layerthorpe was surrendered in consideration of the transfer (YCA Acc. 189).

Sandhill, Colliergate

Earliest mention 1733 as a place where common carriers could be found (Gent). After 1742 when the landlord, William Barwick, moved to *The White Swan* between Petergate and Goodramgate and called that house *The White Swan and Sandhill* it was probably renamed *The Old Sandhill* (YCo 29 6 1742) a name it certainly had by 1763 (YCo 11 1 1763). After this it was occasionally still referred to by its original name.

Sandhill, Goodramgate

An alternative name for *The White Swan* which became *The White Swan and Sandhill* in 1742 (YCo 29 6 1742). In use in the official licensing records between 1822 and 1826 (YCA F30A, F31). Also called *The New Sandhill* in 1821.

Sandhill Tap, St Andrewgate

Shown as *The Old Sandhill Tap* in 1852 (OS), mentioned in 1858 with a different landlord to *The Old Sandhill* (Dir).

Saracen's Head, St Andrewgate

Mentioned between 1818 and 1838, but it was being called *The Turk's Head* by 1828 (Dir), a name which it had fully adopted by 1840 (YG 6 6 1840).

Saracen's Head, Stonegate

Previously Brigg's Coffee House, by 1809 it had become *The Saracen's Head Coffee House* (YCo 3 4 1809) and by 1818 'Coffee House' had been dropped from its name (Dir). Last mention 1867 (Dir).

Sawdust 'ole, King's Square

A familiar name for *The Grapes* (YG 1 3 1946), which was also known for a time as *The King Edward VII.*

Sawdust Parlour, Swinegate

The premises, situated on the east side of the street, half way down from Church Street, were originally a stable (Cooper3 p. 84). Possibly a nickname but it has not been possible to identify the proper name. A meeting place for carvers and artists who there composed epitaphs to their departed colleagues e.g. for Joseph Batman, died 1879, and for John Bellerby

John Bellerby has departed hence
Woodcarving in Heaven to commence.

(JWK2 pp. 35,60). Closed by 1897 (Cooper p. 79).

Scawin's Railway Hotel, Tanner Row

When Mrs Sarah Scawin took over The Railway Hotel from George Britton in 1841 (YG 9 10 1841), she personalised it with the addition of her surname. In 1852 she added a new wing (YG 20 3 1852) and the hotel then had 80 bedrooms, a stable, a billiard saloon and a coffee room. After the centre of railway activity had moved to a site outside the walls 'Family and Commercial' was exchanged for 'Railway' but the hotel could not recapture its former success. It was purchased by the NER who spent £1079 15s 4d in 1892/3 converting it into offices (NER).

Scruffy Murphy's, Micklegate

Previously *The Bar Hotel*, by 1996 it had been given a makeover and this themed name (Thomson) which lasted for seven years. It became *The Micklegate* late in 2002 (YEP 22 2 2003). A Grade II listed building (CAMRA2).

Sea Horse, Castlegate

Mentioned in this street in 1855 in error for *The Sea Horse*, Cattle Market (Dir).

Sea Horse, Fawcett Street (Cattle Market) ¶

Mentioned in 1838 when the street was called Fishergate (Dir). When it was offered for sale in 1845 and again in 1862 the premises contained brewhouses (YG 29 3 1845, 22 2 1862). On the latter occasion it is described as 'newly erected'. In 1902 it had 12 bedrooms enabling up to 25 travellers to be accommodated. In addition there were a dining room and a drawing room upstairs. On the ground floor were two smoke rooms, a private room, a licensed kitchen and a private kitchen. The full range of meals could be supplied (CC). It had stabling for 25 horses which eventually housed the Brewery's horses. Because of this its name was changed to *The Shire Horse* in 1974 (YEP 31 1 1974). The old sign, a carved wooden fairground beast, was restored by Dick Reid in 1982 and sent to the Castle Museum (YEP 8 4 1982). By 1995 The Sea Horse again (Thomson).

Sellers' Vaults, Sellers' Dram Shop, Fossgate

Alternative names for *The Board*, a reference to Charles Sellers, licensee in 1858 (Dir).

Seven Stars, Church Lane, Low Ousegate

Mentioned in 1897 as a house which had closed (Cooper p. 79). No other evidence has been found to confirm its existence.

Seven Stars, Trinity Lane

The premises, previously *The Square and Compasses, The Cup and Compass, The Cricket Ground, The Cricketers' Arms,* became a beerhouse after the demise of the latter. It appears under this guise in 1851 and the name was first recorded in 1857. By 1872 *The Half Moon* (Dir), although it was under its previous name that it was purchased by Hotham & Co. in 1875 (Davison p. 43).

Shakespeare Tavern, Little Blake Street (Lop Lane)

Previously *The Theatre Coffee House*, given this name, presumably because of its proximity to the Theatre Royal by 1818 (Dir). Demolished in 1861 in the creation of Duncombe Place (Cooper pp. 19/21). Cooper suggests that it was earlier called *The Barrel* (Cooper p. 79), a name which also appears in 1823 with Robert Smith as licensee of both houses (Dir).

Shakespeare Tavern, Little Stonegate
Previously *The Horse and Jockey*, also known as *The Horse and Groom*, by 1861 it had become a beerhouse, identifiable by this name in 1872 (Dir). It was acquired by Hotham & Co. in 1875 (Davison p. 43) after which it disappears from all records.

Shakespeare Tavern or Tap, Walmgate
Mentioned 1828 and 1830 (Dir).

Shamrock, George Street
Although mentioned in 1897 (Cooper p. 87) it does not appear in any street directories under this name. As the directories include *The Phoenix* and *The Newcastle Arms,* this must be an alternative name for a third pub which is shown only as a beerhouse but was, in fact, called *The Albert*.

Shamrock, Goodramgate
Mentioned as an earlier name for The Bay Horse (Cooper p. 49).

Sharpshooter, Grape Lane
Mentioned in 1828 (Dir). A familiar name for *The Rifleman*.

Ship Inn, Acaster Malbis
First mentioned by name in 1823 (Dir) but known early in the nineteenth century when the premises were occupied by Michael Drew. The sign at this time bore the legend

My Honest Friend, I Tell you True,
Good Ale's Sold Here by Mickey Drew.

Originally the building was part of Lord Wenlock's estate but was sold at auction on 15 December 1898 'together with all the Manorial and Sporting Rights of the Property, and the Salmon Fisheries in the River Ouse to which it lies adjacent'. All this was bought for £1650 by Robert Couch Kent of Acomb (Appleby pp. 43/4) who became the licensee (Dir).

Ship, Acomb
Mentioned in 1771 (YCo 29 1 1771).

Ship Inn, Carmelite Street
A beerhouse, mentioned in 1855, it had gained this name by 1876 (Dir). It may have also been called *The Whale Fishery* but given the more familiar name from the depiction of a whale fishing boat on its sign. Later *The Garden Gate*. Mentioned in 1879, in error, as *The Slip.*

Ship, Feasegate
An alehouse, to be sold 1763 (YCo 3 4 1763).

Ship, Heslington
Mentioned 1823 (Dir). Next *The Fox, The Yarburgh Arms, The De Yarburgh Arms* and *The Deramore Arms*.

Ship, Far Water Lane
Facing the Staith, for sale 1766 (YCo 18 3 1766).

Ship, First Water Lane (later King Street), King's Staith ¶
Mentioned 1787 & 95 (YCA K69, Cooper2 p. 45). Rebuilt in 1851 as part of the first clearance of the Water Lanes area when First Water Lane was widened and renamed King Street. In 1902 it had three bedrooms, all used by the family. On the ground floor it had a smoke room and a bar, both very small, a taproom and two private kitchens, from which food could be supplied if required. The family and customers shared the sole WC. There was an internal communicating door with the house next door which was used for access when the river was in flood (CC). It was closed and became a restaurant in 1976 (YEP 19 11 1975). Also known as *The Ship Victory*.

Ship, Micklegate
The Adelphi, then a temperance hotel was built in 1851 on the site of an earlier public house, *The Royal Oak,* which by 1647 was given this name (Johnson p. 7)

Ship, Middle Water Lane
Mentioned in 1795 (YCA K69) and 1818 (Dir).

Ship, Monk Bridge
Mentioned in 1795 (YCA K69).

Ship, Skeldergate
Mentioned 1774 (YCo 5 7 1774). Licence lapsed 10 October 1889 when the building was required for other purposes (YCA Acc. 189). By 1897 it was a miller's warehouse, (Cooper p. 67).

Ship, Strensall ¶
Earliest mention 1840 (Dir).

Ship, Walmgate
Mentioned in 1783 (YCA K69).

Ship Victory, King's Staith
An alternative name for *The Ship* which has an earlier existence than the battle of Trafalgar of 1805 in which Nelson's flagship was the Victory. The sign, after a more recent repaint, must have portrayed the most famous ship in the nation.

Shire Horse, Fawcett Street
Previously and later *The Sea Horse*, given this name in 1974 when the brewery's horses were stabled there (YEP 31 1 1974). A grade I listed building (CAMRA2).

Shoe, Friargate (Far Water Lane)
A familiar name for *The Slipper*. Both names were in use in 1823, The Shoe in Friargate and *The Slipper* in Far Water Lane, the editor of the street directory having not realised they were the same street (Dir).

Shoe, Goodramgate
Mentioned in 1782, 85, 87, 95 (YCA K69, Cooper2 p. 44). Later *The Slipper* and *The Golden Slipper.*

Shoulder of Mutton, Goodramgate
For sale in 1765 (YCo 5 2 1765).

Shoulder of Mutton, Haymarket

Mentioned in 1841 (Dir) and 1843 (YG 4 2 1843). Next *The Tower of London* and *The Haymarket.*

Shoulder of Mutton, Heworth (Green) Moor ¶

Earliest mention 1838 (Dir). In 1902 it had three unfurnished attics, two bedrooms and a club room on the upper floors. Below were a smoke room, a bar parlour, a dining room, a serving bar and a kitchen. There was also a cellar (CC). On 12 February 1951, permission was given for its removal to new premises, The Heworth Hyrst Hotel, formerly a private house. The new premises were opened on 14 January 1955 (YCA Acc. 189).

Shoulder of Mutton, Shambles

Mentioned 1818 (Dir). Closed on 1 January 1898, one of three licences surrendered in consideration of a new licence being granted to the Tadcaster Tower Brewery Co. for a new house, *The Jubilee*, Balfour Street (YCA Acc. 189).

Shoulder of Mutton, Middle Water Lane

Mentioned in 1783, 87, 95 (YCA K69, Cooper2 p. 45). When it was for sale in 1844 the premises included a brewhouse (YG 15 6 1844). Renewal of licence refused at Brewster Sessions 1855 (YG 1 9 1855).

Simpson's Coffee House, Petergate

Mentioned in 1761 (YCo 4 1 1773). For sale after the death of the proprietor in 1771 (YCo 6 8 1771).

Sir Colin Campbell, Alma Terrace

Previously Lawson's Beerhouse, by 1881 it had been renamed *The Wellington* (YG 4 6 1881) but when it was bought by Samuel Smith in 1887 it was described in the sale note under this name as 'an old established beerhouse' (CAMRA2). Sir Colin Campbell (1792–1863) was the son of Colin Macliver, a Glasgow carpenter, who took the name Campbell in 1807 after an error by the Duke of York. He served as an ensign under Sir John Moore in Portugal and then throughout the Peninsular campaign. After further service in the West Indies, China and India, now a Major-General, he took command of the Highland Brigade at the Battle of the Alma. After suppressing the Indian Mutiny in 1858 he was created Baron Clyde. Four years later in 1862, he was made a Field Marshal. (DNB). After the sale the pub became *The Wellington* once again (Wilson p. 7).

Sir Sidney Smith, Tanner Row

Mentioned in 1818 (Dir). Sir [William] Sidney Smith (1764–1840) entered the Royal Navy in 1777 and by 1821 had reached the rank of Admiral. He was awarded the GCB in 1838 and when he died he was buried in Père Lachaise cemetery, Paris. In his career he had been theatrical and fond of self–laudation but nevertheless was brave and energetic (DNB). He was soon forgotten for by 1843 the pub was renamed *The Sun Inn* (Dir).

Six Bells, Oxcar Lane, Strensall

Earliest mention 1991 (Thomson).

Slip, (Heworth Moor) Malton Road ¶

Mentioned in 1843 (Dir) but sometimes known as *The New Slip Inn.* It closed on 31 July 1968 (YEP 31 7 1968), still without an electricity supply. It was heated and lit entirely by gas (YEP 11 5 1968).

Slip Inn, Carmelite Street
Mentioned in 1879 (Dir), in error for *The Ship.*

Slip Inn, Clementhorpe ¶
Mentioned in 1843 (Dir). It takes its name from the slipway, 215 feet in length, built in the street by the Ouse Navigation Trustees and let by ticket. It opened in 1836 and was capable of accommodating three keels at once. It closed in the 1930s, the last relic of York's ship building and repair industry. In 1902 the public house, described as recently rebuilt, had three bedrooms, all used by the family. On the ground floor were a taproom, a serving bar, a small smoke room and a living kitchen, from which food could be supplied if required. There was also a cellar (CC).

Slip Inn, Hungate
Mentioned in 1879 (Dir). It appears in three places in this street directory, twice as The Slip and once as The Ship, the latter being an error.

Slipper, (Far Water Lane) Friargate
Mentioned 1795 (YCA K69) to 1879 (Dir). According to TP Cooper it was formerly known as *The Boot and Shoe* (Cooper p. 79). Mentioned in 1823 as both *The Shoe* and under this name (Dir). Between 1828 and 1841 it was known as *The Star and Garter* (Dir). When it was for sale in 1861 the premises included a brewhouse (YG 6 4 1861).

Slipper, Goodramgate
Previously *The Shoe*, using this name by 1818 (Dir). Later *The Golden Slipper.*

Slug and Lettuce, The Courtyard, Back Swinegate
Licence granted in December 1997, opened in 1998 (YEP 5 12 1997).

Smith, Micklegate
A familiar name for *The Whitesmiths' Arms* (YCA K69).

Smiths' Arms, Dunnington
Mentioned in 1840 but by 1849 was using this name (Dir). Also known for a period as *The Horseshoe.*

Snickleway Inn, Goodramgate
Previously *The Square and Compass, The Board* or *Cooper's Vaults* and *The Anglers' Arms.* Given this name in 1994, to 'reflect its historical associations', a reference to Mark Jones's book 'The Snickelways of York' – note the variation in the spelling (YEP 14 6 1994).

Soldier's Rest Inn, Fulford Road
Mentioned in 1867 and 1872 (Dir). Demolished between 1900 and 1905 (Wilson2 p. 122).

Sportsman, Caroline Street ¶
A beerhouse, mentioned in 1867 (Dir). In 1902 it had two bedrooms and a sitting room upstairs. On the ground floor were a smoke room, a taproom and a kitchen which was also used as a serving bar. All the rooms were small and the family shared their WC with the customers. There was also a cellar (CC). It closed on 22 May 1939, its licence having been voluntarily surrendered on the transfer of the licence of *The Red Lion,* Micklegate to *The Winning Post* (YCA Acc. 189).

Sportsman, Hungate
A beerhouse, previously *The Dog and Gun*, it had conclusively gained this name by 1852 (OS). As it was previously mentioned under this name in 1834 (YG 15 11 1834), 1841 and 1843 (Dir), it appears that both names refer to the sign which must have depicted a sportsman with his dog and gun. In 1902 the Chief Constable listed it under its former name, which must have been its official name, but also giving its familiar name. It had 11 bedrooms, of which only five were furnished and, of these, two were available for travellers. Below were a smoke room, a taproom, a dram shop and private kitchens from which food could be supplied if required. There was also a cellar. At one time it had been two houses separated by a passage which still existed (CC). It was referred for compensation in 1911 (YG 11 3 1911) and closed in 1912 (YCA Acc. 189).

Spotted Cow, Lawrence Row, (after 1890 Barbican Road) ¶
Mentioned in 1828 (Dir), its building almost certainly coincidental with the new cattle market which had opened outside the walls on 4 October 1827. In 1902 it was described as a recently rebuilt house. It had eight bedrooms and provided sleeping accommodation for 24 travellers. There was also a sitting room upstairs. Below were a large bar, a smoke room, a dining room and a kitchen which supplied the full range of meals to cattle dealers. There was also a cellar (CC). It was put up for sale in 1992 and became a Chinese restaurant called the Royal Dragon (YEP 24 3 1992).

Spotted Dog, Aldwark
Mentioned by TP Cooper as an earlier name for the Bay Horse (Cooper p. 77). Could he be confusing it with the next?

Spotted Dog, St Andrewgate
Mentioned in 1834 (Dir), a confusion with the previous or the next?

Spotted Dog, St Saviourgate
Previously *The Pointer Dog, The Dog* and *The White Dog*, it had been given this name by 1818 (Dir). It closed after the occupier left for Hull after eight years as tenant (YG 7 8 1858). He had apparently unsuccessfully tried to let it but in 1859 sold the furniture and other effects (YG 22 10 1859).

Spotted Dog, 112 Walmgate
Mentioned in 1822 (YCA F30A), by 1867 it had become *St Peter's Vaults.*

Spotted Dog, 128 Walmgate
Previously and later *The Bay Horse*, in 1876 and 1879, during the tenancy of William Howell, it was using this name (Dir).

Spotted Leopard, Coney Street
Mentioned in 1834 (Dir), an alternative name for *The Leopard.*

Spread Eagle, Goodramgate
An alternative name for The Eagle, mentioned in 1867 (Dir). This was based on the appearance of the eagle on the sign, derived from the heraldic charge of *an eagle displayed.* This is a very early device which was portrayed with its wings and legs spread outwards to fill as much space as possible on the shield.

Spread Eagle, Walmgate ¶
Previously *The Malt Shovel*, *The Old Malt Shovel* and *The Bricklayers' Arms*. By 1867 it had been given this name (Dir). In 1902 it had four bedrooms, none available for travellers, and a sitting room upstairs. On the ground floor were a smoke room, a bar and a kitchen which was used as a drinking room. Food could be supplied if required (CC). The renewal of its licence was unsuccessfully opposed in 1903 (Peacock p. 65). It became a free house in 1977 when it was sold by Bass North (YEP 21 4 1977).

Square and Compass, Goodramgate
Mentioned in 1818 (Dir). Also known as *The Masons' Arms*, based on the tradesman's tools displayed on the sign (Dir 1823). Later *The Board* or *Cooper's Vaults*, *The Angler's Arms* and *The Snickleway Inn*.

Square and Compass, Long Close Lane ¶
Mentioned in 1822 (YCA F30A). In 1902 it had three bedrooms and a sitting room upstairs. Below were a smoke room and a kitchen used for both living and drinking. There was also a cellar. There was only one WC accessed by passing through the urinal. The Chief Constable in describing it as a very poor house, dirty and partly furnished, thought that it was worthy of special consideration, with a view to closing it, by the Licensing Justices (CC). Although the renewal of the licence was opposed in 1903 it was allowed to continue its business (Peacock pp 65/6). At the Brewster Sessions in 1906 it was described as one of the six worst houses in York (Peacock p. 92) and at this time the licence was not renewed on the grounds of non–necessity. It lapsed on 16 February 1907, compensation having been paid (YCA Acc. 189).

Square and Compass, Middle Water Lane
Previously *The Compass*, mentioned 1825 (YCA F30A) to 1830 (Dir).

Square and Compass, Trinity Lane
Mentioned in 1818 (Dir). Sold in 1819 on the bankruptcy of John Kilby (YG 28 8 1819). Next, by 1831, *The Cup and Compass*, then *The Cricket Ground*, and *The Cricketers' Arms*.

Square and Compass, Wesley Place
Mentioned in 1838 (Dir). Described as newly built in 1848 (YG 16 9 1848). In 1902 it had six bedrooms, of which only three were furnished and used by the family, and a sitting room upstairs. Below were a badly lit smoke room, a dram shop and a private kitchen and washhouse. Food could be supplied if required. There was also a cellar and the family shared their WC with the customers (CC). It was referred for compensation in February 1911 (YG 11 3 1911). This was agreed at £450 for the lessee and £115 for the tenant (Benson2) in July 1911 (YG 8 7 1911). The licence expired on 4 October 1911 (YCA Acc. 189). At various times between 1851 and 1872 it was also known as *The Joiners' Arms* (Dir), based on the implements shown on the sign.

Square and Compasses, Front Street, Acomb
Mentioned in 1793 on the north side of the street but by 1817, when it was referred to by both its former name and its new name of *The Marcia*, it was on the south side (AMCR). Later *The Poacher*.

Stag, Rufforth

An alternative name for *The Buck*, although, strangely, the recorded use of this occurs in 1861 (Census) by which time it had become *The Blacksmiths' Arms*.

Stag, St Sampson's Square

Sign of the Stag, to be let with shop attached (YCo 8 2 1838), an alternative name for *The Reindeer*.

Stanhope Press, Swinegate

Mentioned in 1823 (Dir; YCA F30A). Alternatively known as *The Printing Press*.

Star, Blossom Street

At Holgate Lane end in 1750 (YCo 9 10 1750), an alternative name for *The Sun*.

Star, Fossgate

Owned in 1580 by Elizabeth Taylor, who, by her will, gave to the churchwardens of St John, Ousebridge, the annual rent charge of 3s 4d to be paid by succeeding owners of the house (Cooper2 p. 9).

Star, North Street

For sale 1782 (YCo 24 12 1782), an alternative name for *The Sun*.

Star Inn, Stonegate

The oldest extant public house in York, mentioned in 1644 as the address on a sermon printed nearby (Cooper2 p. 8). It was once open to the street but, by 1733, it was hidden by a dwelling house built in front of it. Consequently on 5 February that year it was agreed that a beam sign could be erected across the street to advertise its presence, the landlord paying rent to the owners of the properties to which it was fixed (Cooper2 pp. 12/3). On 25 March 1828 the City Commissioners decided that the beam sign should be removed (YCA M18/1) but wiser counsels have obviously prevailed as the sign is still there. When it was let in 1831 the premises contained a brewhouse (YG 22 10 1831). In 1902 it was described as being approached by a passage from Stonegate. It had six bedrooms, three set apart for travellers. On the ground floor were two smoke rooms, a snug, a serving bar, a large club room and a private kitchen (CC). A Grade II listed building (CAMRA2). Called *The Star and Garter* in 1828, probably mistakenly (Dir). By 1921 the name *Ye Olde Starre Inne* was in use (Dir). Also known for a short period as *The Star Inn and Turf Coffee House*.

Star Inn and Turf Coffee House

When William Knapton moved from *The Turf Coffee House* to *The Star Inn*, Stonegate, in 1803 he gave it this name (YCo 13 6 1803). It was taken by Joseph Wilkinson in 1804 (YCo 16 4 1804).

Star and Garden, Nessgate

A mistake for *The Star and Garter* on the map compiled by Dr White in 1782.

Star and Garter, Friargate

Previously and later *The Slipper* (YCA F31) mentioned 1828 to 1841 (Dir). Name based on the insignia of the Order of the Garter, founded in 1348.

Star and Garter, King's Square
Mentioned in 1783, 85, 87, 95 (YCA K69, Cooper2 p. 44) and 1810 (PR Holy Trinity, King's Court).

Star and Garter, Nessgate ¶
For sale in 1749 (YCo 26 9 1749). A restaurant and dining room were opened in 1865 (YG 16 7 1865). In 1902 it had five bedrooms, one available for travellers, a sitting room and a kitchen upstairs. Below were a smoke room, a dram shop, a small snug and another kitchen. There was also a cellar. With the exception of the dram shop all the rooms on the ground floor were dark. It was demolished to widen the street to allow a double track for the proposed electric tramway system in July 1904 (YCA Acc. 189), work completed by 1905 (YG 3 6 1905).

Star and Garter, Petergate
In 1812 it was occupied by Emmanuel Siddal under an agreement, which had started in April 1881, to pay an annual rent of £35 5s 0d for seven years (YCA E78A).

Star and Garter, Stonegate
Mentioned in 1828 (Dir) but, in reality, *The Star*. Possibly a mistake by the compiler of the street directory.

Starting Gate, Tadcaster Road, Dringhouses
In 1974 The York Motel was built in the gardens of Dringhouses Manor (Pocock p. 62). This later became The York Beefeater Restaurant and by 1993 had been given this name (Thomson). Closed and sold for residential development 28 November 2002 (YEP 28 11 2002).

Steam Hammer, Skeldergate
Mentioned by TP Cooper as having closed by 1897 (Cooper p. 79). Possibly a beerhouse not listed in the street directories under a specific name. There were three of these, two mentioned in 1858 and a third in 1876 and 1879 (Dir).

Stockton on the Forest, Malton Road
Previously *The Hopgrove*, in 1997 it was given this name, causing much controversy, as the new owners had a policy of naming their pubs after the locality in which they were situated (YEP 17 5 1997).

Stonebow, Stonebow
Built on the site of *The Board*, Fossgate, and opened in July 1957 (YCA Acc. 189). Renamed The Boulevard in 1986 (YEP 2 12 1986). Later *The Northern Wall*.

Stott's Coffee House, Petergate
Mentioned in 1772 (YCo 13 10 1772) and 1781 (YCo 6 11 1782).

Sun Inn, Acomb Green ¶
Previously *The Grey Orville* and *The Grey Horse*, by 1838 it had gained this name (Dir). Transferred from the Tadcaster Licensing District 1 April 1937 on the extension of city boundaries (YCA Acc. 189).

Sun, Blossom Street

Nearly opposite the entrance to Holgate Road, previously, according to some, *The Boar* (Knight p, 350, Cooper2 p. 6). It is probable, however, that The Boar, mentioned in 1485 and 1487, was not this house but another *Boar* in Castlegate (see below). It was in existence under this name in 1731 when its sign was included on John Hayne's engraving 'York from SW'. The furniture, brewing plant and fixtures were sold in 1857, after which the pub was demolished and the land offered for building (YEP 14 3 1857). The land was use to create access to a new street, East Mount Road (Cooper pp. 23/4). Also known as *The Star.*

Sun, Micklegate

'The signe of the Sune' within Micklegate Bar, mentioned in a lease in 1604 (YCA E27 F 10b.)

Sun, North Street

For sale in 1782 (YCo 24 12 1782). Mentioned in 1787 and 95 (Cooper2 p42, YCA K69).

Sun, St Peter the Little parish

Mentioned in 1783 (YCA K69).

Sun Inn, Tanner Row

Previously *The Sir Sidney Smith*, given this name by 1843 (Dir). In 1884 the directors of the Tadcaster Tower Brewery thought it their worst house and confirmed they would apply for the removal of its licence to a new pub, to be built on land they had bought in Leeman Road (Avis pp. 89/90, 96). The licence was allowed to lapse sometime after 14 November 1892 and, in fact, three other licences were surrendered to gain just one for *The Jubilee* (YCA Acc. 189). It was reported in 1898, however, that the licence had been transferred to Leeman Road (YG 3 9 1898). The Sun Inn next became a private house and was offered for sale in 1908 (YG 6 6 1908).

Sussex, St Helen's Square

An alternative name for *The Royal Sussex*.

Swan

In April 1487 William Maunsell, who had been city ostler was now at the sign of the Swan, within the city walls (Attreed p. 547).

Swan, Askham Richard

The name used in the licensing records between 1822 and 1828 (YCA F30A, F31) for an establishment which in 1823 and 1857 is called *The Black Swan* (Dir).

Swan, Bootham

Mentioned in 1540 (Benson p. 166).

Swan(n) Inn, Clementhorpe

While it is recorded with this name in the licensing records until 1892 when Palliser Addyman transferred the licence to his son Albert (YCA Acc. 189), it does not appear in the street directories until 1909 (Dir). A beer house, in 1902 it had four bedrooms and a WC upstairs. On the ground floor were a smoke room, a dram shop and a bottle and jug department. There was also a cellar. Across a small yard was a private kitchen with bedrooms above (CC). In the 1930s it was refurbished by Kitson, Parish & Ledgard, Tetley's architects. It was granted a full 'on' licence on 14 February 1961 (YCA Acc. 189) and in the mid 1980s it became one of Tetley's Heritage Pubs (CAMRA).

Swan, Deighton
Mentioned in 1823 (Dir), then by 1872 the colour of the swan had been determined and it became *The White Swan*. This fuller title was still being used in 1876 but old habits die hard and for the rest of the century it is recorded under its original name.

Swan, Front Street, Acomb
A familiar name for *The Black Swan* (Dir 1843).

Swan, Peasholme Green
Mentioned in 1787 and 95 (Cooper2 p. 44; YCA K69), a familiar name for *The Black Swan.*

Swan, Stockton on the Forest
A familiar name for *The White Swan* (Dir 1895).

Sycamore, Water End, Clifton ¶
The Green Tree, mentioned in 1825 (YG 22 10 1825) and 1830 (Dir) is possibly an earlier name for this pub. It first appears as The Sycamore Tree in 1838 and again in 1841 and 1848. In 1843 it was called The Sycamore Cottage but in 1846 it had become just The Sycamore, a name it was using in 1851 and 1855, the last time the pub is mentioned (Dir).

Sycamore Cottage, Water End, Clifton
See *The Sycamore.*

Sycamore Tree, Grape Lane
Mentioned in 1830 (Dir).

Sycamore Tree, Minster Close (Yard)
Mentioned in 1731 at the east end of the Minster (YCo 24 8 1731). Removed during improvements to Minster Yard in 1828 (YG 19 7 1828). Alternatively known as *The Green Tree* (Cooper p. 21).

Sycamore Tree, Water End, Clifton
See *The Sycamore.*

Talbot, Church Lane, Spurriergate
Mentioned in 1769 when Thomas Blackburn advertised that he could supply victuals and spirituous liquors (YCo 21 3 1769). Shown on Dr White's map 1782 as an alehouse without a name.

Talbot Inn, Church Street ¶
Previously *The Blacksmiths' Arms* and *The Harcourt Arms.* Given this name in 1865 by the licensee, George Osborne, just before he moved to *The Plough*, Fulford. In 1902 it had four bedrooms, none available for travellers, a club room, a drawing room and a sitting room upstairs. On the ground floor were a smoke room, a taproom, a bar parlour, a scullery and a kitchen from which food could be supplied. There was also a cellar (CC). It was bought by Shepherd Developments in 1972 and replaced by a shop and office building called, appropriately, Talbot House.

Talbot, Low Petergate

George Fawcett, free as an innholder in 1604/5, established an inn (Benson p. 166) in one of the most ancient timber buildings in the city (Drake p. 319). In 1639 it is described as 'a very faire inne' (Palliser p. 20). Mentioned in 1688 in John Webster's diary (Malden) and again in 1704 when the Innholders' Company held a social gathering there (BI MTA.17.1 p 134). Taken down in 1730 (Benson p. 166), part of the site recently occupied by York College for Girls.

Talbot, Micklegate

Mrs Martha Ellis of 56 Knavesmire Crescent, widow of a former licensee, found with her throat cut (YG 26 12 1908). An error in the newspaper for *The Falcon.*

Tam O'Shanter, Lawrence Street ¶

Previously *The St Nicholas,* it became *The Tam O'Shanter* by 1854 when it was to let with immediate possession (YG 1 April 1854) and was alternatively known as *The Burns' Hotel* (CC). It has been claimed that it is named after the racehorse Tam O'Shanter which won the Chester Cup in 1876 (Pepper p. 147) but as it was using this name by 1855 and it has the alternative name which relates it to the author of a poem of the same name it is clearly the poet not the racehorse which provided the inspiration for its renaming. In 1902 it was described as a fairly good house with nine bedrooms and providing good sleeping accommodation for travellers. On the ground floor were a smoke room, a dram shop, a taproom, a private room and a kitchen from which food could be supplied (CC).

Tang Hall Hotel, Fourth Avenue ¶

A large mansion house, previously the home of the Starkey family, was bought by JJ Hunt & Co and was opened as a public house to serve the Tang Hall estate, its licence transferred from *Harker's York Hotel,* St Helen's Square, on 6 January 1930 (YCA Acc. 189). The old pub was closed in May 1978 and a modern building was erected on its site, which opened on 8 March 1979 (YEP 18 6 1979).

Tankard, Holy Trinity, King's Court, parish

Mentioned in 1783 (YCA K69).

Tankard, Rufforth

Earliest mention 1822 (YCA F30A). Given a complete refurbishment in 1937 by Sam Smith's Brewery designed by the Leeds architect H Lane Fox (CAMRA).

Tap and Spile, Monkgate

Previously *The Black Horse,* in 1988, after a £100,000 facelift, it was reopened as *The Tap and Spile* (Star 28 7 1988). A Grade II listed building (CAMRA2).

Tavern in the Town, Church Lane, Spurriergate

Opened on 27 March 1969 (YCA Acc. 189) in a building which had previously been Brett's Brewery. It was converted by Chef and Brewers architects' department (Nuttgens p. 89). Next *The Riverside Inn* and *Yates' Wine Lodge.*

Telegraph Arms, North Street

A beerhouse, first mentioned without a name in 1851, but by its last appearance in 1867 it had gained this name (Dir).

Thackwray's, Goodramgate
See *The Board*, Goodramgate.

Thackwray's, Coppergate
An alternative name for *The Three Tuns,* in use from 1898, when Thackwray & Co., brewers, acquired the premises and opened its central office there (Davison p.42), until 1929 when the firm was bought by John J. Hunt & Co. (YEP 23 10 1970).

Theatre Coffee House, Little Blake Street (Lopp Lane)
At the upper end of the street, opened by Patrick Byrne from *The Unicorn*, Petergate, in 1778 (YCo 18 8 1778). Next, by 1818, *The Shakespeare Tavern* (Dir).

Thomas's Hotel, Museum Street ¶
Built on part of the site of *Etridge's Royal Hotel* which had been demolished to make improvements to the approaches to the new bridge being built at Lendal (YG 7 4 1860). Part of the old building had been bought by William Thomas of *Thomas's* Family and Commercial Hotel in Low Petergate who removed there in 1858 (YG 13 11 1858). His newly built hotel had opened by 1861 (Dir). The year before William Thomas's death in 1877 it was sold to Thomas Lightfoot, a brewer of Bedale (YG 1 7 1876) before becoming the property of John Smith & Co (YG 26 5 1900). In 1902 it had eight bedrooms, five set apart for travellers, a drawing room and a coffee room upstairs. Below were a smoke room, a billiard room, another drawing room and a bar. There was also a cellar and two cellar kitchens. Customers were also served through a small window in a side passage (CC). A wine bar and bistro was opened on the premises on 2 February 1979 (YEP 21 1 1979). A Grade II listed building (CAMRA2).

Thomas's Hotel, Low Petergate
Previously *Baynes' Coffee House, Baynes' Hotel, Tomlinson's Hotel,* and *Jackson's Hotel,* although also known as *The Grapes*. William Thomas, for 11 years steward at the De Grey Rooms, purchased it in 1853 (YG 27 8 1853). Thomas moved to Museum Street in 1858 (YG 13 11 1858) where he opened a new hotel.

Three Arrows, Gillygate
Later *The Earl of Dublin* and *The Cricketers' Arms*, mentioned between 1840 (YG 22 8 1840) and 1848 (Dir). Also known as The Sign of the Arrows(YG 10 10 1843).

Three Bucks, Foss Bridge, Fossgate
Mentioned in 1765 (YCo 24 12 1765).

Three Coneys, Coney Street
Mentioned in 1641 and 1679 in St Martin's parish (Cook pp. 98, 118). Later *The Three Crowns and Coneys or The Three Crowns.*

Three Cranes, Church Street (Girdlergate)
Mentioned in 1783, 85, 87 in Holy Trinity, King's Court, parish and in 1795 in Girdlergate (YCA K69, Cooper2 p. 44).

Three Cranes, St Sampson's Square ¶
Mentioned in 1749 when Thomas Heckford was the licensee (Johnson p. 43). In 1902 it had an attic, two bedrooms, both occupied by the family, and two clubrooms upstairs. On the ground floor were a smoke room, a dram shop, a small snug, a small bar and two kitchens from which food could be supplied. The urinal was inside the house (CC).

Three Crowns, Coney Street

Previously *The Three Coneys* and *The Three Crowns and Coneys.* Mentioned by Francis Drake in 1736 as one of three principal inns in the city. The other two were *The Black Swan* and *George* (Drake p. 331). A large inn to be let 1742 (YC0 13 4 1742).

Three Crowns and Coneys, Coney Street

Previously *The Three Coneys.* Mentioned in 1739 (Benson p. 166). Later *The Three Crowns.* This name suggests that the sign at the time portrayed three crowned kings or Old Norse *kunungr*, the word from which Coney Street is derived.

Three Cups, Coney Street

To let and goods for sale 1743 (YCo 6 9 1743).

Three Cups, Foss Bridge

Earliest mention 1733 as a place where common carriers could be found (Gent). One of two pubs with the same name listed in St Dennis parish in 1787 (Cooper2 p. 46). The other was located in Walmgate only 40 yards away but that one changed its name in 1905 to *The Red Lion* to end a confusing situation. It was rebuilt c.1830 (RCHME V p. 238). In 1902 it had five bedrooms, two set aside for travellers. Below were a smoke room, a snug, a dram shop and a private kitchen from which food could be supplied. There was also a cellar but no urinal (CC). The renewal of its licence was successfully opposed at the Brewster Sessions in 1906 on the grounds of non–necessity. There were another six pubs within 100 yards of it and it was also said to be one of the worst six houses in York. (YG 7 3 1906). The licence would expire on 5 April 1907 or earlier if compensation was paid (YCA Acc. 189), a situation reported in February that year (YG 16 2 1907).

Three Cups, Walmgate

Mentioned in 1783, 87 and 95, one of two pubs with the same name listed in St Dennis parish in 1787 (Cooper2 p. 46). The other was located at Foss Bridge only 40 yards away. The name of this pub was changed in 1905 to *The Red Lion* to end a confusing situation (YCo 18 11 1805).

Three Horseshoes, Walmgate

Mentioned 1743 (YCo 15 3 1743) and 1813 (YCo 12 4 1813).

Three Jolly Butchers, Girdlergate (Church Street)

Mentioned in 1818, by 1828 it had been renamed *The Curriers' Arms* but became *The Jolly Butchers* by 1834 (Dir). Later *The Ebor Vaults.*

Three Kings, Micklegate

Mentioned in 1554 as the third place at which the Corpus Christi plays were performed (YCA CC4/2). Mentioned in a lease in St Martin cum Gregory parish, next to *The Sun*, in 1604 (YCA E27 f. 10b).

Three Legged Mare, High Petergate

Opened on 10 July 2001, the second pub in York Brewery Company's chain of tied houses (YEP 14 7 2001). Following the hanging theme inspired by *The Last Drop* its name relates to the gibbet, with this nickname, which once stood on the Knavesmire.

Three Legs of Man, Monkgate

To be let at Lady Day 1770 (YCo 16 1 1770). For sale 1816 (YCo 14 10 1816).

Three Tuns, Coppergate ¶
Mentioned in 1783, 87 and 95 (YCA K69; Cooper2 p. 45). In 1902 it had a six day and early closing licence. The three bedrooms were all used as storerooms and no–one resided on the premises. There were four smoke rooms, a dram shop and an office on the ground floor, all of which were small. There was also a cellar (CC). A full 'on' licence was granted on 11 February 1960 (YCA Acc. 189). A Grade II listed building (CAMRA2). Also known as *Thackwray's* after it became the central office of that brewery in 1898 (Davison p. 42). The sign is based on the arms of the Brewers' Company – *Gules on a chevron engrailed Argent between six barley sheaves in saltire three kilderkins [tuns] Sable hooped Or.*

Three Tuns, Peter Lane
A beerhouse, mentioned in 1838, which by 1843 had gained this name (Dir). For sale in 1846 (YG 7 11 1846). In 1863 the building became *The Beehive.*

Three Tuns, St Maurice's parish
Mentioned in 1783, 85 and 87 (YCA K69; Cooper2 p. 44).

Three Tuns, Shambles
Mentioned in 1828 (Dir).

Three Tuns, Skeldergate
Previously *The Labourer,* it had gained this name by 1834 (Dir). By 1840 it had become *The Foresters' Arms*, later *The Prince of Wales.*

Tiger, Haxby
Earliest mention 1840 (Dir). When a new extension was added in 1976 its premises were described as two cottages knocked into one (YEP 9 12 1976).

Tiger, (Jubbergate) Market Street ¶
Mentioned in 1851 (Dir). In 1902 it had five bedrooms, two of which were available to travellers during race meetings, and a sitting room upstairs. Below were two smoke rooms and a bar. The private kitchen, from which food could be supplied, was in the cellar. There was only one WC, shared by the family and customers. The urinal was not screened off from view (CC). It closed for four weeks in May 1988 for a major refurbishment and reopened as *The William Bass* (YEP 11 5 1988).

Tiger, North Street
An alternative name for *The Leopard*, the name it had when first licensed as a beerhouse in 1837 (YG 16 9 1837). First mentioned in 1838 (Dir). The interchangeability of the names was a commentary on the ability of the sign painter to depict a wild animal he had never seen or, alternately, of the pub's customers to recognise the beast intended. The confusion was sorted out by 1848 when it changed its name to *The Crown and Cushion.*

Tomlinson's Hotel, Petergate
Although called *The Grapes* from 1822 to 1874 it was also known as *Baynes' Coffee House* and *Baynes' Hotel* before it changed its name when Mr Tomlinson, who died in February 1828 (YG 9 2 1828), became proprietor. He was succeeded by his wife, Elizabeth (YCA F30A) and four months after her death in September 1843 (YG 30 9 1843) it became *Jackson's Hotel,* then *Thomas's Hotel*. Next, having reverted to *The Grapes* for a

time, *The Londesborough Arms*. It was here that a meeting was held on 23 December 1833, attended by George Hudson amongst others, to discuss bringing a railway to York.

Tower, Haymarket (King's Square)
Mentioned as The Sign of the Tower in 1781 (YCo 18 12 1781).

Tower, Haymarket (Peasholme Green)
An alternative name for *The Tower of London*, in use in 1851 (Dir).

Tower, Peasholme Green
An alternative name for *The Clifford's Tower*, in used between 1818 (Dir) and 1826 (YCA F31).

Tower of London, Haymarket
Previously *The Shoulder of Mutton*, using this name between 1846 and 1855. When it was for sale in 1851 the premises included a brewhouse (YG 31 5 1851). Later *The Haymarket Tavern.*

Trafalgar Bay, Nunnery Lane (¶ see Britannia)
First mentioned in 1834 (Dir) some 29 years after the sea battle off Cape Trafalgar in which Lord Nelson defeated the French and Spanish fleets and lost his life. The map on the sign (from at least 1980), however, clearly depicts Trafalgar as it actually is, a headland and not a bay. This suggests there may be another source for this reputedly unique name. It was a custom at the time of the origin of the pub to prefix or suffix racehorses' names by their colour and a bay colt with this name, by Gohanna out of the sister to Skyscraper, was runner up in the Derby in 1806 after a close race. At that time it was owned by Lord Egremont but a year later in May 1807, when it won two valuable challenge matches at York for prizes of 1000 gns and 500 gns, it was owned by George Augustus, Prince of Wales (later Prince Regent and by 1820, George IV). It was later named Harpocrates (Orton pp. 287, 296/7). If this theory is correct the origin of the name is still ultimately Nelson's famous victory. When the pub was offered for sale in 1842 the premises included a brewhouse (YG 26 11 1842). In 1902 it had three bedrooms, two set aside for travellers, and a sitting room upstairs. On the ground floor all the rooms were licensed. They comprised a smoke room, a dram shop, a serving bar and a kitchen from which food could be supplied. The family shared its WC with the customers (CC). At the Brewster Sessions in 1903 the renewal of its licence was unsuccessfully opposed. At this time JJ Hunt & Co paid £60 a year for the lease but only charged their tenant a rent of £32 a year (Peacock p. 64). Another attempt was made to close it in 1926 when it was declared redundant (YG 14 3 1925) but later that year, after an appeal, the licence was renewed (YG 30 5 1925).

Travellers' Rest, Earswick
Mentioned 1872 and 1881 (Dir).

Travellers' Rest, Jubbergate
A beerhouse, mentioned between 1836 (YG 5 3 1836) and 1846 (Dir).

Trellis, Coffee Yard
Previously *The Chequer*? Mentioned in 1795 (YCA K69), a general sign used by houses with no specific name and synonymous with The Chequer.

Trellis, Goodramgate
Mentioned in 1783, 85, 87 and 95 (YCA K69; Cooper2 p. 44).

Trinity House Hotel, Trinity Lane ¶
Mentioned in 1872 when occupied by Robert Simpson, Wine and Spirit Merchant (Dir). In 1902 it had a six day licence. On the upper floors were three and two bedrooms, both occupied by the family. On the ground floor were a smoke room, a bar and a private kitchen from which food could be supplied. There was also a cellar but no urinal; the customers used a long narrow passage at the side of the house (CC). The renewal of the licence was unsuccessfully opposed at the Brewster Sessions in 1903. At this time, when beer was 1d a pint, it was selling between £7 and £8 worth of two beers (Peacock p. 64). It was finally referred for compensation on 12 March 1923 and closed on 1 October that year (YCA Acc. 189). Also known as *The Board* (CC).

Trumpet Inn, Townend Street
Previously *The Free Gardeners' Arms*, it had gained this name by 1858 (Dir). In 1902 it was described as a very small house, a cottage. It had two bedrooms, neither available for travellers, and a sitting room upstairs. Below were a smoke room and a kitchen which doubled as a taproom. The food for both the customers and the family was prepared in this room. There was also a cellar (CC). It was referred for compensation on 10 June 1908 and the licence was extinguished on 5 October that year (YCA Acc. 189).

Turf Tavern, Tadcaster Road, Dringhouses
Mentioned 1834 (Dir). Originally in a building next to The Hollies (York Marriott Hotel), the home of Major John Close, but, through his influence, it was moved to new premises in Railway View (Pocock p. 29).

Turf Tavern, Railway View, Dringhouses
Moved here from Tadcaster Road between 1902 and 1909 (Dir). Transferred from the Tadcaster Licensing District 1 April 1937 on the extension of city boundaries (YCA Acc. 189). Permission granted in 1954 to transfer the licence to a new pub of the same name at the junction of Thanet Road and Jervis Road (YEP 8 3 1954). Closed 7 March 1955 (YEP 9 3 1955). Also known as *The New Turf Tavern*.

Turf Tavern, Thanet Road
Licence transferred from *The Turf Tavern*, Railway View, on 8 March 1955 (YCA Acc. 189).

Turf Tavern, Market Street (Jubbergate)
Previously *The Horse and Jockey*, it had gained this name by 1851 (Dir). Later, by 1876, *The Alexandra*.

Turf Coffee House, Davygate
Mentioned in 1783 and 95 (YCA K69). In 1803 William Knapton moved to *The Star Inn*, Stonegate and called that house *The Star Inn and Turf Coffee House*. Nevertheless the original establishment continued to trade under its old name for many years. For sale in 1857 (YG 7 3 1851). By 1867 it had become *The Cricketers' Arms*. Next *The London Hotel*. Known in 1824 and 1826 as *The Coffee House* (YCA F30A).

226

Turf Coffee House, Jubbergate
Previously *The Horse and Jockey* it had gained this name by 1837 (YG 19 10 1837). Described as newly rebuilt when it was to let in 1848 (YG 8 7 1848). Next by 1851 *The Turf Tavern* and later *The Alexandra*.

Turk's Head, College Street
Mentioned in 1818 (Dir). Although the building was demolished in March 1892 (YG 5 3 1892) the licence did not elapse until 10 October that year (YCA Acc. 189). The sign is often interchangeable with *The Saracen's Head*.

Turk's Head, King's Square (Haymarket)
Previously *The Turk's Head Coffee House*, it had gained this name sometime prior to 1789 (YCo 29 6 1789). Used universally between 1818 and 1843 (Dir). An alternative name for *The Old Turk's Head*.

Turk's Head, Low Ousegate
Previously *The Turk's Head Coffee House*, mentioned in 1783 and 87 (YCA K69).

Turk's Head, Petergate
Mentioned in 1743 as a meeting place of the governors of York County Hospital (YCo 2 8 1743). Death of proprietor, George Woodhouse, in 1755 (YCo 11 11 1755).

Turk's Head, St Andrewgate ¶
Previously *The Saracen's Head*, this name first appeared in 1828 (Dir). The old name was last used in 1838 (Dir) and by 1840 the new name had been completely adopted (YG 6 6 1840). In 1902 it had a box room and four bedrooms, all occupied by the family. The whole of the ground floor, including the kitchen were licensed. All the rooms in the house were very small (CC). It was referred for compensation on 9 March 1927 which was confirmed on 13 June that year. It closed on 5 April 1928 (YCA Acc. 189).

Turks' Head Coffee House, Coney Street
Mentioned in 1748 (YJ 25 11 1748).

Turk's Head Coffee House, King's Square
Part for sale in 1750 (YCo 23 1 1750). Although called *The Old Turk's Head* by 1783 and later *The Turk's Head* it was still using this name in 1824 (YG 17 7 1824). By 1846 it had become *The Old Turk's Head* exclusively.

Turk's Head Coffee House, Low Ousegate
First mentioned in 1750 (YCo 13 2 1750) and shown on Dr White's Map in 1782. Called simply *The Turk's Head* in 1783 and 1787.

Two Angels, Marygate
Mentioned in 1770 (Benson p. 167).

Unicorn Inn, Lord Mayor's Walk ¶
A beerhouse, first mentioned in 1852 when the York Interment Institution held a meeting at which 150 people were present (YG 21 8 1852). In 1902 it had four bedrooms, a taproom, a small smoke room and a small kitchen which was also used as a serving bar. The family shared its WC with the customers (CC). At the Brewster Sessions in 1956 it was decided to close it as it was very small, the sanitary accommodation was not good and

trade was not very great (YEP 5 3 1956, 29 5 1956). Compensation was paid on 24 October and the premises closed on 31 October 1956 (YCA Acc. 189).

Unicorn Inn, Monkgate
Mentioned in 1791 (YCA E55). The Unicorn coach for Malton left here daily at 5 pm in 1840 (Cooper p. 67). Last mention in 1846 when the inn and cottages were offered for sale (YG 21 11 1846).

Unicorn, Petergate
To be let 1766 (YCo 18 8 1766). Patrick Byrne moved from here in 1778 to take over *The Theatre Coffee House* (YCo 18 8 1778) to be replaced by John Coupland (YCo 15 9 1778).

Unicorn, Tanner Row ¶
Mentioned in a lease in 1804 (YCA E96 ff. 30/1). Sold in 1819 on the bankruptcy of John Kilby (YG 25 9 1819). By 1838 and still in 1841 it had changed its name to The Oddfellows' Arms but had reverted to its former name by 1843 (Dir). In 1902 it had an attic, four bedrooms, one set apart for travellers, a nursery, a sitting room and the kitchen upstairs. On the ground floor were a smoke room, a dram shop, a bottle and jug department and a private room. Food could be supplied if required (CC). It was familiarly called *The Corner Pin* for many years but formally adopted this name in 1985 (YEP 28 10 1987).

Upholders' Arms, Trinity Lane
An alternative name for *The Upholsterer's Arms*, in use in 1822 (YCA F30A).

Upholsterers' Arms, Trinity Lane
An alternative name for *The Greyhound*, in use during the occupation of John Duffield in 1822 (YCA F30A) and 1823 (Dir). Also called *The Upholders' Arms.*

Varsity, Lendal
The former Lloyds Bank branch premises were converted into licensed premises in 1999 and opened in early 2000 (YEP 17 11 1999).

Victor J's, Finkle Street
A café–bar, first mentioned in 1998 (Thomson).

Victoria, Bootham Square
A beerhouse, mentioned in 1834, had gained this name by 1838 only a year after Princess Victoria's accession to the throne. By 1843 it was called *The Princess Victoria* but then the name alternated between *The Victoria,* 1846 and 1851, and *The Queen,* 1849 and 1855 (Dir). Later *The Queen's Head.*

Victoria, Fossgate
Mentioned in 1841 (Dir).

Victoria Inn/Hotel, Victoria Place, Heslington Road (also East Riding Place, later Cemetery Road) ¶
Mentioned in 1838 (Dir). In 1902 it was described as a good suitable house used by cattle dealers on market day. It had five bedrooms, providing accommodation for 16 travellers in addition to the family. There were also two smoke rooms, a taproom, a serving bar, a dram shop and private kitchens from which food was supplied to dealers on fair days. There was also a cellar (CC).

Victoria, Lawrence Street
Previously *The Wheatsheaf, The Princess Victoria* but it was using this name in 1841 (Dir). Its official name would appear to have been *The Queen Victoria* but it was more generally known by the shorter name. Later *The Queen's Head, The Queen* and *The Rook and Gaskill*.

Victoria Vaults, Nunnery Lane/Dove Street ¶
First mentioned in 1857 as *The Victoria* (Dir). It was purchased in 1884, complete with a brewery, by Messrs Cooper and Close, Wine and Spirit Merchants for £1200 (YG 2 & 22 Aug 1884). By 1889 it had gained this name (Dir). In 1902 it had four bedrooms, one of which was available for travellers, and a private WC upstairs. On the ground floor were a smoke room, a large bar, a bottle and jug department, and a kitchen from which food could be supplied. The urinal was inside the house and there was no WC for customers (CC).

Victoria Hotel, Railway Street
A beerhouse and coffee rooms, mentioned in 1857, it had gained this name by 1872 (Dir). In 1902 it had five bedrooms, a commercial room, a smoke room and a bar. There was also a cellar in which the private kitchen was situated. Inside the premises, entered from the smoke room, was a combined urinal and WC for the customers (CC). It was granted a full 'on' licence on 11 February 1960 (YCA Acc. 189). It closed in 1970 (Dir).

Viking Hotel, North Street
A new hotel, now The Moat House, was granted an ale licence on 6 January 1965 (YCA Acc. 189).

Villiers, Skeldergate
Previously *The Plumbers' Arms*, and *The Cock and Bottle* by 1965. It was later given this name and, closing after being inundated by floods in January 2001, re–opened under its previous name on 6 April that year (YEP 10 3 2001).

Volunteer's Arms, Watson Street (¶ see Locomotive)
A beerhouse mentioned in 1867 (Dir). In 1902 it had three bedrooms and a club room upstairs. Below were a smokeroom, a snug, a bar and a private kitchen. There was also a cellar (CC). On 30 May 1962 it was granted a full 'on' licence (YCA Acc. 189).

Volunteer Circus, Watson Street
An alternative name for *The Volunteer Arms*, mentioned in 1881 (Dir).

W Bar, Micklegate
Previously *Walker's Bar*, renamed 2002 (YEP 19 1 2002).

Wag(g)on, Lawrence Street
A familiar name for *The Waggon and Horses*, First mentioned in 1791 (YCA E55) and used intermittently until 1851 (Dir).

Waggon and Horses, Jubbergate
Mentioned 1818 (Dir) to 1828 (F30A). Next *The Coach and Horses.*

Waggon and Horses, Gillygate ¶
Mentioned 1811 (YCo 25 3 1811). In 1902 it had six bedrooms, one set apart for travellers, and a sitting room upstairs. Below were a smoke room, a taproom, a ladies' market room

and private kitchens from which food could be supplied (CC). A Grade II listed building (CAMRA2). Name changed 17 April 2003 to *The Gillygate.*

Waggon and Horses, Lawrence Street ¶
First mentioned under this name in 1795 (YCA K69) but recorded in 1791 as *The Waggon*, its familiar name. In 1902 it had 10 bedrooms in which 20 travellers could be accommodated in addition to the family. On the ground floor were two smoke rooms, a dram shop and a private kitchen from which dinners and other meals could be supplied. There was also a cellar (CC). A Grade II listed building (CAMRA2).

Walker's Bar, Micklegate ¶
The Petit Trianon was taken over by Neville England and turned into a bar with this name. It opened on 1 November 1973 (YEP 16 10 1973). Until 1970 the premises had been *The Board*, at one time owned by Walker and Scott, wine and spirit merchants. In 2002 it was renamed *W Bar.*

Walnut Tree, Heworth Village
The Britannia, on the opposite side of the road closed on 19 July 1967 and its licence transferred to this new public house (YEP 19 7 1967, YCA Acc. 189).

Watermill, Walmgate
Previously and later *The Windmill*, but strangely this mill changed its method of propulsion in the licensing records between 1822 and 1826 (YCA F30A, F31).

Watermans' Arms, Friargate
Mentioned in 1838 (Dir).

Well House, Fishergate
Mentioned in 1741 when Joseph Netherwood was prosecuted for selling ale without a licence. In August 1796 it was auctioned as a dwelling house, garden and stables, known as The Well House public house. *The Light Horseman* was built on its site (Kaner p. 15).

Wellington, Alma Terrace
A beerhouse, previously Lawson's Beerhouse, by 1881 it had become *The Wellington* but when it was bought by Samuel Smith in 1887 it was described in the sale note as *The Sir Colin Campbell*, 'an old established beerhouse' (CAMRA2). After the sale and certainly by 1902 it had regained its former name. It that year it had four bedrooms and a club room upstairs. On the ground floor were a bar parlour, a snug, a taproom and a private kitchen (CC). It was granted a full 'on' licence on 9 February, confirmed 5 April 1949 (YCA Acc. 189).

Wellington Coffee House, Fossgate
Mentioned in 1822 (YCA F30A) and 1834 (Dir). By 1838 it had become *The Queen's Head.*

Wellington Inn, Goodramgate
Earliest mention 1818 (Dir). Later *The Marquis of Wellington*, *Lord Wellington* and *The Duke of Wellington.* By 1843 it had firmly reverted to its earliest and simplest name. When it was for sale in 1881 the premises included a brewhouse (YG 21 5 1881). In 1902 it had four bedrooms, one let off to travellers when necessary, and a sitting room upstairs. On the

ground floor were a dram shop, a dark smoke room, a singing room and a kitchen from which food could be supplied. There was also a cellar (CC). Compensation was granted in 1913 (YG 19 1 1913) and it closed on 6 October that year (YCA Acc. 189).

Wenlock Arms, Wheldrake ¶
Previously *The Blacksmiths' Arms*, rebuilt and given this name in 1856 (Wheldrake p. 11). It was described the next year as a large and commodious inn, a new and very good building (Dir). Name after the Lords of the Manor of Wheldrake since 1820, the Lawley family who were ennobled as Barons Wenlock in 1839 (Wheldrake p. 21).

Whale Fishery, Hungate
Sometime between 1835 (YG 14 3 1835) and 1838 (Dir), Christopher Bean moved from *The Curriers' Arms* in Church Street to open this new public house on the corner of Carmelite Street named to commemorate his former profession of harpooner in the polar region (Cooper p. 46). He had abandoned this calling by 1823 when he became licensee at *The Three Jolly Butchers* in Church Street (Dir). If he is the Christopher Bean, waterman, who died in 1865 at the age of 67 he had left the rigours of the frozen seas at a comparatively early age. He put his new pub, complete with brewhouse, on the market in 1843 (YG 19 8 1843) but was still there in 1844 (YG 20 1 1844). By 1846 he had moved to another house in the same street, *The Crown* (Dir). His old premises were rechristened *The Cotherstone.* He next appeared as a beerhouse keeper between 1855 and 1861 in an establishment in Carmelite Street (Dir) which by 1876 was called *The Ship.*

Whale Fishery, Carmelite Street
According to TP Cooper, after Christopher Bean left the pub with this name in Hungate he took the name with him to a new house in Carmelite Street (Cooper p. 46). However he first went to *The Crown* (see previous entry) before appearing in Carmelite Street in 1855, in a house which was by 1876 to be called *The Ship.* Its sign would probably have been a whale fishing boat and *The Ship* its familiar name. Later *The Garden Gate.*

Wheatsheaf, Castlegate ¶
Mentioned in 1754 when Thomas Hunter moved from there to The Blue Boar (YCo 14 5 1754). Between 1851 and 1855 it was renamed *The Castle Hotel* (Dir).

Wheatsheaf, Davygate
Previously *The Barleycorn*, it was using this name by 1822 (YCA F30A). On 20 Sept 1898 the Streets and Buildings Committee of the Council agreed to purchase from Tadcaster Tower Brewery Co. all their interest in the pub for £700 to enable the street to be widened (S&B) and, as a result, at the Brewster Sessions in 1899 the licence was allowed to lapse (YCA Acc. 189). The part of the pub not required for street widening was conveyed to James Melrose who included it in the site on which he built Century House, now occupied by WP Brown's department store.

Wheatsheaf, Grape Lane
Mentioned in 1823 (Dir) in error for a pub with the same name in Silver Street.

Wheatsheaf, Hessay
Mentioned 1822 (YCA F30A) to 1909 (Dir).

Wheatsheaf, Hungate ¶

Mentioned in 1783, 85, 87 and 95 (YCA K69, Cooper2 p. 44). Rebuilt on another site in the same street in 1885 (YG 6 1 1885). In 1902, described as newly built, it had two attics and four bedrooms with sleeping accommodation for four or five travellers in addition to the family. Downstairs were two smoke rooms, a bar and a kitchen from which food could be supplied. There was also a cellar (CC). A closure attempt was made in 1911 (Peacock p. 247) but it stayed open until compensation was granted on 27 April 1937. It finally closed on 26 February 1938 (YCA Acc. 189).

Wheatsheaf, Lawrence Street

Mentioned 1818 to 1834 (Dir). Next *The Princess Victoria, The Victoria, The Queen Victoria, The Queen's Head, The Queen* and *The Rook and Gaskill.*

Wheatsheaf, Nunnery Lane

Previously *The Golden Ball,* it next became *The Barley Sheaf* but used this name as an alternative in 1841 and 1843. Next *The Crown* but had become The Wheatsheaf again by 1872 (Dir). In 1902 it had three habitable attics, four bedrooms and a sitting room upstairs. Below were two smoke rooms, a dram shop and a private kitchen, there was also a cellar (CC). It was referred for compensation on 26 February 1937 and closed after it was paid on 31 January 1938 (YCA Acc. 189).

Wheatsheaf, Silver Street

Mentioned 1822 to 1826 (YCA F30A, F31).

Wheatsheaf, Stonegate

Mentioned in connection with a burial in 1749 in St Helen's, Stonegate, parish (PR) and when it was to be let in 1754 (YCo 20 8 1754).

Wheatsheaf, Walmgate

Mentioned in 1755 (YCo 39 12 1755), 1771 (YCo 19 3 1771) and 1787 (Cooper2 p. 46).

White Bull, Davygate

Mentioned in 1763 (YCo 7 6 1763), 1778 when J Bosomworth was the licensee (YCo 31 3 1778) and 1783 (YCA K69).

White Dog, Bedern

Mentioned 1813 (YCo 5 4 1813). For sale in 1827 (YG 21 7 1827). Last mention 1828 (Dir).

White Dog, St Saviourgate

Previously *The Pointer Dog* and *The Dog,* it had been given this name by 1807 when the house was to be let for 14 years (YCo 17 8 1807). Although it had become *The Spotted Dog* by 1818 (Dir) it was still occasionally called by this name (YG 16 4 1836).

White Dog, Stonegate

'Nigh the Minster Gates', it was for let in 1748 (YCo 4 10 1748). When Matthew Todd became the licensee in 1833 he renamed it *The White Hart* (YG 26 10 1833).

White Hart, Stonegate

Previously *The White Dog,* it was given this name by Matthew Todd in 1833 when he moved from *The Golden Fleece* (YG 26 10 1833). Called *The White Hart Coffee House* in 1834 (YG 18 10 1834). Last mention in 1861 (Dir).

White Hart Coffee House, Stonegate
See above.

White Horse (1), Bootham
Benson mentions a house of this name here in 1502 (Benson p. 166), but has confused it with *The White Horse*, Fossgate.

White Horse (2), Bootham ¶
Reportedly there has been a pub on this site since 1502 (YEP 21 3 1987) but this is an error (see above). The earliest mention of this house is in 1770 (YCo 23 1 1770) but there had been an earlier establishment with the same name (see above). Rebuilding plans for CJ Melrose were approved in 1894 (S&B 18 12 1894) and the new house opened the next year (date on oriel window). Built hard against the walls of St Mary's Abbey with no back yard, the rooms of the new pub, particularly the cellars, were damp in 1902. There were four bedrooms, all used by the family, and a kitchen upstairs. Food was supplied to the customers, with some difficulty, from this latter room. On the ground floor were two smoke rooms and a dram shop (CC).

White Horse, Coney Street
Opened in the old Judges' Lodgings in 1810 by T Crow (YCo 4 6 1810). Also known as *Crow's Coffee House.* Advertised for let in 1814 (YCo 15 8 1814).

White Horse, Coppergate ¶
Mentioned in 1733 as a place where common carriers could be found (Gent). In 1901, in the ownership of JW Craven, the confectioner, it was rebuilt on a smaller scale (CC). By 1968 it was in the possession of York Corporation and closed in October that year (YEP 11 11 1968). It was subsequently demolished for the Coppergate Development.

White Horse, Fossgate
On 6 February 1520/1 John Butterfield, innholder, bequeathed his house in Fossgate, the sign of the White Horse, to the Master of Trinity Hospital (Smith p. 72). Mentioned in 1548 (Smith p. 145).

White Horse, Grape Lane
Mentioned in 1733 as a place where common carriers could be found (Gent).

White Horse, Main Street, Huntington
Mentioned 1823 to 1963 (Dir).

White Horse, (St) Marygate
Mentioned 1855 (Dir).

White Horse, Skeldergate ¶
Mentioned in 1688 in John Webster's diary, near St Mary Bishophill Senior (Malden). and then in 1745 (Yorkshire Gazetteer 26 2 1745). In 1902 it had six bedrooms, all occupied by the family. On the ground floor were a smoke room, a dram shop, a bar parlour and a kitchen from which food could be supplied although it was very seldom asked for. There was also a cellar. The family, the customers and the occupants of an adjoining shop all shared the WC (CC). It closed on 7 October 1931 (YCA Acc. 189).

White Horse, St Sampson's Square
An earlier name for *The Nag's Head.*

White Horse, Upper Poppleton
Earliest mention by name 1832 (YCA F30A) although the house was leased to William Knapton, publican, in 1802 (Davies2 p. 23).

White Horse, Walmgate
Mentioned in 1823 (Dir), an alternative name for *The Bay Horse*.

White House, The Mount ¶
Previously *The New Inn* and *The Gallows* it had become, by the 19th century, a starch factory and kennels for the York and Ainsty Hunt. In 1855 it was given a new licence as a beerhouse under the name of *The White House* (YG 1 3 1855). Last mention in 1858 (Dir). The proprietors, The Station Hotel, had allowed the licence to lapse (RCHME III p. 106).

White Lion, St Sampson's parish
Mentioned in 1783, 85 and 87 (YCA K69, Cooper2 p. 43).

White Rose, Cornlands Road, Acomb
The licence of *The Clock Inn,* Walmgate, was transferred here on 3 June 1957 on the closure of that pub. At the same time the licence of *The Old George*, Pavement (in suspension) was surrendered (YCA Acc. 189).

White Swan, Bootham Bar
Mentioned in 1743 (YCo 24 4 1743).

White Swan, Deighton
Previously *The Swan*, a name it was still using in 1909 (Dir), later to be replaced by the full name.

White Swan, High Jubbergate
Mentioned in 1770 (Benson p. 167).

White Swan, Blossom Street (without Micklegate Bar)
Mentioned in 1733 (Benson p. 166) and 1769 (YCo 31 3 1769).

White Swan, Goodramgate
See *The White Swan*, Petergate.

White Swan, Pavement (later Piccadilly) ¶
Earliest mention 1733 as a place where common carriers could be found (Gent). In 1902 it had 25 bedrooms, 16 of which were set aside for travellers. There were also a drawing room, three sitting rooms, a commercial room, a coffee room, a smoke room, a bar, a vault, a servants hall, a larder, a pantry and two kitchens from which the full range of meals could be supplied. All in all the Chief Constable considered it a very good commercial hotel and market house (CC). It was demolished during the construction of the new street, Piccadilly, and rebuilt on a much larger scale in 1912 (YG 20 4 1912) having been bought by People's Refreshment Houses in 1911 (YG 11 2 1911). It closed between 22 January and Christmas 1982 (YEP 21 1 1972, 5 11 1972) and finally closed by 1990 (Thomson).

White Swan, Petergate
Referred to in the Churchwarden's Accounts of Holy Trinity Goodramgate in 1703 (Benson2). Mentioned in 1733 as a place where common carriers could be found (Gent). When in 1742 William Barwick of *The Sandhill*, Colliergate, became the licensee, he renamed it *The White Swan and Sandhill*. At one time it had entrances on both Petergate and Goodramgate, the latter having taken over as its address by 1795 (YCA K69). By 1786 'Sandhill' had been dropped from its name (PR HTKC p. 121). 'Old' was added to its name by 1885 (Dir) when it is first mentioned as *The Old White Swan.*

White Swan, Stockton on the Forest
Mentioned in 1823 (Dir), closed in 1947 (Inf from S Burton, present owner of the building). Although predating the Beerhouse Act 1830 this was its status in later years (Dir 1895). Familiarly known as *The Swan*. See also *The Rose and Crown* which may have been an alternative or temporary name for this estalishment in 1884.

White Swan and Sandhill, Petergate
In 1742 William Barwick of *The Sandhill*, Colliergate, became the licensee of *The White Swan* and he renamed it The White Swan and Sandhill. By 1786 it had reverted to its original name (PR HTKC p. 121).

Whitesmiths' Arms, Micklegate
Mentioned in 1766 (YCo 9 9 1766) and 1787 (Cooper2 p. 43). Also known as *The Smith.*

Wild Man, Petergate
Mentioned in 1727 in connection with a burial at St Michael le Belfry (PR). A place in 1733 where common carriers could be found (Gent). Last mention 1752 (YCo 5 5 1752).

Wild Man, Water Lane ¶
A pub with a sign depicting a large naked man, illustrated in a drawing published in 1841 (Bedford), has given rise to this identification (Cooper p. 53) but it is not mentioned in any other contemporary source.

Wilde's Bar, Grape Lane
Opened in July 1991 by the owners of Oscar's in Little Stonegate (YEP 6 7 1991).

William Bass, Market Street
Previously *The Tiger*, it closed for four weeks in May 1988 for a major refurbishment and reopened with this name *The William Bass* (YEP 11 5 1988).

Windmill, Askham Bryan ¶
Mentioned by name 1902 to 1909 but in 1857 John Gilson is recorded as a miller and beer retailer (Dir) which may be an earlier reference to this pub.

Windmill, Blossom Street ¶
Mentioned in 1769 (YCo 24 10 1769). When purchased by EP Brett in July 1893 for £3750 the premises included a brewhouse. In 1902 it had 21 bedrooms, 16 of which were let off to travellers. The rest of the premises consisted of a bar, a taproom, a coffee room, a commercial room, a large dining room and private kitchens. There was also a cellar. Across the yard was a large bar or canteen (CC). A Grade II listed building (CAMRA2).

Windmill, Hull Road, Dunnington
Originally a beerhouse, first mentioned by name in 1872. Between 1889 and 1909 the pub is referred to as *The Mill*, its familiar name (Dir).

Windmill, St George's Field ¶
On Dr White's map in 1782 as an unnamed alehouse. Name mentioned in 1783 (YCA K69). Demolished in 1856 when the basin at the head of Browney Dyke was created (Cooper p 57).

Windmill, Trinity Lane
Mentioned in 1783 and 1785 (YCA K69).

Windmill, Walmgate
Mentioned in 1818 (Dir) but strangely, according to the licensing records, changed its name to *The Watermill* between 1822 and 1826 before reappearing under its former name in 1828 (YCA F30A, F31).

Windmill, York Road, Wigginton ¶
Mentioned 1857 to 1937 (Dir). Familiarly known as *The Mill.*

Winning Post, Bishopthorpe Road
A new public house built by John Smith & Sons which opened on 22 May 1939 (YCA Acc. 189). At the same time, and in consideration of the licence being granted, that of *The Sportsman*, Caroline Street, was voluntarily surrendered.

Wolstenholme's Dram Shop, Petergate
Opened c.1869 (Dir), by 1887 it had become *Haigh's Vaults*, next *Petergate Wine and Spirit Stores and Bar*, *The Board* and *The Hole in the Wall*.

Woodman, Bishopthorpe ¶
Possibly the successor to *The Black Swan* last mentioned in 1843. Earliest mention of this pub 1853 (YG 1 1 1853).

Woodman, Elmwood Street
Mentioned in 1867 (Dir).

Woodman, Heworth Green, Malton Road ¶
Mentioned 1828 to 1855 (Dir). The building, on the site of a leper hospital, was demolished between 1924 and 1926 to make way for a new approach road to the widened Monk Bridge.

Woolpack, Fawcett Street (Cattle Market) ¶
Previously *The Fat Ox*, it had been given this name by 1867 (Dir). In 1902 it had six bedrooms, four set apart for travellers, a sitting room and a dining room upstairs. Below were three smoke rooms and a private kitchen from which food could be supplied. There was also a cellar. There was no WC for the customers and the urinal entrance was on the street (CC). A Grade II listed building (CAMRA2).

Woolpack, St Saviour's Place ¶
Mentioned in 1838 (Dir), in 1902 it had two attics and two bedrooms and did not provide accommodation for travellers. On the ground floor were a smoke room, a taproom with a

low ceiling, a small dram shop, a clubroom and a licensed kitchen from which food could be supplied. There was also a cellar. The urinal was inside the house (CC). It was rebuilt in the 1930s and sold in 1975 to an insurance company (YEP 18 6 1975) who closed it and turned it into offices (YEP 3 7 1975).

Wright's House, Nunnery Lane
First licensed as a beerhouse in 1863. Although more than £1000 had been spent on it and electric light installed, an application in 1901 for a full licence was declined as there were five other houses, four fully licensed within a radius of 250 yards (Peacock p. 22). In 1902 it had two attics, two bedrooms, a bathroom and a WC upstairs. Below were two smoke rooms, a bar and a private kitchen. Altogether it was considered to be a very suitable house for the business (CC). Renamed *The Edward VII* by 1905 (Dir).

Yarburgh Arms, Main Street, Heslington
Previously *The Ship, The Fox,* later *The De Yarburgh Arms* then *The Deramore Arms*. Mentioned 1855 to 1893 (Dir). George Bateson succeeded through his wife, Mary Elizabeth Yarburgh, to the estates of her family, including Heslington Hall, in 1875 and, in accordance with the wishes of one of her forebears, changed his name to Yarburgh. A year later George changed his mind and took the surname of Bateson de Yarburgh (Murray2 pp. 68, 69). By 1895 the pub had followed suit, adding the 'De' to its name.

Yates' Wine Lodge, Church Lane, Spurriergate
Previously *The Tavern in the Town*, and *The Riverside*. Reopened with this name in 1989 (YEP 12 12 1989).

Yates' Wine Lodge, Low Ousegate
Previously *The Board, Hillyard's Wine Lodge* and *The Lodge*, later *Dukes of York* and *O'Neills*. It was given this name after 1975 (Dir).

Ye Olde Grey Mare, Clifton
Previously *The Grey Horse, The Grey Mare, The Old Grey Mare.* It had gained this name by 1953 (Dir). A Grade II listed building (CAMRA2).

Ye Olde Malte Shovel, Walmgate
During the time *The Old Malt Shovel* belonged to Brett Brothers Brewery, who sold it to JJ Hunt & Co in 1896, a tessellated pavement was installed in the entrance which described it as *Ye Old Malt Shovel*.

Ye Olde No 5, Bridge Street ¶
Previously *Rooke's Dram Shop* (Dir). Also known as *New Bridge Street Hotel*. A Beerhouse with a six day licence (YCA Acc. 189), it had gained the alternative name of *The Board* by 1830 but by 1902 it was more generally called *Ye Olde No 5*. In 1902 it had four bedrooms, three set aside for travellers, a box room and a private WC upstairs. On the ground floor there was a smoke room used by the family and a small and badly lighted dram shop. Below there was a cellar and kitchen from which food could be supplied. There was no WC or urinal for the customers and it was considered to be a very poor house, badly accommodated (CC). A full 'on' licence was granted on 14 February 1961 only to be surrendered on 24 August 1966 (YCA Acc. 189).

Ye Olde Starre Inne, Stonegate ¶
By 1921 the antiquity of The Star was recognised by the adoption of a mock old English form of its name viz. *Ye Olde Starre Inne* (Dir).

Yearsley Grove, Huntington Road
A large private house, once owned by the Robson Family, was turned into a hotel by 1937 (Dir), becoming a public house after World War II.

Yew Tree, Lawrence Row, Barbican Road
An earlier name for *The Green Tree*, in use in 1838 (Dir).

York Arms, High Petergate ¶
Previously *Carr's Coffee House*, *The Chapter Coffee House*, *The Eclipse*, *The Board* and later *The Chapter Coffee House* again and, finally, by 1861 it had gained this name (Dir). In 1902 it had two attics, four bedrooms, one of which was available for travellers, a club room and a sitting room upstairs. On the ground floor were a smoke room, a bar and two kitchens, one licensed, from which food could be supplied. There was also a cellar. The family shared their WC with the customers (CC). In 1938 the pub was extended into an adjoining property (CAMRA). A Grade II listed building (CAMRA2).

York Tavern, St Helen's Square
Opened in 1770 (YCo 31 1 1770) and subsequently sold to the Corporation (Cooper p. 22). For a period known as *The Royal Sussex Hotel,* it was known as *Harker's York Hotel* from some time shortly after 1850, although The York Tavern was always its official name.

York Hotel Tap, Davygate
An establishment adjoining *The York Tavern* but apparently separately licensed, mentioned in 1872 and 1876 (Dir).

York Glass Works
York Glass House
York Glass Maker's Arms, Cattle Market, Fawcett Street
Some of the various names by which this public house was known, in addition to *The Glass House* and *The Glassmakers' Arms*, its eventual consistent name. It appears as The York Glass Works in 1838, 1843 and 1857, The York Glass House in 1841, 1849 and 1858 and the York Glass Makers' Arms in 1861 and 1879 (Dir).

York Minster, Marygate
Previously *The Minster*, it was using this name between 1838 and 1846 (Dir). Later *The Gardeners' Arms* and *The Minster* again.

York Minster, Micklegate
It appeared under this name on John Cossins' New and Exact Plan of the City of York, published in 1727 (Murray3 p. 18) but by 1736 it was known by the shortened name of *The Minster*. Also known as *The Minster Coffee House*.

Yorkshire Coffee House, Coppergate
An alternative name for *The Yorkshireman Coffee House*, in use in 1846 and 1848 (Dir).

Yorkshire Tavern, North Street
An alternative name for *The Yorkshire Hussar*, in use between 1848 and 1851 (Dir).

Yorkshire Hussar, North Street

Mentioned in 1841, but for a period called *The Yorkshire Tavern.* Rebuilt in 1896 (Johnson p. 48). In 1902, it had four bedrooms, only two furnished and none available for travellers, and a large dining room upstairs. On the ground floor were a smoke room, a bar parlour, a bar and a private kitchen from which food could be supplied. There was also a cellar (CC). Later *The Other Tap and Spile* and *The First Hussar*.

Yorkshireman Inn, Coppergate ¶

An abbreviated form of *The Yorkshireman Coffee House,* in use by 1841 and regularly from 1851 (Dir). It was for sale with a brewhouse in 1869 (YG 23 10 1869). In 1902 it had five bedrooms, one available for travellers, and a sitting room upstairs. Below were a smoke room, a taproom, a bar, a small private room and two kitchens from which food could be supplied. There was also a cellar (CC). It closed in 1970 (YEP 16 3 1977).

Yorkshireman, Parliament Street

According to TP Cooper a former name for *The Albion* (Cooper p. 77).

Yorkshireman Coffee House, Coppergate

Mentioned in 1836 (YG 13 8 1836). For sale with a brewhouse in 1851 (YG 31 5 1851) after which it became known as *The Yorkshireman Inn* (Dir). Also known as *The Yorkshire Coffee House.*

REFERENCES
AMCR	Acomb Manor Court Rolls
APCM	Acomb Parish Council Minutes
Ash	Ash, A & Day JE *Immortal Turpin* (1948)
Appleby	Appleby, CA & Smith, DB (ed) *A History of Acaster Malbis* (2000)
Appleton	Appleton, Avril E. Webster, *Looking Back at Heworth* (1999)
Attreed	Attreed, LA, *York House Books 1461–1490* (1991)
Avis	Avis, A, *The Brewers' Tale* (1995)
Bedford	Bedford F, Jnr, *Sketches in York* (1841)
Benson	Benson, G, *York Part III, From the Reformation to 1925* (1925)
Benson2	Benson, G, *The Taverns, Hostels and Inns of York and their signboards* (1913)
Benson3	Benson, G, 'Coins, especially those relating to York' *YPS Annual Report* 1913 (1914)
BI	Borthwick Institute for Historical Research
Brayley	Brayley, CEW *The Annals of Bishopthorpe* 10 (n.d. but c.1963)
Briddon	Briddon, IH & Pickering, J *A History of Fulford* (nd)
CAMRA	*Historic Pubs in and around York* (2000)
CAMRA2	*Pilot Suggestions for New Listings* (n.d. but c.1991)
CC	Chief Constable's Report (1902) YCA 258
Cook	*Cook, RB (ed), The Parish Registers of St Martin Coney Street, York* (1909)
Co-op	*Jubilee History of the York Equitable & Industrial Society* (1909)
Cooper	Cooper, TP, *The Old Inns and Inn Signs of York* (1897)
Cooper2	Cooper, TP, *Some Old York Inns* (1929)
Cooper3	Cooper, TP, 'York Annals', Ms in York City Library
Davies	Davies, Robert, *Walks Through the City of York* (1880)
Davies2	Davies, Barry *The Public Houses of Poppleton* (1999)
Davison	Davison, A, 'A Genuine and Superior Article: The last two Centuries of Brewing in York' *York Historian* 10 (1992)
Dawes	Darcy Dawes Account Book, YML Add Ms. 6371
Dir	Street Directories
DNB	*Dictionary of National Biography*
DNL	Cygnet Group *Down Nunnery Lane* (1992)
Drake	Drake, Francis, *Eboracum* (1836)
Dunkling	Dunkling, Leslie and Wright, Gordon, *Dictionary of Pub Names* (1994)
Duthie	Duthie, Ruth E 'The Ancient Society of York Florists', *York Historian* 3 (1980)
EH	English Heritage Brochure on 37 Tanner Row
ER	Electoral Register
Fairfax	Fairfax_Blakeborough, J, *Northern Turf History* vol 3 (1950)
Fiennes	Morris, C (ed), *The Journeys of Celia Fiennes* (1947)
Finnegan	Finnegan, F. *Poverty and Prostitution, a Study of Victorian Prostitutes in York* (1979)
Gent	Gent, Thomas, *Ancient and Modern History of Ripon* (1733)
Hargrove	Hargrove, William, *History and Description of the Ancient City of York* (1818).
Gregory	Gregory, Sister 'The Bar Convent and the Bay Horse Inn' *YAYAS Times* 44 (2001)
Johnson	Johnson, A, *The Inns and Alehouses of York* (1989)
JohnsonB	Johnson, BP, 'The Curriers' Account Books', *Yorkshire Architectural and York Archaeological Society Annual Report* 1951/2
JWK	Knowles, John Ward, 'Cuttings Books 1852-91', York City Library
JWK2	Knowles, John Ward, 'York Artists' Manuscript at York City Library
Kaner	Kaner, Jennifer, 'Wells on the River Bank, revised', *YAYAS Times* 42 (Dec 2000).
Knight	Knight, CB, *A History of the City of York* (1944)
Knipe	Knipe, William, *Criminal Chronology of York Castle* (1867)
Larwood	Larwood, Jacob & Hotten, John Camden *English Inn Signs* (1985)
Lyth	Lyth, John *Glimpses of Methodism in York* (1885)

Malden	Malden, J, 'A Secret Diary', *York Historian* 17 (2000)
Mennim	Mennim, AM, *The Merchant Taylors Hall, York* (2000)
MI	Monumental Inscription
Mitchell	Mitchell, Tessa *Strensall in the mid 19th century* (1989)
Murray	Murray, H, Riddick, S & Green, R, *York through the Eyes of the Artist* (1990)
Murray2	Murray, H, *Heraldry on the Buildings of York* (1985)
Murray3	Murray, H, *Scarborough, York and Leeds, the Town Plans of John Cossins 1697– 1743* (1997)
Murray4	Murray, H, 'The Mayor's Esquires', *York Historian* 6 (1985)
NER	North Eastern Railway Contract Summaries Book
Nuttgens	Nuttgens, P, *York* (1970)
Orton	Orton, J, *Turf Annals of York and Doncaster* (1844)
OS	Ordnance Survey
Pace	Pace, NB (transcribed), *The Parish Register of St Olave, York* (1993)
Palliser	Palliser, D & M, *York as They saw It* (1979)
Peacock	Peacock, AJ *York 1900 to 1914* (nd)
Pepper	Pepper, Barrie, *A Haunt of Rare Souls* (1990)
Pick	Pick, W, *Pedigrees and Performances of the most celebrated Racehorses* (1785)
Pocock	Pocock, Michael, *Halfdane's Heritage* (1998)
Poole	Poole, David 'Linnet Singing' *YAYAS Times* 26 (1991)
PR	Parish Register
PRO	Public Record Office
Raine	Raine, Angelo *Medieval York* (1955)
RCHME	Royal Commission on Historical Monuments, England, City of York
Riley	J Ramsden Riley *The Yorkshire Lodges* (1885)
S&B	York City Council, Minutes of Streets and Buildings Committee
Smith	Smith, DM, *A Guide to the Archives of the Company of Merchant Adventurers of York* (1990)
SS125	Sellars, M (ed), 'York Memorandum Book Pt II' *Surtees Society* 125 (1915)
Star	A free newspaper issued by the YEP
Thomson	*The Thomson Directory* or *The Thomson Local*
VCH	Tillott, PM (ed), *Victoria County History: The History of York* (1961)
Vernon	Vernon, Anne, *A Quaker Business Man* (1958)
Wheldrake	Wheldrake Local History Society *Wheldrake: Aspects of a Yorkshire Village* (1971)
Wilde	Wilde, D, *Osbaldwick, a Suburban Village* (1980)
Wilson	Wilson, Van, *Fulford Road District, The History of a Community* (1984)
WRRD	West Riding Register of Deeds
YCA	York City Archives
YCh	*York Chronicle*
YCL	York City Library
YCo	*York Courant*
YE	*York Express*
YEP	*Yorkshire Evening Press*
YG	*Yorkshire Gazette*
YGS	*York Georgian Society Annual Report*
YH	*York Herald* or *Yorkshire Herald*
YI	*York Illustrated* (1895)
YJ	*York Journal*
YML	York Minster Library